WEALTH OF RICHES

Oyewola Oyeleke

Homefront
Corporation

Email: info@wealthofrichesbooks.com

Phone: 9177542759

Website: www.wealthofrichesbooks.com

Edited by Professor Terry Benjamin

Writer By Nature

Wealth
of
Riches

How to have the all-
round success

Oyewola Oyeleke

Contents

Foreword

"There is no greater wealth in this world than peace of mind." (From an Unknown Writer)

When the student is ready the teacher will appear. If you're holding this book in your hands, you are ready for the next level of life. This is the book you need to read at this time in your life. Wealth of Riches: How to have all-around success FOREVER by Life Coach and Financial Advisor Oyewola Oyeleke is for you at this time because deep down in your soul, you know that wealth is more than money in the bank. This book will help you develop a wealth mentality for today and tomorrow, and help you cultivate and grow human qualities that will make you a "money magnet". You will meet many mentors and teachers in this book. Some from the real-life experiences of the author. Some are from quotes from valuable books the author has read, all curated to make you a financial success story.

As the author writes: "When you become wealthy, in the truest sense, money will stay with you. You will live in abundance that goes far beyond money."

You will meet Billie Bob Harrell, Jr., the 31-million-dollar Texas lottery winner, and see how money was not enough to save his life. Even before you become rich in your pocket, you must become rich in your spirit as illustrated in the following Les Brown quote from the book: "There is greatness in you." And this acceptance of your "greatness" enables you to feel worthy of the wealth you will accumulate during your lifetime.

The author makes a powerful statement in this book: "Truly wealthy people know how to make, manage, and hold onto money because of the unique ways their minds work. They have mastered the secrets of wealth generation and can, therefore, bring forth money whatever it takes, whenever it is needed, and where it is been produced." This mindset of "wealth sustainability" is a lesson fully presented in this book. In this book are the histories of Henry Ford, Michael Mack, King Solomon, General Dantaneil, Felix Didier, Willie Jolley, and many others that serve as wealthy mindset case studies.

The author looks at different types of wealth: financial wealth, social wealth, time wealth, and physical wealth. This book discusses misconceptions about money management that prevent many from enjoying wealth for a lifetime. Those who have fallen to the disaster of 'easy come, easy go' when it comes to money will be helped greatly as this book examines and explores the "science of wealth". This book also identifies the wrong roads to riches and helps establish things to be avoided like poor time management, procrastination, greed, and criminal activity, and fully explores wealth's sacred and practical laws.

The author spotlights the Law of Attraction, the Law of Respect, the Law of Nurturing, the Law of Knowledge, the Law of Giving and Distribution, the Law of Commitment, the Law of Believing, the Law of Dedication, the Law of Resilient, the Law of Action, the Law of Risk, the Law of Focus, the Law of Vision, and the Law of Management.

As you can see, this is not the book for those looking for a quick fix or an easy solution, but the author has created a roadmap to the greatest riches ever for those truly intentionally achieving financial control and economic freedom. This book is designed to open your mind as Martha Stewart, an American retail businesswoman and TV personality is quoted as: "Without an open-minded mind, you can never be a great success."

Here is the essence of this book, according to this brilliant writer and motivational teacher: "Dear Reader, I believe that this book has opened your eyes and helped you see beyond the concept of trying to be rich, chasing money in hopes of becoming and secure for the future, rather it is who you are and what you have made yourself to be. If your wealth is not sustainable and not coming out of a grounded-in-wealth mindset, it is not true wealth."

If education is wealth, Wealth of Riches: How to have all-around success FOREVER by Oyewola Oyeleke is a gold mine, a gift that will keep giving value, power, and a roadmap to success. You will become what the book talks about as you hold it in your hands - the more you read and study and apply it daily, the more living becomes an exciting experience.

Professor Terry Benjamin

Writer by Nature

Author, Content Creator, and Keynote Speaker.

Preface

To be vital in this new age requires a deep understanding of what makes you relevant in these times and tides. Wealth is not the currency you spend, neither is it the amount of money you have as many take it to be, searching for money to become relevant and have a good life is not the new game because life has evolved. Wealth is about having all it takes to be happy and fulfilled which is what we all look up to. This is not the age to miss the mark, the world is changing, and you cannot continue to take money above the important things in life as that is the least in the hierarchy of achievement, having money is what many believe to be success and prosperity.

The book, 'Wealth of Riches' is about revolutionizing the mind of those who are serious and want to be wealthy and successful in life, they are not in the game of "have money become the king" No. You will understand that having just money and struggling to be rich is the least that you will want to go for, not for yourself and your family, but to be an impact on every people and generation to come. They become assets of immeasurable value to society.

I have said several times that managing yourself to become wealthy isn't a day job. Sometimes it's tough to keep up with the elements that make you different from a money man, living a new life than what you knew you to be; smart, productive, result oriented. All these things can throw you into a brand-new life where you begin to lead and achieve greater results. No matter where you are, the good news is that it's never too late to turn things around and reset. And these simple tips in this book can help get you started.

The book, Wealth of Riches came into being as a result of correcting the misconception of success and prosperity. We had long missed the meaning of success and prosperity as having money. Money is not success, and it is not prosperity if you don't have the character and ability to live right and influence people positively. So many young people are already on the wrong path heading straight to failure because they have been taught that money is the most important thing, and their focus has always been 'get money, get money, get money!

I have seen so many people, young and old, male, and female who do not understand the way to succeed. Struggling through life and heading to a dead end. But now is the apocalypse, the good insight that will bring you to a good end.

Dedication

My dad raised me well, Prince Oyelola Oyeleke. An easygoing but principled man. He gave me a good direction by which to follow and live. He has that strong but subtle voice that spoke to me with deep love and clear direction to succeed through every good method he knew. He wanted me to know that a giant is me; that giant must not lay low. He told me several times that I am a trending superstar that must shine for all to see.

I will forever be grateful for the love, care, prayers, hard training, and guidance that kept me focused and determined to succeed in life, even as he continued telling these words to my earing, he never compromised discipline.

My dad taught me morals above possession; truthfulness, right standing, honesty, patience, contentment, dedication, and hard work. These are the things that have remained with me and guided me to bring forth this book.

Acknowledgment

Often it is said, "No man is an island." And often in families and communities people help one another to succeed with never a thought of needing a thank you or payment in return.

But saying "Thank you" is probably the smallest but warmest I can tell all those who have contributed in one way or the other to the successful completion of this book. This is why I have made these little words to tell you all that you are the best, you rock!

Firstly, everything is to God Almighty that takes all the glory – He gave the strength, the wisdom, the ability, the health, and the life to start and finish. Without Him, nothing is.

To my man of God, Rev. Chris Oyakhilome Ph.D., my life coach, and spiritual father, I love you sir, and will forever dwell in your guidance and counsel.

To the hundreds of Churches, pastors, and people of all places who have generously given their time and shared their hearts, minds, and souls with me over the period of the work. The prayers, calls, and words of encouragement have greatly impacted my chosen field.

I am grateful to Archbishop Macfonse Akinnugba, Exarch of West Africa, you have always been a great help in so many ways, I thank you so much, sir.

I am expressing my love and appreciation to my mum, my prayer mama, no day goes without praying, advising me, and making me laugh. My sisters and their families, I love you all. My in-laws, Barrister Tadema, Mr. Shola Olaloku, and

Mr. Tosin Kolawole. My friends, and well-wishers, thank you all so very much.

My mother-in-law is a mother indeed, Mummy Nwauzu, I love you ma, to my other in-laws, the Nwauzu family, and I am proud to have you all as my family.

And finally, I want to express my love and appreciation to my darling wife, Nkechi, and our kids David, Alvin, Deborah, and Alice, their love and support for me to do great things are just out of this world, you have endured me at the worst and have inspired me to be my best.

INTRODUCTION

Money itself flies around from one place to another, from hand to hand, physically and electronically. It moves and many will chase it from one end to another. Many are trying to get money to make themselves happy, while others want to have it for superiority. If you are one of those that chase money, you will chase it to the end of your life. If you want to have all the wealth you require, the best way to lay hold of all the money you need is to have you become a money magnet.

After reading this book, you will see wealth in a brand-new way, and how easy it is for you to live a wealthy and successful life. You will realize that "wealth" is more than money but a way of life in itself. To become wealthy in this effervescent way, I am going to show you in this book.

To become, you must first know what wealth is, how it functions, and what makes it multiply in the one who owns it, then you can become a person of value and influence. You will become a person that will have all that it takes to live a happy and successful life. You will know that how much money you have doesn't define your value or your worth. You will see money as simply an instrument to ensure that you will live the successful life you have imagined for yourself. You will also have this all-around success mentality in every season of your life.

My first unforgettable lesson on finance was when I was 6 years old. My dad got me a piggy bank made of grey clay and ground ceramics. He asked me to care for the little bank; to make sure it doesn't crack or break and must be neat at all times, that is the first sign of respect and responsibility he handed to me, a pathway to becoming a success in life, he asked me to put 50% of every money I receive or earn from him or any other person that came to our house.

We have this tradition in Africa, especially when we have visitors, my mum will provide good food and lots of drinks. The food and drinks prepared for one or two visitors are usually enough to fill more than a dozen people, always more than what our guests can finish. But as an act of gratitude, love, and respect for how we took care of them, the guest would give the kids money to let our parents know they were satisfied and ready to leave. This was the traditional way of saying "Thank you" to the hosts.

After we received this money, we would decide how we wanted to spend it. I would often want to buy "Ekona Gowon", also known as "Gowon's Finger", a candy made from sugar, honey, and lemon or lime juice., but my dad took that way of life from me, my present-hour priority should be how to grow money and not satisfy my childish craving- "Every money that comes to you must be accounted for because they know how much was given from each visit, the amount of money you receive, the one in your piggy bank and the money you spend. you will be held responsible for every penny.

He was already talking to me as if I was grown already, I was only 6 years old, but I later realized that he started at the very right time and with the right kind of training. As he continued training me, he will mention that I keep track of all income and expenditures." Those were the words of my dad, with a strong voice and a direct look like a boss to his workers, he was speaking to a six-year-old boy. He was teaching me about financial matters and strategy, addressing me like I was a full-grown adult who is about to manage his business. It was then I realized I could not spend money just any way I wanted anymore, I immediately said bye to Ekona Gowon and its cohorts of candy and cookies. I know that I had to be responsible for every money that comes to me and give an account of every money that goes out.

Apart from teaching me about the rules that govern the success of the piggy bank, he told me that the smooth running of any piggy bank is depended on the attitude of the custodian, how much I follow the rules of finance, how much I become disciplined and consistent, how much I look for means to ensure that the piggy bank gets its regular funds.

The other surprising thing was when he told me that I will break the little clay bank on my 7th year birthday and use the money to start a new circle, 10% to be given out to help any person in need, 10% to give to God as my tithe, 10% to buy all I need for my birthday celebration; that means I am spending the money and not from him

I can recall my dad asking me to give an account of my income and expenditures. He wanted to know how I spent my money within three months. My mom looked on and was very amused, almost laughing out of control as if all this was a joke. I had to laugh along with her, realizing that I couldn't buy all the things I wanted to buy, but being comfortable with that reality. Still, I felt a little sad because I felt restricted. But my dad didn't let up on his lesson even as his red eyes looked at my sad face. I knew he was not joking with me as I told him I knew I had #600 with him but I couldn't tell him what I had in my piggy bank.

I was not as happy as I thought a little kid should be, but I knew I was learning valuable financial lessons. My dad taught me how to do the things that would bring in money. There were many things around me that I was just not aware of. But these money lessons were not just from my dad. I learned a deep and valuable lesson from my French teacher, Mr. Grapier Akana. He told me that my time is worth all the diamonds in Russia. He let me know that my smile could win hearts, build character, improve my reasoning, aid my patience and uplift my mind. And that all these things were more valuable than money. The money came when all of these things were in place, all these qualities attracted money. I was taught to work at those things that would bring in money.

As I grew up and learned more in school, my understanding of money and my mindset about how money was acquired changed. Still, I was fixed on the things that I thought would guarantee me a good life: a decent-paying job, a good car, a nice apartment, and a good woman by my side. I knew it was important to stay out of trouble, build a good credit rating and work hard. Although I knew all this and worked at all this, it was still difficult for me to translate my efforts into tangible wealth. I began to struggle, and I saw that I was not alone, I saw many young people going through the same ordeal as me. But with God on my side, I began to see another path.

My success was assured when at age 37, I met a mentor who helped me shape my life. I began to translate the principles and concepts I had learned into a way of life, and not chase after money.

As I watched my mentor and listened to him, I began to learn that money was the result of wealth. I started seeing many avenues on the road to success. In less than two years, I became comfortable, not lacking anything. I did not doubt that I would attract all the money I would ever need.

This book, Wealth of Riches: How to Have All-Round Success Forever, is my way of teaching those who read, listen, and learn from my experiences. I want to teach the true value of money, that it is just one component of being wealthy. Wealth is more than money.

During the writing of this book, I was confusing wealth with material riches. Many of whom I told I was writing this book on wealth thought the same. When I began to do more thinking, research, writing, and prayer, I began to see that money was a byproduct of where I focused my energy. I had to think to grow rich.

The most important and difficult first step was to review the attitudes and behaviors that kept me from developing a wealth mentality. I had to see myself as a financial success story. I had to believe it to see it. In this book, I will review the building blocks of the complete financial planning process that brought me to where I am today. I will show you where all this can fit into your life at all levels. The concept of building wealth and having lasting prosperity begins with you, you are the money magnet.

When you become wealthy, in the truest sense, money will stay with you and surround you. You will live in an abundance that goes far beyond money.

The financial planning, I will be teaching you will guarantee a mindset that will laser focus on those things that will ensure wealth for you and your loved ones. You will come into a new fullness of yourself that will guarantee you a wealth of riches, not just money. You will have a hunger to learn more about wealth building. You will develop a new attitude, a fresh approach to new possibilities, and the idea of being financially comfortable. You will become what you were destined to become and have all the wealth you ever dreamed of.

Anyone can find dirt in others, but I want to be the one that finds the gold in you.

Yours in service,

Oyewola Oyeleke

Financial Advisor, Life Coach

Chapter One:
Is it wealth or riches?

"This real measure of our wealth is how much we'd be worth if we are not measured by riches"

John Henry Jowett, British Protestant, Preacher, and Author

Billie Bob Harrell, Jr. couldn't contain his joy when he won the 31-million-dollar Texas lottery in June 1997. All at once, his dream of escaping poverty and living a good life for the rest of his days seemed to have materialized overnight. For many years, Billie had struggled to provide for himself and his family. Being a religious man, he had been prayerful that one day he would experience a turnaround, that his finances would change for the better. Every Saturday and Wednesday, he would buy a few lottery tickets. He was looking for a way out, a probable doorway to prosperity.

The much-anticipated financial turnaround came to Billie on a day he had least expected. Everyone at his workplace was talking about someone that won the big bang, but he wasn't in the mood to talk about another man's lucky entry into riches, much less imagine that he could be the winner.

When he found out that he was indeed the winner, he walked around in a trance, hitting his head with his palm like someone that is trying to hit a spider out of his head through the ears; it was just too good to be true. When it finally dawned on him that he was rich, he began to cry and laugh at the same time, and began to imagine all the luxuries of this world he will enjoy going forward.

Billie resigned from his job at Home Depot that same hour and took his family on a Hawaiian vacation. The next day, he got his first credit alert. They had the best vacation anyone could dream of. After that, he went on a spending spree: buying houses and cars for himself and members of his immediate family and even for some of his friends. He made donations to his church and some other churches he felt needed money for bigger ministry exploits. He also reached out to a handful of organizations that asked for his financial help.

Life was good for Billie, he never said no to the hundreds of requests and pleaded for assistance, he just wanted to share the season of bliss he had suddenly come into. He often thought in his head that it would one day get better, I didn't realize it would get this much better, and very fast.

Unfortunately, as these sudden financial windfalls turned out, Billie found himself going rapidly downhill. From his high perch of financial success, Billie found himself falling into anxiety and uncertainty. Due to the pressure of his newfound fame and fortune, he was under a lot of stress and strain. Everyone was pulling on him with money requests and he found it hard to say no. It was once said that there is a real sure way to be successful, but there are so many ways to the ant hole; the quickest way to failure is trying to please everyone, in every way possible.

Caught up in this uncanny disease that wants to make him please all and sundry, and wanting to enjoy life to the fullest, Billie's whole world began to crumble. He found his whole life falling apart and soon he and his wife divorced, this was the first straw that broke the camel's hump. But because he still had some money, he was able to rebound somewhat. It didn't take him too long to get a much younger, classier, and prettier woman to marry him. But the depression that was upon him didn't ease up. He sought relief in counseling, confessing to a health professional that winning the lottery ruined his life. Instead of finding solace in his newfound fame and riches, he sank even further into the unsatisfaction of a lifetime.

One day in May 1999, Billie decided he had had enough, he could no longer live the way he had been living since after the winning. Even in his new home, he could see no light at the end of the dark tunnel he found himself in the everyday torment. He locked himself in a bedroom, took off all of his clothes, and shot himself.

Recognizing True Wealth

The story of Billie Bob Harrell, Jr. echoes in the lives of many who have gotten riches and lost them for instance, falling into a tragic and surprising ending. You may have probably heard some people who were once rich say, I was once there, I had several great cars, big houses, and loads of money.

You may have been rich before, but if you don't have it anymore, then you are poor. There is no achievement in being rich before, but now impecunious. You have to be clear about this: there is a big difference between wealth and riches. What do you have and what are you looking to have? What are you aspiring to be, now and forever?

Many think that every person who has money or property is wealthy. What you have to understand is that many millionaires are struggling to keep their heads above water, sinking into a private hell, that is not the "good life". They had believed in the 'Great Good Dream', thinking that all would be "sunny days and rainbows" because they had money. That they would live in everyday bliss without a worry in this world. Soon, they had to face the hard truth that there is fantasy and that there is reality, and they are two distinctly different states of being. They were rich but they weren't happy or couldn't sustain what they have. Achieving the American Dream or the Great Good Dream had turned out to be a nightmare for them.

Things looked good on the outside, but they were dying inside, unhappy without hope for what tomorrow will end up being like. It must be repeated time and time again: wealth and riches are not the same, and that is why we have this book, to teach us how to know the difference and to make the right choice and live happily ever after.

The first difference between being rich and or wealthy is satisfaction and sustainability. The rich man is never satisfied with what he has, he will always want more money to meet up with the standard or make him go beyond it. The rich man is also never going to be able to sustain what he has because he only has money, he does not have the power to make it available forever, time and chance can take everything from him if he is not careful and may not be able to recover again.

The rich man has money for his flexing, money is here to spend (that's his satisfaction) and not necessarily what will become of him the next time thunder after the storm comes (not sustained). The wealthy man has both satisfaction and sustainability (not based on just what he has for his enjoyment and spending- which is his bases for his happiness and comfort, but that which he has that is sustained and forever unfinishable) which is oftentimes deposited in him.

A truly wealthy person can maintain his status, finances, and success, and be happy every day of his life because he is self-sufficient. He can get whatever he wants, not because of the opportunities that the world threw at him, but by what he has made himself to become, a "truly wealthy" person, and the world (the system of the cosmos) can't take away who he is from him.

The rich guy's mindset is fixed on the joy of the present moment, the struggle to get more money than any other person is his priority, so he does anything and everything possible to meet up. Such a person is always subject to the ups and downs of life, the profit, and the losses, the boom and burn, and all the plague that can hit on anybody and at any time. But the truly wealthy man is always on the come up thither, moving upward and forward in his daily walk with success. All his needs are met without any struggle because he is the money machine, he is the solution to every one of his needs; he knows what to do to get all needs met and ensures that he doesn't have any reason to lack.

He knows that wants and needs are two distinctly different things, he doesn't have wants anymore, but rather he takes care of his needs as required. He is truly happy because he has learned to be happy with what he has at every moment and is not stressing about what he doesn't have, what he has lost, or what he hopes to get. He knows how to get in where he fits in no matter the geographical location, economic situation, or social pressures all around him.

On the second hand, the rich man is only "rich" if the money keeps coming, his money comes via work, trade, other areas of investments, or every other means he knows to get money. He may be living the Great Good Dream, but it is fueled by what he can get outside of himself. This way of life is not sustainable. He can buy all the things that money can buy, but what happens when there is no money? Unfortunately, the "good life" he enjoys is going to be only for a temporary period, he will sooner or later lose the capacity to sustain it as money can't buy everything that makes a man happy.

When I think of a "rich man" I think of someone that has money, good enough to keep him going and enough for him to spend. I think about someone who is ostentatious and will eventually want to be known as a "rich person", the expensive clothing, big and blinking chains, and every luxury money can buy, that every other person can see. These are people who surround themselves with the trappings of an assumed 'rich man': the fancy lifestyle, but the wealthy man is who he is, he does not need to tell you or show you what he possesses or what he carries with him, but from his words, his personality, his charisma, his love, and leadership passion will fish him out.

Thirdly, Rich people usually become "rich" from a compilation. Every penny from every source outside of themselves is added. These outside sources belong to the world and are subject to the winds of change that move the world around. These seemingly good things that come from getting a better paying job, a bigger business, earning more from savings, earning more from trade, and the like can be taken away in a blow or with time.

What you should want to have should be that which you will have from inside you, that grows inside you and remains with you, no matter what the circumstance of life brings, your wealth will be unshaken forever. Building people and creating networks, educating yourself and building capacity, and establishing a problem-solving and solid mechanism that will forever be needed by humanity are all varieties of wealth.

Some become "rich" through inherited assets. Some win the lottery or money from a wager. Some earn money by having prestigious and lucrative jobs. Some have saved their money and stumbled upon a quick get-rich scheme that worked out for them. Some could be lucky, or got that "found" money, getting income from unexpected and unanticipated sources, and many others you can think of. These types of riches are very deceptive because you feel comfortable seeing these resources and assets come to you, your bills are settled as at when due, and you can buy what things you so needed. But you must learn how to live above board, to be utterly prosperous and then a distributor of wealth and opportunities.

Still, the question is: Does having such a financial windfall make one wealthy? Again, that is why it is so important to understand the difference between wealth and riches.

Imagine a person deep in the quicksand of life: How long can they keep themselves from sinking? How much would they be worth if they didn't have money? Or look at it another way: Can the substance of their lives sustain them? Will all be lost once the person's earning power is gone for whatever reason? If misadventure or illness strikes, will they be able to stand and thrive? Or will they come to the end of the road?

These are personal questions for you and me. It is often said, your network equals Your net worth. Lisa Nicholas, a transformational coach, and author once said: *"You will never find your next best version of you sitting inside of your comfort zone."* You have to get outside of yourself. So, the question is: How many people are part of your network? How many people are encouraging you and working with you to go beyond yourself and step into your greatness?

Like Henry James, a legendary American novelist, once said: "It's time to start living the life you've imagined for yourself." As Les Brown, motivational teacher, and author, often says, "There is greatness in you."

We're speaking here of your influence over the elements of life, outside of your capacity to make money, how many people have you influenced to the point where they are ready to bring a matchbox when you need to light a fire? Most importantly, and most significantly, can what you have been passed on to future generations? can you pay it forward in any significant way? Can you travel and stay for some time on a pleasure island and still be able to fund the matters of your life and that of others? See, this is the inward substance we are going to be dealing with. I am asking you to make a choice: wealth or riches?

Knowledge Fuels Sustainability

Think about people in history who may have been considered truly wealthy, and you'll see where I am going. Think of the Rockefellers, the Carnegies, the Campbells, the DuPonts, these are popular names in the lineup of the wealthy. You would find this thread of sustainability running through the tapestry of their histories. Their wealth spans multiple generations. You may ask, why is that so? What makes the rich continue to be rich? What is the difference between these dynasties and those who stumble upon riches through inheritances and lottery winnings like people like Billie H. Harrell, Michael Carol, and Evelyn Adams, those folks who won millions of dollars, but couldn't hold onto their riches for long? What differentiates them from some professional athletes who made quick millions within a short time and then it's gone like smoke in the wind? It might be because truly wealthy people are knowledgeable people, - they know what many so-called rich people do not know.

To know is to own, - The custodians of knowledge are those who hold the power to lead those who must by all means follow. I was speaking at a conference some years back and told the class of young entrepreneurs that "the more you learn, the more you earn". This custodian of knowledge knows the direction that leads to the good life, you may have loads of money, but if you do not have the "loads of knowledge", you are still an underdog that must follow the lead.

In the book- The Wealth Choice: Success Secrets of Black Millionaires, Dr. Dennis Kimbro writes: "There need not be a poor person on the planet. The earth is replete with resources that we have yet to tap. As a result, we grow comfortable with our lack of prosperity and opportunity. Financial riches are lying everywhere, waiting for the observant to discover them. Wealth begins in the mind, and those who are hostile to it will never possess it" (Kimbro, p71).

Truly wealthy people know how to make, manage, and hold onto money because of the unique ways their minds work. They have mastered the secrets of wealth generation and can, therefore, bring forth money wherever and whenever it is and to wherever it is needed.

On the other hand, rich people only get money from different sources they have entered into or arranged to bring them their present state, status, and reality, and this determines their level of living. Consequently, and sadly, even when they appear to be enjoying life, they are often restless and dissatisfied. They are always on guard, waiting for the next financial move that will either keep them rich or shatter them into oblivion, otherwise; peradventure things didn't work out as planned, it is doomsday, calamity will strike.

Many rich folks will be lucky to keep their heads up and keep up their financial standard, rolling their money from day to day, and even building it to become bigger, but they are still regarded as unsuccessful people because money is not the yardstick to measure success, prosperity is. And you will also agree with me that prosperity is the state of being happy and content, having everything, including money.

My point here: building true wealth begins with knowing how to effortlessly generate riches from every source within the bank called 'you'. This is the only way to build sustainable riches. With this mindset, money never stops coming in for you, you find yourself comfortable because you lack nothing. The essence of what I am talking about is this: make all you can, save all you can and give all you can, you must make yourself the priority of your establishment, you become everything that matters in life, building you to become knowledge personified, you make yourself powerful with ideas, skills, strength, resilience, and focused. But there will be challenges and setbacks, you may get knocked down, but you won't stay there long.

As a motivational teacher and author Willie Jolley often says: "A setback is a setup for a comeback." The past president of the United States, Donald Trump, comes to mind here. As the story goes, several years ago, Mr. Trump was deep in debt. But oddly, he didn't change his money habits, and nor did he shrink from the limelight. He never told anyone how much debt he was in, but he still talked about the life of wealth and affluence, he talked in the millions, the multi-investment opportunities he is vying to conquer, and how he plans to be the next president of the United States all at the same time, he is possessed with wealth and the millions he was determined to make on all his successes, from his many ongoing property acquisitions and business deals kept running after him.

His mindset held him up even though he seemed to be going down because of some failed business deals and miscalculations. He knew wealth began in this mind of his, and it must continue there for him to remain wealthy and strong, and then it could show up in his pocket as riches.

He is wealthy from the inside out. You must know where real wealth comes out from, and how to bring it out and make it tangible. You must be that diamond in the rough that anytime the heat gets on to, it becomes more precious. Many truly wealthy people continue to succeed because of their knowledge, their network, and their focused thinking.

Motivational teacher and author Charles "Tremendous" Jones once said: "There are essentially two things that will make you wiser-the books you read and the people you meet." These truly wealthy people valued knowledge over money at the start of their journey to sustainable riches that would enhance their life, career, and businesses. Because of this prior planning, true riches naturally flowed into their lives. They worked on themselves and made themselves a "magnet", they became the brain behind great ideas, the force that establishes giant industries, and the vision that gave birth to what many would call riches.

They used their wealth 'innate powers' to pull riches for themselves. They dared to be great. They have answered the "wake-up call" to be all that they can be. They have learned to live their dreams and not their fears, something motivational teacher and author Les Brown often talk about in his classic 1992 book, Live Your Dreams. Brown writes: "To change so that you can live your dreams, you must grow in consciousness.

This process of personal growth involves four stages of increased awareness in the areas of self-knowledge, self-approval, self-commitment, and self-fulfillment" (Brown p80).

Now, let us look at a classical example of Henry Ford, a renowned industrialist, business magnate, and founder of the Ford Motor Company who successfully bounced back stronger, after nearly losing everything that he had built over the years. It was Ford who once said: "Two classes of people lose money; those who are too weak to guard what they have, and those who do not know that they have anything. This is quite powerful and true; I will add to what Ford said, 'those who do not know who they are and those who played chess with what they could have become, they all lose in the end."

Ford was rich at the start of his life, and with a wealth of knowledge on how to be successful, he made great strides during the recession of 1920 to 1921. History tells us many businesses failed in almost every venture. Much poverty and misery in America in the months that followed the first World War. Still, Ford's daily language was about buying more land and buildings for new factories, increasing production for the new car models, increasing budgets, and always talking in the millions of dollars. There was a period when people hardly could comprehend what having a few Thousands of dollars will look like.

He made his team discover new ways to overcome hard times in crisis, when many began to lose hope, Ford drew from his will to sustain himself and his company through the trying times, he talked about hundreds of ways to make millions when people dare talk in hundreds. He was big and wealthy on the inside and no wonder he was not deterred by the catastrophe flying around the world at that time.

An example of this grit, closer to our times, is Michael Mack, an attorney and founder of Bankruptcy Credit Foundation who had to practically dig himself out of personal bankruptcy. He had been doing well professionally and financially until he made a bad investment move. Consequently, he lost all his assets and had to file for Chapter 7 bankruptcy in 1998.

Many people saw nothing but gloom and doom for Michael, but he remained unmoved because his wealthy ways were ingrained, just within him was everything that the people thought had left him. His "wealth". It wasn't based on what he had or what he had lost, but on what is inherent in him.

Things didn't quite go well, his marriage took a hit and ended in divorce. Still, he kept on going. "I almost dropped out of life, but I knew I am wealthy," Michael said. "I have it inside; what was lost should be a portion and not everything, my everything lives in my mind."

That mindset was the start of a new beginning for Michael. He moved into a one-bedroom apartment. He started working as a telemarketer by day and a bartender at night. he went about the business of building his wealth from the scratch. "The great turnaround was the fact that I started building riches all over again, from the wealth that was deposited in me." I never pursued money in my comeback stage in life, rather, I invested heavily in myself.

He goes on to say, " I brought out my wealth mind, I rearranged it and packaged it to begin a new circle of prosperity for me. I built the inside to become so wealthy that it started resonating outside without much effort. I could see abundance and brightness again, and in record time. everything became easy to achieve. I could afford anything and buy whatsoever I wanted. I started raising people from every sphere of life; these men became my giants. It was like an arachnid's web; I was well connected with resources beyond ever getting broke or needing anything again." Currently, Michael Mack has created various foundations that helped people out of financial mishaps and personal and corporate bankruptcies.

Wise King's Example

The Holy Scriptures furnish us with compelling examples of a person who understood what it meant to build great wealth that transcends mere riches. King Solomon was extraordinarily wealthy as a result of his uncommon wisdom as the Holy Scripture describes.

What was the secret of his wealth? When he newly became king, God appeared to him in a dream and asked him what his heart's desire was, and what he wanted most as a king. Anyone could quickly think of more money or fame, these could make a such person become the strongest and richest king of his time, or, maybe he could have demanded more power and influence to rule over more nations and territories, so he could be named the king of kings, but King Solomon asked for wisdom; wisdom to rule well, to oversee the affairs of his kingdom, and to be wise enough to be a good leader. He wanted the wisdom and knowledge that makes everything possible, that knowledge that will make him stand out among kings and men. That simple request made him become the wealthiest man ever recorded by the word of God, a man that became timeless in greatness.

Throughout his writings, King Solomon lists wisdom and knowledge (understanding) as two of his most important possessions. He was a king and definitely, a king should be rich in gold and silver and money, but he sorts after wisdom. This enabled him to obtain and sustain his true wealth and happiness. Just as it happened for King Solomon, wisdom and knowledge can create great wealth for anyone who truly desires it.

Recently someone humbly asked me what he could do to create wealth. My immediate response to him was to start learning everything he could about wealth. My thinking is that once he knew, then he could begin formulating a strategy and work frame to build wealth. But the knowledge must come first; otherwise, even if money comes to him, he would not be able to hold onto it. It would slip through his fingers like one under a rushing tap water.

I am most grateful to my life coach who instilled in me an unmatched and unquenchable thirst for knowledge. That kind of knowledge will make every man successful. No matter their background or strength or purpose in life. This is the greatest gift (other than life itself) that I have gained from personal experiences. It is this thirst for knowledge that led me to uncommon successes, knowing full well that nothing can make me see lack again here on earth and beyond life.

Proverbs 4: 7: Wisdom is the principal thing; therefore, get wisdom; and with all thy getting get understanding. The principal thing is the consortium of every good thing that entails wealth and happiness, which includes riches, prosperity, success, income, and ownership.

When you have this wisdom, you will be exalted as one who has more than meets the eye. King Solomon also talked about honor when he embraces wisdom as a base for his wealth, obtaining information that is beyond most people's comprehension is what will put you ahead of them automatically.

Talking about the role of knowledge in the process of wealth creation, cannot be overemphasized as soon as you get the facts, information, and skills through experience or education, you will go beyond where you are currently in terms of wisdom and understanding.

A man of knowledge has, without retreating or without faltering, gone as far as he can in unraveling the secrets of power and education. He has gone above the limits of what any other person knows. This makes this man a master of information. To become a man of knowledge one must challenge and answer every question, thus providing answers and solutions to every need of life. If you master knowledge, you will be a problem solver. A problem solver is invariably a wealth creator, he is the custodian of knowledge.

The New Living Translation of Proverbs 24:5 makes a clearer description of who a man of knowledge is: "The wise are mightier than the strong, and those with knowledge grow stronger and stronger." No wonder he is a "solution provider," a person who lives an examined life and progresses through stages of awareness and information dissemination.

Henry David Thoreau, philosopher and author said it best: "I know of no more encouraging fact than the unquestioning ability of man to elevate his life by conscious endeavor." In other words, life is what you make it.

A man is termed wealthy because of what he knows that others don't know. He has solutions to the needs of others that they are ready to pay for. He knows where to get resources. He knows who needs services, in short, he knows the people's problems and knows how to solve them, and in turn, collects money from each of them which added together makes him rich. "The habit of depending on the self, a determination to uncover inner personal resources, develops strength as well as wealth," according to Dr. Dennis Kimbro in his self-help classic, The Wealth Choice: Success Secrets of Black Millionaires. Therefore, the first stage of wealth acquisition comes from the amount of knowledge you can control.

But this is not a somber process. It can be joyful because you are living your life to the fullest: In Life Force: How new breakages in precision medicine can transform the quality of your life & those you love, Tony Robbins writes: "Live life fully while you're here. Experience everything. Take care of yourself and your friends. Have fun, be crazy, and be weird. Go out and screw up! You're going to anyway, so you might as well enjoy the process" (Robins, p619).

The whole world needs help. Every living creature is seeking a way to fulfill its needs. The only reason people seek work is that they want to have money in their pockets to take care of all their needs and most of their wants. Is there one person on this earth who can solve all of the world's problems? This person would have the whole world in his hands if he can. Everyone would come to that person for help and solution, they will pour money into his coffers for all the services he or she could render. I am not saying I can make you the master of this world, but I can help you develop the mindset, that wisdom, knowledge, and understanding will give you wealth in a platter of gold forever.

In your own words

....
....
....
....
....
....
....
....
....
....
....
....
....
....
....
....
....
....

Wealth is not Money Having money is a good thing, but don't be a fool to remain there, get big, be wealthy.

Wealth is not money, rather, it is what is deposited into your spirit that makes you function with ease, capabilities, and prosperity.

To be wealthy is not narrated in monetary value, but what you are worth all-round.

Anyway, it is good to have money, and when it Is changing lives, then you have transcended.

Chapter Two:
General D's Definition of Wealth

"True wealth is not of the pocket, but the mind."

Kevin Gates, American rapper, singer, and entrepreneur

I often advise people that if they want to be poor, start looking for money, and if they want to be poorer, they should spend their money alone. Some people are running helter-skelter searching for money to soothe their deep thirst for riches. That hunger for riches has put many in precarious situations, trying to get rich quicker and by any means possible has made them dangerous. That's why we have this popular 50 Cent saying, "Get rich or die trying." This defective expression has sent many down a dangerously wrong path in life.

We have older men who can soil or even totally cut off their consciences just to have money. They know they are being so wrong, unethical, and selfish, but they can't help themselves. Because of their selfish desire, they have stopped caring about the legacy that is supposed to be left for future generations.

It doesn't stop with men; we now see mothers who will sell their daughters for a token, who does not care what morals mean anymore but is ready to go far away in pursuit of money at the expense of their family. And, of course, we have the younger generation of ladies and guys who are all too ready to dive into the most barbaric and satanic acts to satisfy their perverted lusts for money.

But, as we have seen in our previous chapter, being rich does not necessarily mean having comfort and satisfaction, if this mindset is well-driven, more people will be wealthy without going through the death tunnel to by all means get money.

Here's a story to help you understand where I'm coming from. General Dantaneil published a memoir of exploits in the military in 1983, after the United States invasion of Grenada. The memoir was more about his successes in the military and after, what it is like to be rich and later become wealthy- this made me gasp for air as if I was already drowning in the euphoria of the lessons, it was indeed an eye opener for me.

There was great excitement as he looked around the dock, General D was with his comrades in his new GLZ 09 white yacht traveling on Miami beach to South Pointe Park where they were to continue the 'party for the achiever' cocktail party. The atmosphere was so relaxing and enjoyable as the reunion after the general's retirement from the service party continued.

He is surrounded by wads of great minds, strewn across his king-sized bed near the cabin. He can consider himself a success as he feasts on the choicest foods and wine in his immaculate, well-decorated suite painted in white and gold. With him were his most trusted friends who served together with him as naval Seal in the US marines, well-trained military personnel, and trusted friends who fought with him in the different battles back in the 80s and 90s. The yacht was filled with captains of industries, investors, and top businessmen and women.

He basks in the euphoria, the reality that he is now a wealthy man and a man of influence to many brings joy into his heart. General D has served in the US military with distinction, earning several medals and awards for excellence, commemorating his 40th year of service to the nation, he is not just celebrating his military achievements but his brand-new success. Not just closing his military career successfully, but to appreciate the newly wealthy and happy life he just found out, with over 3 gross of his friends who have gathered all around Miami and on the yacht with him, he had employed over 2,000 professionals working in his fast-growing private security outfit, he has raised dedicated men and women helping him to achieve the success that will never be outlived.

General Dantaneil caught the attention of his friends as they continued to celebrate his successes and great achievements just 3 years after retirement, they were busy enjoying themselves with roasted ribs laced with manuka honey and oysters, picking from the biggest plate of vela tacos and vegetables back at the fireside. He doesn't want for anything but casually throws out a question to the assembled friends laughing loud and having a skull session about their military experiences: what would you do if ten million dollars were given to you right now? Asked; General Dantaneil.

There was a long silence on the slow-moving white yacht, and the answers from his friends were almost all the same, it went with my idea if I was asked the same question. These answers would have been your answer if you were on that yacht.

Felix Didier from Cote d'Ivoire in Africa, trained as an amphibious under the third infantry division of the US marines raised his hands before others could finish thinking of what ten million dollars look like. With a smile that looks like a scowl, his right-hand hanging in the air like a nursery school student that is sure of giving the teacher the right answer. He was the general's right-hand man at the peacekeeping mission in Sudan and was quick to answer before he was told to continue. "I will invest it in the stock market, make my money and never be broke again."

His shallow smile made everyone quiet for about six seconds before the crowd started clapping and murmuring as though they all will do the same thing Didier said, nodding their heads in agreement.

Others gave their answers one after the other, and their answer was all similar to Didier's'; as if there was no other way to manage this million-dollar windfall than to trade in stocks, buy properties, or invest in a business, a few said that they will trade in cryptocurrency, some said the best way to go is to start an online business selling services or subscriptions.

For me, I will employ capable professionals who will manage the money for me, they will invest a part in every growing business and buy properties with some other portion of the money, Edgar Wilkinson added that he was going to invest in his life-long desire which is to be in politics.

After the outpouring of the different ideas of what to do with ten million dollars dried up, they all were waiting for the general's response to their answers and what he will do with the money since he started the confab.

Anyone will have something they will want to push such money into, as he continued, General D as many that worked with him in the military called him. There are a hundred and one ways to spend much money on; business, investments, properties, stocks, trading, and so on, so there could be profit added on it, at least no one is going to be dumb enough to say they'll keep it under a carpet or dump it in a savings account, that will not be a wise way to become wealthy.

It is what we learn by a natural law of increase that you will also want to deploy if you were asked the same question. Every man will want to plant a seed and get a multiplied harvest on it, to make what they have in their hand become much more than what it was.

Do you realize that none of you have mentioned a key component that has helped me transition from riches to wealth, this same component has built many rich people to become influencers and solution providers which is "Investing in Yourself"? Many do not know that there is no success without you, and there is no result without your input. Do you also realize that Many have not prepared themselves to be the source of wealth that will turn whatever comes to them into riches and prosperity? You cannot handle the amount of money that you are not at first, it's proportion. Until you have prepared yourself ahead of wealth, you cannot be wealthy, no matter what amount of money comes to you.

You may say that the amount mentioned is too large to develop just you, but when we look at the principle of seeds and harvest, the belief we have is that we must plant a seed to bring forth the branches, and in it comes the fruit and the harvest, .. Sure, we all know that every seed brings a harvest, but we want a big harvest, isn't it? but we can define it differently, what if we focus on the Sower that brings in the harvest, the intelligent Sower can bring in a big, healthier harvest, rather than the seed that brings whatever the land gives it, a good Sower can transform it to be a different kind of harvest.

What if you are vast enough to know the kind of seed to sow, what particular type of land to sow a seed on, on what particular type of soil will be best for that type of seed, and in what season will bring forth the best harvest?

Seeds oftentimes grow by themselves, not needing someone to plant and till them,\. It will grow and bring out its natural harvest, but you will always see a bigger and more bountiful harvest if you have a good and knowledgeable farmer to handle such a venture, that same seed that brought out a basket full of the harvest without a good farmer will in the same season and the same soil yield a bigger harvest of 10 baskets full in the hands of a good and trained farmer.

What if you are that Sower, the one that is meant to plant and nurture the tree that will bring the many fruits for harvest? That means the first and the most important element to build and invest in should be the human resources which is you. That means to make yourself the first in line to invest knowledge, and you become that superhuman that will turn $10m into a lifetime fortune, you will be full of every knowledge and authority in the field that will make money grow into wealth.

I tell you; you will transform the last penny into a cash cow that will easily become great gain, you will be the determinant of what the money will become, and how it will evolve, that is my definition of wealth, and that is what I learned that made me who I am today.

This is my personal experience in the financial world, not until I became a smarter and wiser investor with precision and skill, I could not have been able to handle the money that came to me, it would have been bigger than my head can carry and inversely become my nightmare. Such money will not come to me because I cannot handle it. But fellas, I know too much to be less than a multi-millionaire, my capacity has increased, and I can only deal with the biggest harvest. it is not the amount of money that determines my worth, it is the amount of knowledge about everything that says my worth and makes wealth a reality for me.

When you allow money bigger than you to come to you, it will enslave you and even put you in a bigger problem than you were when you didn't have such because you will begin to work for it and make you a slave to it. Such incapacitation will not allow money to remain with you for long and possibly have you destroyed if you are not careful. But if you are big, you will become the master of any money, anything in your hands will invariably become your tool, it will conform to your level because it must naturally want to level up to meet up to whatever you want to make it become. If you are big, you will not need money to achieve anything, because money will be the least of the element that will make you wealthy.

I have been a senior officer in the military for over three decades now, and I have seen a lot of money, my salary is pretty good, I also invested in some businesses that were working and yielding good profits for me, and I worked with the rich and business-minded folks at different times, paying some good heads to work for me. I was comfortable because I had money to use, which made me feel good, but when I discovered the power of inherent wealth, I knew I was just a money handler that must transition to a money machine. A wealthy man is different from a money handler because the money handler survives through money, the wealthy make money survive through him.

I was never fulfilled because I worked to have this money all that time, I never realized the power of me being 'the money. The money that the world chases after becomes my tool and errand bird, it was transformed into a tool that will bring more to me.

I began to focus and invested in myself like never before; my education became paramount, and I wanted to know everything and anything, I learned from every field and every piece of knowledge. I also invested in my personality, to become big inside and out, my utterances were improved, and I began to talk wealth, speak wisdom, and talk positivity at all times. My mind was what I invested in most. I began to push myself into a different circle of the wealthy, I made friends with those that know too much, and I knew that the friends that will not teach me anything will never lead me anywhere. From where I was and with everything I had, I became a student of knowledge, totally humbling myself to correction, rebuke, reproof, and instructions as 2 Timothy 3:16 narrates. A lot of investment was made in that area (my personality) more than I ever did with any other area of investment.

My point is this, invest in your personality like your life depends on it because it does depend on it. The man that is big inside cannot be small outside, that is not possible. That is what made me the successful person I am today, not because of the investments I made in a business but the investment I made in myself first.

The elegant white yacht became like a bathtub full of ice, now cold and empty as if it was not that same fun group that was jumping and dancing with a glass of wine on the hand of everybody with the clinging sound, laughing and shouting so loud for joy and merriment, enjoying the good food and drinks. Do not accept the money I am offering you my friends, be afraid to take it if you are not wealthy inside. The money I am offering is not just for you to become rich because if that is the determinant, you will become a slave to it, but should be for you to build wealth; and that wealth should be "you".

Build Wealth in People

General D also talked about becoming wealthy through people. When you make yourself a shining star for others to follow, a tangible asset, and an example of a wealth builder, that is when you are transformed to become wealthy, at that point, you have raised a system that works through the people you raised. If you cannot connect with people, and raise them to be successful, you miss out on a good portion of what makes anyone's life successful.

Wealth in people becomes a reality when you have not just ordinary people with you, but successful people surrounding you. But to achieve such a feat, you must first lead yourself into that level of trust and capacity, then, become an example by helping others grow and become successful.

Walter Bennis, an American scholar, organizational consultant, and author once said, *"The point is not to become a leader because you have money, but a leader that commands followership because you are the example and the best to follow"*.

I told a group of some fine young men who attended a bachelor's eve party in Pennsylvania in the summer of 2019, then I was told by the MC that I will say a word or two to the about-to-be husband – the good-looking bachelor who is about to metamorphose into husband hood and his friends paid rapt attention as I took the microphone as if they were all waiting to learn what leadership is for the first time, some had read my book on leadership titled 'Strong Meat' and were ready to learn how to be wealthy by raising men. They all turned to me at once… my subtle voice was convincing already as I started with my first sentence, "Not all men are husbands, and not all husbands are leaders, many are just males in the house because of the third leg. leadership is not achieved by your sex or age, neither is it by money, but by being the best in loving people genuinely and showing a good example to follow, leadership is about making everyone else better" entrusting people with responsibilities because you cannot do it alone.

 The point is to make yourself great." For you to be great, you have to make others around you greater.

The keywords were simple and as a compass to help navigate to a better person and a good leader who will build a life around the people he loves and live with passion and purpose. This singular and focused mindset is best illustrated in Stedman Graham's book, - Identity Leadership: To lead others you must first lead yourself; where he writes: *"Success flows from understanding who you are. Success is the result of becoming clear about your identity, discovering what you love to do, and learning how to do it so well that you create value in the world"* (*Steadman, p37*). So, when your focus is to build wealth, money will be the last thing on your list, but rather build a consortium of wealthy people, goal-getters, transformers, and inventors. It is sweet to be a father of achievers than to be a money bag that he alone is glorified because of his cash.

It was Jim Rohn, an American entrepreneur and motivational teacher and author, a mentor to Tony Robbins and many other self-help superstars, who once said: "Success is something you attract by the person you become in others." When you see a man surrounded by flocks of successful people, know that such a person is wealth personified, he has raised a standard that cannot be reduced as far as others are growing.

Building wealth through people can be in form of building networks. A network of people in your life is the best thing that can ever happen to a person that wants to be successful and be successful for a long time. Experts agree that the most networked and connected people are often the most successful and wealthiest. When you invest in your relationships — professional and personal — it can pay you back in dividends throughout the course of your life. Networking is essential since it will help you develop and improve your skill set, make you stay on top of the latest trends in your industry, keep a pulse on the job market, meet prospective mentors, partners, and clients, and gain access to the necessary resources that will foster your career development, indeed, it will bring the best brains to your domain and use at your disposal.

Remember, your network is your net worth, and it can support you by helping you find connections in the industry you are trying to break into or helping you find leads into different opportunities, it can help you save your greatest and most precious asset, which is 'time' - when everyone is adding their time to help you build a conglomerate. Take the time to build meaningful relationships with those in your professional circle, so when the time comes to do great things, you will not be there alone, you can tap into those valuable connections for referrals, insights into leads, and other valuable information.

Wealth is a byproduct of mindful living.

To be truly wealthy starts with who you truly are and how you can quickly identify it and put it to work. In Success Guide, a networking journal, George C. Fraser, author of the classic Networking Beyond the Cultural Stereotype: Building Powerful Partnerships to Win, writes: "The happiest and most contented people are those not in pursuit but the fulfillment of their dreams or ideals.

How would I define wealth or prosperity without being aware of what's happening in the present moment, what will happen in the future, and what you have to learn from your past experiences? The power of awareness of what is going on around you is important. If you don't know the trend of things and the present-hour reality, you will be forgotten in the mist dew. Prosperity isn't measured in numbers, fame, or money-it's not a line drawn somewhere just above the million-dollar mark. Prosperity involves choosing your destiny and living out your potential in your way."

Mindful living is one sure way to go, it helps us become more aware of our habits and to work toward changing those that don't serve us and serving others right. By increasing our self-awareness, how we interact with our world, and the way we live that has to be corrected and connected with success and perfection. We don't live anyhow anymore, because our personality will have to roll over from mediocrity to excellence. We must begin to be aware that we are now in the upper class, our mind must continue to tell us the new reality of whom we have become and continue to live in that direction nonstop.

As you prepare yourself for success and wealth, your mind must be channeled aright, and your thinking faculty must be oiled to perform optimally, that is, to know where you are heading with this newfound life, and how to live in such a powerful new atmosphere. Mindful of what wealth is, you must intentionally build your mind to live in that new realm of power and affluence. You cannot desire wealth and think poorly, your mindset must change drastically and in a big way too.

Studies show that mindfulness can improve confidence, resiliency, and focus. It's also impactful on stressors such as performance anxiety and fear of judgment. But the benefits are not just mental: One study found that mindful living helped people transition from poor and average conformity to an excellent and goal-getter mindset, which invariably improves both performance and mental endurance. It's often said that success in life depends on a high measure of physical correctness and mental toughness. It's the mental toughness and correctness that's the mindfulness, and this is the goal to achieve wealth.

 The power within us is very powerful, but many are not mindful of this, that is why so many potentially great people remain ordinary and fail to accomplish what they are meant to be in life. Until you know and be very mindful of what you can achieve, you may never get there. That is why it is very important to discuss mindful living so you will not just desire to be rich but begin to align yourself to become wealthy in the face of every opposition and drawback.

Sometimes, when you want to give up your dreams and continue living that ordinary, you just want to quit school or stop building others, mindfulness will interrupt this process and realign you to what your start-up goal is. Because you are mindful every single minute, you are conscious of what you have set up to achieve and you are not about to let it slip. Pressure may mount to push your baggage aside, but because you are mindful of what's in the bag, you will hold on to it firmly, and drag it with you to the top.

Contentment, the Heartbeat of Wealth

Contentment is the seedbed and spine of wealth. This is where true wealth resides. It is not humanly possible for a man to have all his wants satisfied. It is an established economic principle that humans' wants are insatiable and never-ending.

No man, for instance, can say he has gotten all the money he wants; he will always be hungry for more. However, with the attitude of contentment, you will be thankful for all you have been blessed with, without getting so desperate and filled with anxiety that you chase money at all costs. This is to your detriment or at the expense of others. Moreover, contentment will spur you to share what you have-especially with those in need, that less fortunate-not because you have an overabundance or because you are satisfied, but because you have a wealthy mindset-you know there is more from where that came from. A wealth mindset believes that there is always enough to spend and spare. This is the byproduct of contentment.

Contentment makes you believe that you are blessed, and therefore capable of blessing others. This is possible because, with a contented mind, your focus is on your needs and not your wants. With this, you can always find joy in knowing that you have all you need to succeed and make a difference in the lives of others.

Contentment motivates you to seek only the good things in life, knowing fully well that some things may be appealing but not expedient. With contentment, your motive is never to be a showoff, to flaunt what you have among those who are less fortunate than you. On the contrary, people who lack this cardinal virtue often become obsessed with having and hoarding more money than they need, and the result is often monumental degradation and a poverty mindset, you think you will never get ahead, that you are born to live a mediocre life, well below the poverty line.

Let me repeat that being truly wealthy is not about accumulating more money than everyone around you; that's just ego. If you harbor the wrong notion of wealth, you will end up being constantly miserable, desperate, and forever discontented. Even if you have what would have been enough, you will continue to feel restless and insecure, continuously fretting about the future, making you become a super hoarder and always seeking more.

Some people wrongly assume that the reason they are not happy is that they do not have enough money. Yet the truth of the matter is that greed is the root of their unhappiness. Sadly, since these people think having money is the be-all and the end-all, they had no problem coveting, depriving, or dispossessing others of their possessions for them to have their cravings. They are the "wild dog" in the dog-eat-dog mentality; they are the "big rat" in the all-mesmerizing "rat race".

The irony is that some of the most successful people that are being envied are those who achieved their success and wealth through hard work, dogged determination, integrity, and the top quality of being content. They faced challenges and setbacks in the journey just as anyone else, but the virtue they upheld paved the way for success and wealth for them.

In the classic - Turn Setbacks into Greenbacks: 7 Secrets for Going Up in Down Times, Willie Jolley, the award-winning motivational speaker writes: "I'm so thankful for those tough experiences, for losing my job, for being broke and busted and disgusted, with nothing to hold onto but my faith and a dream. If you've already been through a challenge in your life, the next time you come up against adversity, you're likely to be afraid. If you never had challenges, you could never find out just what you're capable of."

Willie Jolley narrated more of how the comeback to success from the sinking sand that almost destroyed his career was achieved through zeal and contentment, all that he had was enough to make him win life, he never needed too much, but only what is needed.

In your own words

....
....
....
....
....
....
....
....
....
....
....
....
....
....
....
....
....
....
....
....

From General D's Table. Money inside you is wealth, and money around you is Riches.

Leadership is not about titles, positions, or work hours, it is a relationship. This relationship that is built in people will always translate to wealth, because in people comes unending wealth and success.

Chapter 3:
The types of Wealth to build on

. "Wealth is not about having a lot of money; it's about having a lot of options" –

Oyewola Oyeleke – Author, Leadership & Financial Coach

Take my advice, take a deep search into these different types of wealth models, and let them guide you as you build your new life of success and prosperity.

As previously stated, being wealthy is not only when you have money, gold, houses, fast cars, and those other possessions, but it is about having everything that ensures a great and impactful life, that kind of life you can live happily without using money as the yardstick and can be so powerful to bring into reality the solitude of your imagination.

As we look deep into what the different types of wealth are and how they can be useful to make us achieve this goal, riches are usually measured as the net worth of an individual in tangible possessions like cash, properties, investments, money in the bank, etc. However, wealth is beyond money and financial assets. Because, just as I believe there is a danger in conflating being rich with being wealthy, there is also a danger in operating with a notion that there is only one type of wealth that everyone knows to be money but is supposed to be more than that.

Creating and building wealth – especially if your desire is for it to be sustainable and can provide for multiple generations – will demand a lot of hard work, character, and strategy from you in every area of your life.

You are not supposed to be broke, having possession and money is a good thing and it is designed to make anyone comfortable, but if you stay on it alone, you are already heading to frustration and retrogression. All we are working on is to see you become better and more successful beyond having money, not allowing money to overrule you, and making you myopic to see only these material things as "this is all that it is" because there is more to life.

In his book, "You can be rich too", P.V Subramanyam was explicit about those people whose mindset about riches is based on how much money they have, he said that these are the weakest in the chain of wealth people. They are just about to run like a peg-legged pirate that will eventually fall on the sands when the tide changes and take him off the ship to the seashore. You are not designed for mediocrity, and that is why you must be better than mere definitions, not basing your attention on 'money answers all things, rather than 'money answers to all things. because somewhere along the line, money will have to answer to a better thing that you are prepared to have.

When the world starts beating you down, programming you with the idea that life is hard and can only be solved with money. It starts telling you that as soon as you get out of school, you are going to go 'get a job,' – a good and lucrative job in a reputable organization, something that will make you get by." day-by-day, week-by-week, and month-by-month, you gradually forget who you are and the dream you had at the beginning of your life, accepting what you think life has to offer.

Henry David Thoreau, philosopher, and poet, once said: "I've learned this, by my experiment: that if one advances confidently in the direction of his dreams and endeavors to live the life which he has imagined, he will meet with uncommon success in unexpected hours."

Wealth is an intangible thing, but it produces tangible things that make life pleasurable and great. To understand all of this better, the ordered set of related categories used to group wealth according to its particulars, the following is a breakdown of the intangibles we cannot see with our eyes but will make any man a star; a wealthy superstar, and the strategies we can employ with them to make wealth a reality.

In this section of the book, we will look at the different types of wealth you can build your life on, and that they can be categorized into financial wealth (money); social wealth (status); time wealth (freedom); and physical wealth (health and wellness), that will assure anyone's transition from whatever level they are into prosperity.

1. Financial Wealth (money)

Financial wealth, simply put, is financial freedom. Though this is the lowest on the totem pole of wealth, many people solely focus on this because contemporary society teaches and directs the mind to obtain material riches to make them superhuman. Not only does our society do this, but life's theories have convinced the modern man to believe that money is the ultimate symbol of financial freedom and happiness. If you stick yourself solely to this model of wealth alone, you are already only one step away from financial ruin and unhappiness.

In my explanation, financial wealth is not about money alone but everything that makes you financially strong and comfortable. Financial wealth consists of understanding and mastering some fundamentals that are not only money. These include investing (assets vs. liabilities), spending (necessities vs. luxuries), budgeting (consciously allocating monies), financial literacy (through directed reading, listening to podcasts, attending events, etc.), arming yourself with financial principles that have withstood the test of time and that work every time you employ them.

 Picture yourself in the future where you never have to worry about money again, where you are financially secure forever. Imagine how that would change your family situation. It is an amazing feeling, right? Well, it is possible to achieve this kind of lifestyle as long as you commit to the process of mastering financial wealth principles. Here we are talking about three types of wealth. These present some of the biggest traps that prevent many from reaching their goals, financial illiteracy, spending more than you earn, lack of investments, and hanging around broke people.

Financial Illiteracy

Knowledge, they say is power, but what they are talking about is applied knowledge. – the knowledge you know and apply to bring the expected result. For example, a baby can hold a book but that doesn't make the baby smart. The mind of man is deep enough to contain all the information that could build a continent from scratch. Sadly, the mind is often not put to maximum use.

The mind of many has been kept uncharged due to laziness. For this reason, many problems that could have been resolved with mind power are being pushed to machines and other technological solution providers. A good example that everyone can relate to is the use of a calculator. Even though a student can easily do simple mathematical problems like adding 1325 with 5436 to give a total of 6761; someone would take a calculator to do this simple mathematics, instead of using the brain to solve them.

We are almost all guilty of this, Most times, we do not want to go through all that rigor to use our brains to achieve results, rather, to seek help when not necessary, and in such a situation, that moment of development will be stalled that the mind throw away the expansion opportunity, a lesser degree of wit as a task is now left for machines or other solution providers, their minds go to sleep, they let the calculator do all the work and vehemently kill their new level of knowledge.

The truth of the matter is that if the mind is not put to work and trained to understand how it will achieve a particular task, it will remain underutilized and redundant. And it has been said, a mind is a terrible thing to waste.

Spending more than you earn

Spending more money than you earn or have is very sweet; it is a very easy thing to do, and you don't need a college degree for that. Some people become so good at it that, that they are now called "spendaholics" and they boast about this gory attitude that kills one's future and drops them in the pit of a financial mess. Of course, we have to spend money on some things if we want to live a decent life. We have bills to pay and daily upkeep to maintain a decent standard of existence, but we have to continually practice financial intelligence, -how to spend money wisely and how to handle the money that we have, and the one that we have not yet seen. This is where many people are having problems with credit; they spend the money they assume belongs to them in the form of credit and here and then, put themselves in a deep financial mess than someone who took all his money and threw them into the middle of a football match.

In the final analysis, consistently spending more than you earn is an easy way to accumulate debt, thus, decreasing your capacity to overcome future financial challenges and reversals (up today and down tomorrow), and then there is the dreaded reality of having more months than money. All this indicates that you're probably working without a budget, you don't have any savings, and you don't know where the money from your paycheck went. This is one area that doesn't get better if you don't have a plan to make it better.

Lack of investment

More people are thinking they don't have enough money to invest. They simply can't find room in their budget to invest. Others simply assume that only the rich can invest. Of course, we all know this. A lot of us have things holding us back. Maybe we don't know how to get started. Maybe we feel totally out of our element. Or maybe now's just not the right time. There are a lot of excuses for not investing — and most of them don't hold up. If not all our excuses. whichever way, lack of investing is a harm to your financial future. Investing is proof that you don't only eat well today, but you are ready for tomorrow and generations to come.

Investing does not only mean that you are putting money into a good project that will yield good returns for you in the future, rather, investing is also making ready everything that will keep you financially ready and stable for today and tomorrow. This includes investments in yourself, investing in your goals and dreams, and investing in other people. One thing about true wealth is that you have to give to get; a closed hand can't receive anything in it. So, you must invest in profitable ventures which include all that we have highlighted and see that you are not a joker when it comes to doing the right things in the area of your finances, to see your wealth not only grow but be sustained as it should.

There is financial growth in wise investments. Can you put aside $20 a month? $100 a month or thereabout? Then congratulations! You have enough money to start investing for your future goals. And do you see any opportunity to upgrade yourself in education and acquire more skills? Then this is a movement to an upward acclivity.

If you walk closely with financial experts and analysts, you will see the economic impact of inflation on non-investors. Aside from making money via a return, investing can help you stay ahead of inflation. Inflation is the tendency of money to lose value over time. It refers to the rising cost of goods and services with time, and effectively, measures the rising cost of living. The inflation rate has slowly crept up over the past several years and is eating into the paychecks of many low and medium-earners, and even high-income earners. investing your money is a way to try and stay ahead of inflation.

2. Social Wealth (status)

Social wealth or social status is one of the most underrated types of wealth that exist because we naturally do not think of status as a measurement of wealth. We must understand that status has value, we just never have it connected in our minds that this is one powerful form of true wealth and lasting prosperity.

I will explain what social wealth is, and how it can be used to live a great life and be fulfilled forever.

Social wealth is built with some ingredients that are rare to find in human nature. When you find a person with social wealth, which is also called "social status," they have some very distinctive traits, which include integrity, reputation, high-quality character, and good body language. This is not an exhaustive list of all the fundamental traits of people with social wealth, but the listed elements cover the majority of what social wealth and status consist of.

Social status is a person's standing in society about how he is known to be in the area of respect, honor, integrity, and acceptability. A man of honor and integrity is not brought from heaven, rather, it is built with time and consistency, and anyone can achieve that status if they are willing to be strong in correctness and personal standing. It also refers to the level of honor, respect, and deference accorded to a person who has worked for it.

Some people have a better social status than others very few have this social wealth status because it is hard work to get. Social status can be ascribed or achieved. Ascribed social status is that which was assigned at birth, without considering one's abilities. The queen of England did not have to work for this gain, it was bestowed on her. Moreover, oftentimes, sex, age, family background, religion, and race are usually the basis of an ascribed relationship. For example, we consider a person born into a poor family to have a low social status. However, some people also achieve social status through their skills, abilities, and efforts. This may be based on factors like education, job, accomplishments, and marital status. For example, if someone belongs to lower status by birth, but he gets a good education and a prestigious job, he will achieve a better social status in society.

It is important to know that this status is never gotten in a day or bought with money. They come from years of experience, as well as discipline and commitment to the best of what they make life to be, the best that life has to offer through them. Moreover, social wealth largely comes down to how you interact with society. Of course, your material possessions and highly recognized accomplishments may sometimes be considered in conferring status on you, but real social wealth mainly deals with what kind of character you have and how others interact with it, how much they want to have you around, how much you have influenced people positively and deeply without even knowing that you are such an impact and influence on many. How others see you.

You can get the full details of how to build your social wealth in my book entitled GREET: Character That Influences Relationships.

Surrounding yourself with broke people

This is not to sound harsh, but you must watch the company you keep. Even the Bible says bad company spoils useful habits. If you are surrounded by broken and aimless people, it is unlikely that you will be able to raise your head above water, no one is on the boat to give you a hand a pull you in. This is because of two major reasons. One, these people will continually be liabilities to you, draining you of your much-needed mind that should be used to at least get above board, biting away the little resources and life left in you like blood-sucking vampires.

The second reason; is you would hardly get any motivation to exert yourself any further than this motley crew, no Arctic Tern that lived with Chickens ever tells how the north pole feels like.

A hallmark of Biblical wisdom is this: iron sharpens iron. In more worldly terms: if you are the smartest one in your group, you need to find another group that is bigger, smarter, and deeper than you presently are. Nobody can give you something they do not have. There is no growth in the comfort zone, and many times we have to become a "new" person to rise above our current financial circumstances. When you see better, you do better. You need to be around people that can lift you and get with people on the move so you can move on with them. You can't fly with eagles to the horizon when you're stuck on the ground with Turkeys.

3. Time Wealth (freedom)

Time wealth, the power of freedom is when you have your own time to spend just how you want it, where you have the license to spend it freely, and with whom you want to spend it, without hurting your other plans in life.

This is such a powerful dimension of wealth and one that is widely sought after by all people. Yet time wealth continues to prove elusive to many. There is never time to waste and too precious to throw away. It's often been said, you can make more money, but you can't make more time. It is often hard for someone to think of spending some time traveling or relaxing in some place far away, without thinking of work. It is often very difficult to enjoy time alone with family and friends without thinking, "Who is going to pay for all of this?" Especially if you're on a family vacation, how am I going to pay all my upcoming bills? All these questions will usually run up and down the spines of one's desires to go have a better life than they were.

Yet time wealth is so crucial to mental health and human comfort, if you want to be successful and peaceful, it is important to make out time to relax, meditate, learn, enjoy, and explore new things and places. The majority of people in these modern times spend all of their time working hard just to make a decent living. And "free time" seems like a luxury to too many. But we need this time to renew and refresh ourselves. We need this time to create a well-balanced and maximized life; we weren't born for all work and no play. Even a dog has its day.

But time wealth consists of mastering some fundamentals:

- Earning money outside of a traditional job structure

- An understanding that time is finite, and one must make the best use of it
- An understanding of how people trade time for money.

Here are some of the biggest traps that keep people away from achieving time wealth:

- Staying in a "secure" and conventional job structure
- Acting like time is an infinite resource, and thus not thoroughly planning with the time available
- 'Spending time to waste time; bulge less about life to watching TV or browsing social media all day long, partying to distraction, abusing drugs, and engaging in hedonistic practices.

Time is life. No one has all the time in the world, but those who have mastery over time will have more time for the things that will add value to their lives and the lives of those around them.

4.   Physical   Wealth   (health   & wellness)

When you are healthy in your body and your mind, you are sure a blessed and indeed a wealthy man, no doubt. This is a sure point for wealth and success that you can achieve more if you are ready to make your agility and strength take you. Taking good care of your health is not a function of fear of death or incapacitation, but it is a function of brilliance and necessity. A healthy body and mind are the most powerful breeder of success. Being positive and happy is the first key to good health which invariably brings wealth and success.

Physical wealth or "good health" as many know it to be is the glue that holds all the other types of wealth together, and also it is what makes you alive to enjoy that life.

Without health and vitality, we cannot achieve any other type of wealth, no matter how hardworking or very well connected, or at least not in the long term. We have come to realize that health is wealth, on many levels. Unfortunately, too many people fail to understand that health is the first wealth and must be taken as the most important aspect of life to pay attention to. People often fail to invest in their minds and bodies. Some aren't even aware that this is a worthy pursuit. They abuse themselves mentally and physically, and much of this abuse takes its toll on their quest for success and progress, and in their present and their more mature years to come.

I gave this literal demonstration to a taxi driver in New York just after I left the Brooklyn Magazine Festival to travel to Queens to finish up an assignment, and it made a lot of sense to me too. He was telling me about his struggles as an immigrant in the USA and how he works more hours than he sleeps and live a normal life. He was looking pale and struggling to finish the trip. His eyes were yellowish and heavy, forcing the eyelids to pucker, and his skin is pale, looking dehydrated. I knew immediately that this man is not at ease.

I had to cut him off in the middle of his narration which I think is more of complaints and frustrations. His reasons for overworking and not minding how his health was dying slowly was because of the piled-up bills, compounded family needs back home in Africa, many he left behind, who are always with open mouths like Eaglets waiting for their mum to throw food in their mouth. I had to give him some natural examples of what life is all about, using animals and plants as examples, probably it will sink into him better.

Even the strongest of Sharks get feeble and eventually die of malnutrition and weakness from hunger amid plenty in the sea; I began telling him how he can change his life from this state of frustration and pain and catapult himself into wealth and success without this unending struggle like life. As I continued with my examples to buttress my points, -the largest of Elephants got wiped away from a mere infection in its trunk. The strongest of beasts do hunger and die, young Lions become powerless and useless from injuries sustained in defending the pride or in the quest for food, or when hunting their prey. And sometimes old age catches up with them just at their peak as they rule over the jungle. The crops the farmer planted but never gave water to will dry up soon.

More people are chasing after money just like the powerful animals chase after other animals for food, they do all the things that lions do, they chase other animals as prey, day, and night; they catch and tear them apart and gulp them down and leave the carcass for the hyenas and the vultures. But it will get to a time when strength fails, age or ill health soon will set in and tell on them, and the old lion that they have become can hunt no more. He can't kill the beasts strolling by the stream or even near its den.

And the time will even come when he will no longer be able to defend himself or his goods anymore. Helpless and vulnerable, he will roam and roar, and struggle with the simplest tasks of life. He gets cornered by hyenas or some wild beast, and then nibbled at and eaten by vultures.

Why did I give the above illustration to the taxi man? Why is it important for you to care for your health and everything that you have? I asked him, and not behave like those in the animal kingdom now that you are able.

I have seen people who were strong and wealthy, looking healthy and glowing, basking in power and authority, and plenty to spend. But they never saw their health as a priority. They ran Wall Street and flew across every sky, globetrotting; doing everything they know how to do. They made the biggest deals and garnered the juiciest Shark Tank-type contracts. They built empires and conglomerates and accumulated impressive monetary riches and commercial and business and personal properties. Sadly, they didn't put the first thing first.

They neglected their health and became incapacitated in the prime of their lives. Their eyes begin to fail them, their minds became fuddled, and their limbs become weak. Their hands became too shaky and numb to sign another contract paper or check. It was then that they realized that they had done a disservice to themselves over the years of their lives.

So, dear friends, be smart and take care of your health, don't be like the New York taxi man that wants to work all day, not minding that he is deteriorating fast. Live consciously and responsibly, find the time to be good to yourself to the full, and take care of your mind, body, and spirit. Remember, physical wealth also consists of properly handling your nutrition, adequate sleep and rest, good personal and environmental hygiene, frequent exercise, proper mind, and body training, and regular medical checkups.

Health literacy is key. This is where all the happiness before, during, and after all the life pursuit comes to settle.

There are some common health and wellness eye-openers that I will want to share with you in this book, it is for you to take cognizance of what you may have been ignorant of. Those hidden effects that people hardly take seriously, but these effects are what will make a person who has planned and worked hard towards achieving his life goals enjoy them. Health advice is the best gift anyone can give his neighbor because a physically healthy man with sound mental health has already achieved the first level of wealth.

Let us take a peep at the health goals, they will be helpful if you take them seriously. I call them the wealthy man's heart.

Learn to work smart and not hard

Before any task or plan to start and complete a system, you should first take out time to think and come up with strategies that will help you achieve more results with less time and effort, having a clear strategy to prioritize your most important activities so you end each productive day feeling satisfied rather than overwhelmed, overworked, overcommitted, frustrated and your useful time been wasted. This is not a cut corner or the lazy vulture style syndrome, but it is working smart. Work smart is more of working from the head than from the muscles, you think of ways at which to achieve the surmountable task with less work, fewer expenses, less time, fewer people, less space, less energy, and less machine use.

Nobody has over 24 hours in a single day. Still, some very smart individuals manage their time in such a manner that they seem to have more time than anyone else. They get so much done in 24 hours. Others, however, lack good time management skills, their time just seems to get away from them and at the end of the day they have not done much of anything. This poor time management often leads to stress and distress.

Learning to leverage your work with other people's time and effort will help you achieve more with much more little effort and lesser time, let people help you achieve success faster by engaging them with your plans, with a good networking system and synergism. Trust people by giving them tasks to accomplish for you. Stop the workaholic boast and the 'I can do everything myself' gimmick, it won't do you any good than stress you out and make you achieve lesser results with more effort asserted and waste of time.

Hard work and smart work are different tools to complete a certain task. They are two different approaches to reaching the same result, but hard work puts more pressure on you;

your body, your time, and broken results, spending long hours while working smart relieve you of tension, that is to say, you have found more efficient ways to achieve a greater result with a little time spent and lesser or no stress, as your result will prove it on the quantity and quality of your result.

Avoid assumptions and neglect

How many times have you avoided seeing the doctor when you know you should? You assume this tiredness will pass, just like you become better after a few cups of coffee. You self-diagnose and tell yourself it is due to much stress and too little sleep; the sleeping pill will do the trick. But it is important that you take no chances when it comes to your health.

We should never assume that what we feel or what we think is happening to us is minor or temporal, thinking all that you feel or see is all that it is. We should communicate our needs and our feelings clear to those who are specialists in that field where we have needs, like doctors or dentists. We should ask questions from those who have the answers instead of jumping to conclusions about how we think our health status is.

Planning and making an adequate schedule for your medical checkups should be like how you plan your daily meals or even your daily work and even the way you work out your routines. This is not difficult; you can plan to visit your doctor every three months or have a personal nurse that will do routine checks and diagnoses on your body to see where you stand medically.

Many people will take their medication with levity and oftentimes neglect something else that they believe is more important; "I feel better already, I will not need to complete the medication the doctor gave me", these are killer actions that will bring you from hero to zero.

Over the long term, people who abused or neglected their physical health and mental health will pay for it sooner or later, they will put themselves at increased risk of losing all they have worked for and experiencing future regrets, environmental victimization, perpetration, those who are supposed to be entrepreneurs, employers of labor will eventually become the burden of their families and the society.

Do away with damaging habits

As busy as you can be, and as zealous as you are to achieve success and build wealth, seemingly little bad habits must be done with, like skipping breakfast, sleeping late or missing sleep altogether, high sugar consumption, eating junk food, refusing to urinate just because of the pressures of your workload, sparingly taking medications or ignoring the doses, staying dehydrated for too long every day because you don't feel too thirsty, and living a sedentary life with little or no exercise. In the long run, these habits could be detrimental to your overall health and well-being.

These illicit and damaging habits can put a man's general health in total disarray that it gets to a time that only the best of doctors could be able to manage the rot in that body system, and this is what we are fighting against in this book, we want the soundness of health which in return bring all-round wealth and prosperity.

In a TEDx Talk presentation by Eva Bettina Gruber, who spoke beautifully on the topic 'power of bad habits, especially as it can adversely affect anyone's natural abilities and strength if not adequately attended to, even when a man is born into a wealthy home and has arranged good wealth goals, they will not last before they are shattered. Such habits: I mean bad habits cause considerable damage to human existence – loss of great potential and motivation, premature aging of the human body, and the acquisition of diseases of various kinds. Such habits include the consumption of the following killing substances: tobacco, alcohol, drugs, and toxic and psychotropic substances that must be gotten rid of.

I have seen serious-minded people who want to transform their estate into a haven of success and wealth and started from the root which is to change their old lifestyles and habits. Negative attitudes that many don't see as a potential threat to success are quickly noticed, adjusted, and dealt with. Those intermittent lies, being late to appointments and at avoidable instances, lackadaisical attitude towards work and goals, and improper hygiene are choked by the neck and buried quickly.

you must notice those damaging habits that have kept you bound and on the ground for too long and crush them.

Poor mind management

Positive thinking is a powerful medicine for the body and soul; smiling often will keep you healthy and optimistic.

Our 16th U.S. President Abraham Lincoln once said: "Most people are as happy as they make their minds up to be."

I was thinking about the next chapter of this book as I drive through the NJ – 124 to exit 143 Irvington, my mind was hovering over so many things at the same time. How will I manage the next meeting scheduled to start in less than an hour? What will I tell my son after his tennis match that I could not meet up, and at the same time was thinking while still driving to pick up some consignment that arrived at the office? I also suddenly remembered the documents that must be signed, so that the final contract approval will meet up with the budget and allow production to start at the new factory.

All these hovered through my mind that I was lost in thought, also for the waiting supplier to get paid. At the same time, I noticed the wine color sedan, diving down very fast behind me, as if it will hit me from behind if I don't give way, my mind trying to come back to the present hour reality. I never knew that I had already swerved right and almost into the bushes after flying over the pavement, the rumble stripes by the pavement alerted me. The vibration and noise on my unstable tires made me veer back into the road. With my heart in my mouth, I knew I would have had a serious accident because my mind was not well coordinated.

To be successful and wealthy require a positive and well-maintained mind. there is no way a man will be successful in his endeavor and achieve his wealth purpose if all he does is use physical strength, rather than using the mind's power to imagine, think, visualize, and strategize.

There cannot be progress when the mind is unproductive. Our mind is the singular most important factor determining the quality of our life. A nourished, well-arranged mind has the potential of being our greatest asset to wealth creation, or if misused, our worst adversary, and if unused, becomes our disadvantage. If the mind is successfully controlled, it becomes our best tool for achieving wealth.

A poor and divided mind is a product of how unkept and mismanaged the owner handled it. The mind is the first gift of wealth that every man naturally has but produces that tangible and usable wealth if used rightly, and those that manage it wrongly will never amount to good results but rather a waste and non-result.

Let your mind be at rest. There are too many things that are competing for your attention, but you must learn to think of the most important, most useful, and most enriching first. Let your mind stay on one matter at a time, then, let it flutter out the solution and ideas for the envisaged results and desired success before you divert it to another.

Goals for achieving wealth are great but not enough on their own. This is where good mind management starts to make a difference and make you better than your contemporaries. You need to make your mind the most fruitful and powerful resource that you have to become wealthy, take stock of where you are, and look at what's stopping or inhibiting you from achieving your set goals.

You must also train your mind to overrun limitations and fear. The mind is one big world of its own, it can make anyone who uses it well and efficiently will become big, wealthy, and effective.

Your own words

....

....

....

....

....

....

....

....

....

....

Dr. Robert Claud
Wealth is in different ways
than one, your money,
status, time, and health.

The reason we do not
depend solely on money
alone is because life has
thought us that wealth is all
encompassing. It entails
everything that brings
beauty, love, intelligence,
and hard work, and
everything that gives hope,
relationship, and life.

....

....

....

....

....

....

....

....

....

....

Chapter Four:
The Nature of Riches

"Riches enlarge rather than satisfy appetites."

Thomas Fuller, English churchman, and historian.

Riches are often associated with money. To be called a rich person means that you are seen to have a lot of it. when it comes to money you must lose hunger for figures because figures can hold you in bondage to be bigger. money does not exist, it only exists in the mind of the poor, and as long as money exists in your mind it will hold you in bondage and never allow you to experience wealth.

Literarily, all type of exchange is carried out with money, life revolves around it, and nothing tangible happens without the use of money. When you have a reasonable amount of it, you can lay claim to many things, you are respected, and can own the beautiful things of life. The general belief is that being rich has much to do with how much money you have accumulated. You are required to keep that status for a long time and even have more money so you can keep that high level that you have attained.

A typical benchmark for determining if a person is rich is having a million in the amount in the currency you are operating in a liquid fund, you can also add the other pointers to quantifying a rich person with driving a few top-rated cars, having a house or more, and possessing some other valuables or eye-catching assets. oftentimes, a fake banner of being rich is lifted by some status-thirsty individuals to prove a point that they are also there, with those artificial coating to set it up; personal imbroglio on social media, pictures on a fantasy island that seems real, if not for the eye-opener that most come from a background effect, with pictures of God knows who owns the car they posed with, taking pictures on a beautiful building that we all know who owns it. Riches are deceitful.

Having the mindset of riches will usually limit you because you will always want more of it to meet up the game, and in that line, many will become frustrated when they lose a grip of it, many will idolize it and forget how much they have destroyed their environment, many will even do anything to have more of it. That is why it is important to note that money is only a tool, which if you have the right mindset will be available to you.

When you are rich and have money available to you, what will be more important is how you manage this money you have gathered, the ability to know how to operate it so it will not become like a horror movie, to know what to do with the money and how to expand and not condense it. In other words, it is not so much what you have but how much you handle it to be more efficient and useful for you and the world.

Riches equate to money, and money equates to power, and most of the time people tend to struggle to remain in power when it comes to money. You must bend yourself away from the ray of money mentality because it will make your work and work and forget to exert strategy and wisdom, focusing on riches will make you think of yourself more than you will think about how others are surviving, you will bother less if another suffers lose for you to have money. Some people would do everything and anything to maintain or get money and more money and power.

Riches tend to make you forget compassion if you are not cooked to think and act right. That is why it is advised and intentionally taught in this book to become big in your mind and become wealthy. Wealth comes from a spirit that has become blessed and a blessing to others. Riches are deceitful too; it will come to a time when you begin to forget your goals and ambitions and make you lose your composure and the nature you had before.

Are we saying being rich is bad? No; this is just an eye opener to those who have a lifelong dream to become rich because they want to impress or oppress others, they want to have money to live a good life or even help others, but do not know that there is a better level than to be rich, which is been wealthy. Here, you have become masters over money, and you have become a distributor of wealth.

Maximizing Riches

It is not the acquisition of money that brings fulfillment, but how well these riches are used. It is you not working for money but having money work for you. Just having money doesn't mean it will increase and multiply. It is how much intelligence you apply in managing and maximizing your money that determines what eventually happens; how you maintain your millionaire status.

As we have seen earlier, there have been many people who have made quick money or overnight riches but squandered or lost it all in less than two years or less and found themselves back in debt. Such people lacked the ability or wisdom to turn money into sustainable wealth. This invariably confirms that if not handled properly, money can take wings and fly. But this money can also expand to become Wealth for you. You must know what to do with the money when you have it, if not it will flee from you like trash in the wind. This is a natural law.

Getting a lot of money does not cure poverty or bring lasting satisfaction. Some people think that getting a very lucrative job will bring them satisfaction and fulfillment. Recent findings from the Centenary International Corporation and the Bureau of Statistics revealed some surprising facts about the Current Employment Situation (CES). According to the reports, while employment is increasing, so is the number of those leaving jobs as well as those seeking to fill vacant positions. Also, many who have been employed for a long time admitted that their major goal was to get a promotion so they could earn more money. But according to those long-time employees that were interviewed and got their promotions, that did not bring them the needed fulfillment that they sought.

Misconceptions and Mismanagement of Money

Like many other beliefs and practices that are handed down from generation to generation, people's perceptions of money may vary and sometimes are shaped by their family, or their cultural or environmental background. In some cultures and families, it is believed that young children should not be given money to buy things for themselves.

The idea is for that child not to become obsessed with money too early in their life, this will make them get so fixated on money that they begin to believe that life is all about money. This could push them to do the negative things they shouldn't do like stealing to have it, and the idea that you must have it whether by trick or by crook, anyhow you think you can have it, just get it!

This deep love for money could lead them to seek money no matter what it will cost them or cost others. This "love of money" could lead to going into evil acts of over-consumerism, buying things they see and hunger for, things that are not needed but a deep craving will make them want because they have the money to get them.

The mistake with this approach, although well-intended, is that children grow up not knowing that money is around and everywhere, they have not seen much of it and cannot believe that it could be easy to get. they do not know how to manage or multiply money because they have not been taught; they become money spenders, not money makers as they begin to see some money come into their hands. They are now even scared to have much of it or to desire the big things money can buy, they think it is too much and should not be heavily craved for as they were being taught.

They don't learn what money really is and how it really should be used. They know nothing about making profitable investments or paying serious attention to the stock market because they never had a relationship with money. They never knew that money brings in more money.

Many parents in this culture hole simply don't consider it necessary to have the money talk with their children. This could be possible because they do not know better or are scared that schooling their child on money matters will make them have too much knowledge of it and thereby make them go after it like it was pancake and honey, that after the first taste of it, they will become obsessed.

Ultimately, such children grow up as financial illiterates, they find themselves among the masses who spend money faster than they make it. They become "Money Hungry". Some people believe that money is merely for spending. And as soon as they start working and earning money, they start spending it like there is no tomorrow, before long, their earnings become too small to cater to their needs, and the rat race starts aiming for a pay raise or a better job that will pay more to win their high needs, not remembering that it will come back to the same point of dissatisfaction and higher standard of living that they were in before.

There is no rhyme or reason for the way they spend money. It's like "easy come, easy go" is their philosophy. Consequently, and sadly, they develop a pattern of living and random spending that drives them into poverty and ultimately locks them into that environment.

You may see a person who does not have enough money to pay their children's school fees. Still, these people buy expensive cell phones and the latest and the most expensive electronics. These things have no lasting value, and they bring in no income, except they are for business and commerce. This may describe someone who is driving an expensive rental car, like a Mercedes with no reciprocal income. This is a misplacement of priorities, a sure recipe for financial disaster.

The Rich Poor Guy

The look on Danila's face showed that something was amiss. It was obvious, from her fidgety movements, that she was finding it hard to keep herself together. She was about to lose her composure as she attended to the young man standing before her. She was a cashier at a bank, and I noticed that despite her visible discomfort, she did her duty to her customer. From where I stood, I noticed a few drops of sweat on her face despite the AC working at optimum capacity. I also noticed that she stole glances at the young man who seemed to be in his 20s.

What could the matter be? I asked myself this same question that has lurked in my mind aloud: Had she seen any discrepancy in the customer's account? Had there been some foul play in the course of the transaction? Did she suspect that the man was up to something sinister? I was on high alert in case there was a need to press the emergency button. My eagle eyes darted glances in their direction as I continued to work on my file. The young man had come for a withdrawal, and as soon as he received his cash, he left the bank building.

Soon after, Danila came to sit with me and our coworker, Emma, who had been in the reception area since this drama started, just after we had finished a transaction with another customer. Danila couldn't disguise her shock as she breathlessly told us that the young man who had just let her counter had made a cash withdrawal of $10,000 from his savings account with our bank, just after making such a withdrawal a day ago. There was no doubt she knew that disclosing such vital information about a customer was unethical, breaking all rules of customer confidentiality, but we are all bankers, no big deal though. However, there was something that she had to get off her chest, to share with us.

I must admit, I was not pleased with her unprofessional manner, but I was curious to know what she found so intriguing about this particular customer. It was then that Danila revealed that this casually dressed young man had over $3, 000,000 (three million dollars) in his savings account. This was even more shocking because the maximum savings an account holder could have protected by the Federal Deposit Insurance Corporation (FDIC) should be about $250,000, perhaps a little more, depending on the way the owner structured their finances. Another $4,000,000 (Four million dollars) is in the family account in which he is the sole signatory.

This young man's account had far exceeded the legal limit and sent Danila into a tailspin of wonder and confusion. I was stunned because it was indeed rare to find a young man having such a whopping sum in his savings account. I couldn't help but admire this unknown young man. Because I was able to see him through my office window between the bank reception room and the ATM drive-through yard, I took a closer look at him as he stood on the street with his friends, close to an ATM.

He stood about 10 yards away from his red Bentley Bentayga Hybrid SUV in the bank's parking lot. At that moment, I had assumed he was in his early 20s because of his fresh and babyface look; I later learned he was 28. He had a well-trimmed beard and a low-cut hairstyle: his dark skin gleamed like a polished Formica board. His casual dress had a touch of handcrafted gold embroidery, and on his t-shirt was this shiny material I cannot put a name to, his pair of shoes and socks matched the color of his sunglasses. From his appearance, you will know he is a fashionista; his acquaintances are all dressed like him but in different bright colors and styles, I could only assume that he was going out for a party with his friends.

Loud music blared from the parked SUV. This young man had captured my eager attention. As I sat in the reception area with Emma, who was sipping tea, I heard the young man telling someone on his phone that they would be having drinks at a very expensive bar, but he must bring the cash he kept with him the night before. He made it clear that they would be blowing the $10,000 he got from this transaction on drinks and fun in that one night of partying – he was trying to show off his abilities to everyone around the bank premises as he spoke loudly. He even asked if that sum of money would be enough for drinks alone, for that one night, or did he need to get more money.

"Wow, this guy is rich!" I couldn't help but blurt out. This was the moment that Emma had been waiting for: she had some things to share with us about this young man. Danila and I listened with rapt attention as Emma shockingly narrated, "That young man is one of the poor guys in this town; I laughed out so loud that I became ashamed of my outburst; that indeed caught my attention.

Three months ago, he still had up to seven million dollars in his account and over ten million dollars in the family account that he inherited. By now he has spent almost everything on endless nights of partying, and daily shows of shameful spending competitions. Now he has come again today to make another of his usual daily withdrawal for another day's wastages.

He assumes, he is a high-rolling kid..." Although Danila and I were initially attracted to the young man, she became as shocked as I am and more disappointed as to how he handled his money; he seemed to be a spendthrift, throwing his money away on drinks and high times.

Emma had more to tell us. "I used to be his account officer," she went on. "The first day his life insurance claim documents came landing on my table was the day he walked in with his lawyer to open the account. He seemed like a serious-minded person who was desperate to prepare himself for a brilliant future. He lost both his parents in a terrible domestic accident last year and consequently got their entire estate and total life insurance benefits, which amounted to seventeen million dollars. He has since been spending so much without looking back, nothing like investing or building a future. He is the accurate description of a rich-poor guy- rich with plenty of money for a season but poor in wealth creation and his future.

He was spending indiscriminately, like this money will never finish, but people don't realize that the bigger money is the one that gets to disappear quicker than the smaller amount of money because a bigger mirage pool deceives more than the small one, big mirage pools usually disappear after the second stare." it's a known fact.

Emma's words touched me as she described this young man who had so much money but had the mentality of a poor man, someone who has no plan to maintain and expand his income and better his life.

Goose pimples dotted my skin under my Tommy Hilfiger white shirt and red tie. Despite all his money, he could not be counted among the wealthy because money alone is not wealth. Money is a means to an end but only if you know what you have in your hand and use it for a good purpose.

To grow your money, you must know how to have the mindset that says, Because I am a good steward of my money, my money will grow. Wealth is created by people who multiply their money, and they create things that produce more money. Those who don't realize that and have money will see that the money they have today has disappeared as soon as they acquire it. It has often been said, a fool and his money are soon parted. The Bible states: Proverbs 14:7 "Stay away from a foolish man, for you will not find knowledge on his lips. The wisdom of the prudent is to give thought to their ways, but the folly of fools is deception.

Again, Riches Don't Equate to Wealth

I can't say this enough: being rich is not the same as being wealthy. Riches encompass money and other means of exchange that you can use to satisfy your desires, but having wealth is having the mindset, attitude, intellect, acumen, and everything else that directs money from every source and straight to you.

According to T. Harv Eker, in his book. 'In Secrets of the Millionaire Mind: Mastering the Inner Game of Wealth, you must have a money mindset: "Becoming rich isn't about getting rich financially as about whom you have to become, in character and mind, to get rich. I want to share a secret with you that few people know: the fastest way to get rich and stay rich is to work on developing yourself! The idea is to grow yourself into a "successful" person. Again, your outer world is merely a reflection of your inner world. You are the root; your results are the fruits" (Eker, p183).

I like the way my teacher and mentor in high school, John Masaru, clarified this distinction for me. According to him, when you have enough money to buy the countless luxuries and needs in your life, then you can be counted as rich, but when you have built intelligence and intelligent people as your wall, your power and the people's power become your prosperity.

The people you created from the rich deposits from your inner self become your time machine and strength, by then, you have surrounded yourself with sustainable wealth.

When you have come to a point in your life where you do not need anything anymore, that everything that you ever need in your life is settled and taken care of, then you are indeed wealthy.

When you combine this network with applied knowledge, quality investments, business smarts, royalty agreements, and the rest, then you have arrived truly wealth avenue. To buttress this fact, let me add this: a rich man cannot afford to lose all he has acquired, if he does, he will never be the same again; he will be ruined, destroyed to ashes, and sunk. If his house burnt down or robbers stole his money, he would be finished. Basically, and here is the sad fact, he is only "rich" when he has money and while it last, his prospects are uncertain because his life was based on assets with temporary value, this hero suddenly becomes a zero.

On the other hand, since the truly wealthy man's worth is not solely based on money, the property he owns, or the other material things he possesses, he can easily weather any storm or misfortunes, because they are temporal stalls to him. He is never anxious about losing any of his material possessions because he is the wealth machine, he knows that he will find other opportunities to re-align and get something bigger, better, and grander, that is why he fights hard to keep himself strong, careful about his sanity and health, and feed himself with mega blaster education.

His repertoire of options rooted in integrity, intellectual abilities, knowledge, and investment in people will create avenues for him to recover from his temporal losses and get even better. He is moving in the example of the Nobel laureate Samuel Beckett who once wrote: "Ever tried. Ever failed. No matter. Try again. Fail Again. Fail better., and never fail again"

Warren Buffett, an American business leader, genius investor, and magnanimous philanthropist was once asked what he would do to become wealthy if he had to start all over again. His simple answer was that he would drink some water, sit himself down and count what his worth is. He knew that knowledge and a productive mind are all that are needed, and he had the confidence that he would always be wealthy more than over the first stage.

We can conclude from that response that the hallmark of wealth versus riches is the right use of one's intelligence.

Dennis Kimbro brings this concept home when he writes in The Wealth Choice: Success Secrets of Black Millionaires: "Each of us desires the finer things in life-fame, fortune, and respect-but few go beyond just hoping and wishing for them. The easiest thing to do, whenever you fall short of the mark, is to blame lack of ability or circumstances for your misfortunes. The easiest thing to forget, especially when fate has been unkind, is that you were born to succeed, not fail" (Kimbro, p181).

Turning Riches to Wealth and Prosperity

During a media interview, Mr. Ituah Ighodalo, a much-celebrated pastor, businessman, and philanthropist, was asked how he became so successful with claims that he does not have any area of need, he is successful in all his endeavors without cutting corners-as the norm is with most so-called successful people and especially, those that serve God in a hostile environment, who rose from grass to grace. His response was so direct and thought-provoking that I decided to share his testimonies with you.

According to Mr. Ighodalo, success is relative. It is not about having a lot of money or properties or looking around at investments that make you feel happy and fulfilled, all fuzzy inside, as a wealthy or successful person. According to this great man, success means doing things, justly, rightly, and according to specification. It is adding value to yourself and the people around you. He added that success simply involves avoiding compromise in quality, ethics, and good morals.

A student of the Kwame Nkrumah University, Accra expanded on these simple words of inspiration from Pastor Ighodalo. Three major things give power and wealth, 1. People, 2. power, and 3. money. the first one is the most powerful, it is what brings power into reality and money into functionality.

As Dr. Ian Smith, author of Shred-The Revolutionary Diet, explained, "Wealth gives you options to do less of what you don't want to do, and more of what you want to do. So, pursue wealth. Make it important to become wealthy."

Essentially, turning riches into success and wealth requires a conscious effort to set one's priorities right in life. For instance, when you have a certain amount of money you must decide the best way to spend it at that particular time. Is it to meet some specific personal need? Or will you use it in a way that will not benefit you? Whatever option you choose you must understand that it is paramount that you keep your personal needs simple and basic and strive to have what will keep you content. This way, you will have fewer cares in this world. With his mindset, you will be able to meet the needs you have desired as well as help others who may need your help. This, My Friends, is the true essence of success and wealth.

Your own words

....
....
....
....
....
....
....
....
....
....
....
....
....
....
....

Felix Dennis
The incredibly wealthy
founder of maxim
magazine writes:

The incredibly wealthy
founder
of *Maxim* magazine writes:

"Let me repeat it one more
time. Becoming rich does
not guarantee happiness. In
fact, it is almost certain to
impose the opposite
condition – if not from the
stresses and strains of
protecting it, then from the
guilt that inevitably
accompanies its arrival."
Rather get all to become
wealthy, so you will extend
riches to the world

....
....
....
....
....
....

[94   ]

Chapter Five:
Science of Wealth

"Wealth isn't necessarily about money; it is more the wealth that you have within your soul and what comes out through your heart and mouth."

Catherine Pulsifer, author of Change Your Life-Successful People Who Did (Why Not You) Wealth is who you are.

In the New York Times Magazine article, Empire State of Mind, Blair McClendon writes: "High profile singers, athletes, actors and so on often make their real money from endorsement deals rather than their day jobs. What separates the billionaires from their peers is that they turned endorsements into equity" (McClendon p.31). This alchemy of wealth is directly related to the study of science and the building blocks that ensure growth and multiplication. Because all living things are made of cells, we study how cells grow and multiply in the body, and how living things continue to survive, grow and expand as the cells grow and expand. Relating science with wealth creation is a good way to interpret the characteristics and life of wealth creation.

The Science of Wealth

When I was in college, I used to enjoy biology class. It was full of practical illustrations of life, and the study of living organisms and non-living elements, divided into many specialized fields that cover their morphology, physiology, anatomy, behavior, origin, and distribution, learning how life evolves, and how survival manifests itself in all creation. This was more fun than education to me. Studying living and nonliving things in the classroom was so intriguing. Specifically, how living things are characterized, and how things come to be. For a better understanding of wealth, I decided to highlight the characteristics or building blocks of how things come to be and how they survive. I will draw inspiration from some of the characteristics of living things as they relate to creating wealth.

In a holistic sense, wealth is life itself. It communicates and gravitates towards what gives it more life and meaning. That's why a discussion of its birth, nurturing, and distribution is so important for us. You must understand how birth comes about and how it is sustained. To become wealthy, you must hold onto and multiply your income, you must learn what gives it life and it will survive in this world.

King David spoke in Psalm 112:3: *"Wealth and riches shall be in His house"*. You can see that wealth has life, they will live in a house because the house gives it breath and every ingredient that makes it survive. And that is why we will be learning how best to attract this good gift by understanding the science behind it. We want to apply all available resources and illustrations to help us have a good understanding of how wealth creation works. To become more successful than the other person looking for money, you need to think beyond the box and apply more common sense and creativity. To have what others don't have, you must do what others won't do or know to do. You must expand yourself to meet uncommon goals.

On the song "Moment of Clarity" on "The Black Album," Jay-Z, one of a handful of Black billionaires' raps: "I can't help the poor if I'm one of them, so I got wealthy beyond rich and gave back, to me that's the win-win."

Let us dig into the different characteristics of what gives wealth life.

Nutrition

All living things consume food and convert that food into energy for the body. Applied to wealth, nutrition refers to the continued acquisition or intake of knowledge. The Bible talks about "renewing your mind." And wealthy people are identified by the richness and vibrancy of their minds. All wealthy people have well-stocked home libraries. Leaders are readers. They have learned how to sustain their wealth. The legendary motivational teacher and author once said: "Rich people have small TVs and big libraries, and poor people have small libraries and big TVs." How true?

The bottom line: A rich person has his money for a short period, while the wealthy have amassed enough sustainable resources that they don't have to worry about money. They are healthy in this reality. They never stop learning. Whether it's Warren Buffet or Jay-Z, they know where they are going so, they can lead the way. They update their knowledge; they are lifelong learners.

Nutrition for wealth builders is knowledge. This has to do with continuing education and empowerment. Wealthy people are not just known for having money. They are trained to create money. They have this value embedded in them to create money from the inside out. Wealthy people get wealthier as they continue to feed on all types of information from market reports, interactions with like-minded people, and attending training sessions, workshops, seminars, and conferences, which invariably keeps their minds youthful and vibrant.

The late and great Dr. Maya Angelou, a good friend of the billionaire Oprah Winfrey, once said: "You can only become truly accomplished at something you love, and you learn from. Don't make money your goal. Instead, pursue the things you love doing, learn everything about it, and then, do them so well that people can't take their eyes off you."

Wealthy people can control and manage their money to create a sustainable lifestyle. The International Pastors and Partners Conference (IPPC) of the Believers Loveworld INC, aka Christ Embassy is one of the playgrounds of knowledge I am aware of. I experienced this congregation of greatness with the mind-blowing and ever-vibrant Pastor Chris Oyhakilome. I was in the midst of hundreds of thousands of leaders, captains of industries, pastors, and movers and shakers in business and entrepreneurship from all over the world. They came together to discuss and analyze things that the ordinary man on the street will never hear or even consider. There are so many such places of training and learning where deep minds come together to get sharpened. As the Bible says, "As iron sharpens iron, so one person sharpens another" (Proverbs 27:17).

There are hundreds of gatherings and retreats and conferences where deep minds come to get sharpened for untold knowledge and direction. There are hundreds of avenues where the mind can get sharpened with rich nutrition. This is the food for thought and the energy that drives wealth creators, those that will build and nurture the inherent ability to create wealth. In addition, there are seminars, conferences, schools, symposiums, trade fairs, guilds and associations, media gatherings, and so on so someone must attend and get skilled and prepared to take over. Without knowledge, wealth is limited, money cannot grow and expand as it should.

The natural growth of the rich one is restricted when it is just for a short period. To be truly wealthy, you must be in the driver's seat. The weight of this responsibility is not heavy if you know how to carry the load. And to carry such a load does not require muscles or struggles but knowledge, wisdom, and understanding.

Every year, over six million people with outstanding records of success, especially in business, attend enduring workshops and training with top training firms and gurus of wealth creation. They travel from far away countries to attend these meetings, spending lots of money for short hours of training, in many cases. Sometimes this special attention to their personal growth will cost them more than any amount anyone will want to part with, - they think in their minds that such an amount can be thrown into business and yield, even more, why should I waste such an amount on a mere regular training or seminar. The irony is that there are too many people who would not attend this life-affirming training even if it were to be free of charge. They would consider it a waste of time because they are comfortable with their surviving business, and happy with the money they are earning which keeps them at their limited level of growth. It's like thinking that the one room they are in is the entire mansion.

No matter your age, status, or position, you must keep learning and acquiring skills. I often encourage my students and anyone with me with a variation of that quote from Albert Einstein — "never be afraid to learn something every day, and anytime, and from anything, because the moment you stop learning is the moment you start dying."

Pick the right knowledge

All knowledge is spendable currency, depending on the market. I was part of a selected group of students at the Government College, Ojo in Lagos, Nigeria, to visit the zoo in the spring of 1988. A small group of 23 girls and 7 boys attended with our biology teacher, Gregory Madu. He was the lead excursionist with a few staff of the local government board for tourism as we visited the old university zoo. There is a remarkable lesson that I got from that visit. It made me understand that everybody must find their key strategy for their attainment of knowledge, and what works best for them.

I observed this hyena as I cut my grilled steak and threw a portion to this animal. He rushed to it, sniffed it, then turned away from it. I was somewhat embarrassed, thinking that he would be delighted to enjoy the spicy, well-grilled meat that I tossed to him. I was curious as to why this animal would turn away from such a delicacy.

The lesson I learned was that carnivorous animals don't eat processed meat. Mr. Gregory Madu watched me all the while, even though the act of throwing things into the animal's cages was not permitted. He spoke a little above a whisper as he explained that animals such as Hyenas and Lions eat raw meat; they enjoy it more when they kill it themselves. When this meat is fresh with all the blood in it and the warmness of the bones that still carry life in its marrow.

The meal that I threw in that cage is poison to this carnivorous animal and it disgusted the Hyena. In my ignorance, I did that animal a disservice. What the Hyena craved was what I had not given him. This is how it is with our finances: each individual has a particular diet that makes them grow and survive. We cannot all continue on the same path. We must find the diet or path that will make us strong in the journey we must travel to achieve wealth; we all move to the beat of a drum with different dance steps and movements.

There is the sad story of Rowel Andreas of the Philippines, a world-class Citroen mechanic, who traveled all over Asia in the early 70s. Every Citroen car owner knows him or must have heard about him because of his prowess in repairing those expensive cars. He made a lot of money in the early 80s. He made a name for himself "Rowel de Citroen", a name that cornered and conquered every other motor mechanic of that age.

But his business died a natural death as soon as newer models of cars became his competition. The Citroen was no longer in vogue because customers wanted something newer and better than the PSA Peugeot-Citroen model. Andreas was out of business because he could only repair just one type of car, Citroen's model'. He didn't think ahead to when the Citroen would not be in high demand or vogue again, he did not learn other ways to repair any other type of engine or the newer technologies that were coming up.

The moral of this story: You must constantly add knowledge, the nutrition of the mind that will sustain riches. This is the one area where too many people falter and fall flat on their faces, derailing their dreams and aspirations. If you don't seek knowledge, acquire new skills, and new levels of understanding, you will not grow, and sooner lose the vigor and energy to compete and continue in the life of the business. It is the acquisition of knowledge that makes wisdom grow.

Respiration

Respiration means breathing, inhaling, and exhaling God-given air. For any living thing to survive the next minute, it needs to breathe in air and breath out air.

In the area of our discussion, wealth involves taking in and giving back, providing service to mankind, and in return, getting back rewards and benefits. Truly wealthy people are not hoarders or self-centered or self-absorbed people. They are humble and grateful people. As they take in information and knowledge, they are eager to teach and share with others, as they accept contracts and businesses, they also deliver good projects and infrastructures and help with goods and services to better the lives of the people.

Wealthy people don't just have things for the sake of having them, they do because of what others will benefit from it. They know that their wealth is not just a blessing to them but for the betterment of the lives of the people around them and are always eager to give out and bless others. Many of them have philanthropic organizations that promote the welfare of others, typically through financial donations, transfer of knowledge, or provision of service. Being philanthropic develops empathy and broadens our perspectives of the world which invariably builds us into bigger prosperity and wealth. One example is the Bill & Melinda Gates Foundation (BMGF), William Redington & Flora Hewlett Foundation, Robert Wood Johnson Foundation, Li Ka Shing Foundation, Mohammed bin Rashid Al Maktoum Foundation, and the welcome trust are all non-profit organizations and individuals committed to fighting poverty, disease, and inequity around the world, another one I will be introducing you to is the Homefront Care Foundation which I run with my wife, helping the needy and struggling communities with educational materials, medical support, community water projects, and food drive support system.

The process of earning and gaining, while also rendering service and value to others will determine if you are wealthy or not. A wealthy man operates businesses that derive their strength and sustained success from what he gives society from what he gains. The rich man is all about what he can get, not necessarily what he can give.

There are exceptions to this rule, there are rich people who are philanthropic, and many of them don't hesitate to cut corners to ensure their profits are regular and bountiful to the detriment of society. Some may even sell substandard products to unsuspecting consumers, all because they want to make as much profit as they can in the shortest time possible.

In the real sense, however, such people and their businesses and riches cannot be sustained because they negate the nature of living in prosperity. No living thing can survive without taking in and giving out.

What makes a man alive and survive is embedded in his system, that same thing he has inside is broken down into dimensions and layers that produce and release energy which helps him grow bigger and stronger. This enables him to continue to live well and have enough to purge out waste which is a nutrient for other living things. this is the circle of life; it gives and gets back all the positive energy that they are putting out. If there is no letting out, there can't be a getting back. That is what produces stagnation and death that eventually will set in.

When this stagnation sets in, it becomes toxic, and the death of business and life is sure to follow. This is how many rich people fail to become successful because they hold onto what should be freely given out to the world and God, things they are not supposed to take with them, and those things they are supposed to give to help others are held because of greed which in return causes decay.

When you become mature enough to know that the more successful people you have around you, the more your horizon broadens, and money will multiply to become fame and accomplishments. These are not just "lucky people". They create their own "boom". It was in one of my business awakenings classes that I taught the students that - when you pour into men, you will spread wider because, the more the vessels you fill, the more oil you own ."

Even more valuable is one of my often-quoted sayings: "You can have everything in life that you want if you just give enough of what other people want." Wealthy people are always ready and willing to pay it forward. Hendrick Gail Hart, a Swedish professor, once said: "A very successful man amid poor hundreds is too indigent to be accounted as the rich, he will become poorer than those he thought he was Lord over."

A wise man will always become a mentor to others because his wisdom is what makes him bigger, and more valuable for others to become his mentee. By the example of his discipline and lifestyle, he raises men to become like him. He teaches them to take over territories and businesses. His empowering prowess makes him even bigger and more respected because he has raised men who are now respected and honored.

Movement (Internal or External)

'A rolling stone gathers no moss," so goes the popular saying. Wealthy people detest stagnation or complacency in any area of life. They want to keep moving, exploring, and advancing. They are not just learning new skills and acquiring new knowledge but are also eager to apply this knowledge and skills to ensure future progress.

When you see a person that is progressing, know that they are well versed in many areas, not just one. They may have a specific area of expertise, but they are not opposed to discovering other avenues that may sprout from that main concentration. For example, there is Ahmir "Questlove" Thompson who is a five-time Grammy Award-winning musician, musical director for The Tonight Show Starring Jimmy Fallon, culinary entrepreneur, and author of several New York Times bestselling books, Grammy-nominated audiobook creator. His film directorial debut, Summer of Soul, earned him the Grand Jury Prize at the Audience Award at the Sundance Film Festival, Best Documentary at the 75th British Academy Film Awards, Best Documentary Feature at the 94th Academy Awards, and Best Music Film at the 64th Annual Grammy Awards. Simply put, wealthy people, like Questlove, love to know something about everything and everything about something, especially when it comes to their chosen vocation. That is like the "writer" who writes poetry, novels, screenplays, blogs, podcasts, and documentaries and teaches at various colleges and universities.

Continued mental and academic training is key to determining whether you are wealthy or just rich. A rich man may be skilled in an area of specialization, but often only for a short period because they are so fixated on that one thing that brings them money, 'money'. They become easily distracted and soon lose interest in something that would've worked out if they spent a little more time learning them. The rich man is about the get-rich-quick scheme and to remain rich as far as the money is stable and keeps coming, they will never want to explore other grounds of interest that will benefit others, rather what brings them money.

They are often overtaken by the tide of change they hadn't anticipated. They had no interest in the long game. On the other hand, the truly wealthy man has foresight. He keeps putting himself in a physical, mental, and psychological state that ensures future success, and sustained success. He puts all these ducks in a row, and he keeps on trucking. He is never out of style because he creates the style. If he can't find a way, he will make a way.

Wealthy people are self-motivated and self-sufficient, and the example of their lived lives teaches this in formal and informal ways. The legendary Wayne W. Dyer was a man who lived his truth until the very end of his life when he died at age 73. In his final book, 'I Can See Clearly Now', he writes: "If I was to spend my adult life teaching, lecturing, and writing on self-reliance, then I needed to learn to rely upon myself and thus be in a position to never be dissuaded from this awareness. What better training ground for teaching self-reliance than an early childhood that required a sense of independence and a need for self-sufficiency?" (Dyer, p19).

Indeed, the ability to move from what is trending now to what will be the next new and improved trend is to have uncommon foresight. To know the best way to see the future is to create the future. The wealthy note all the trends, but they don't get locked into them. They always have their heads to the sky; they have a vision.

Every day you see people with vision move from one stream of thought to another stream of thought, moving from one enterprise to the next, from one business to another business or company. Because they have multiple streams of income they have created, they never worry about going broke. Making money for them is as easy as breathing in the fresh air. There is no strain on their gain. This tendency to keep moving is for two main reasons: one, they are searching for better ideas, and better ways to serve their customers and consumers; two, they are searching to increase their wealth and to escape the attacks of unworthy competitors.

Please note, that if wealthy people decide to stay in one type of business or enterprise, they continue to explore new terrains and uncover new ideas to run with, and if they want to explore different fronts, they capture each field with distinction. They take the risk and break the rocks to find water, just like Abraham who had to leave his place of comfort to do what God directed him to do. In the Book of Genesis, Abraham was wealthy with everything that makes one counted as prosperous. You cannot remain in one office or trade and think you have arrived, or never tried to add new ideas and acumen to the one business or trade if it's just that one you have. Just because you are seeing some cash roll in, your continued success demands that you keep it moving, adding flakes and flax, new trends and lines, becoming that rolling stone and not the stagnant one that carries moss that has settled on it and threatens to hold it in one place.

It is insanity to think that you can do the same thing over and over again and produce different results. This mindless repetition will only lead to stagnation and the death of all your dreams. This is a sure way to rob yourself of a bright and prosperous future.

Excretion

The simplest explanation for excretion is to eliminate waste. It is that natural process to not hold what the body will not be needed for survival, to not cause disease or death to it. To continue the process of life there must be a way in which the unwanted food in the body is taken out before it becomes toxic and poisonous. This waste can be passed out through almost all the parts of the body, the ear, nose, eyes, skin, anus, and so on. To continue our discussion, we need to understand the process of food and water intake and how it is processed by the different organs of the body and afterward, the process of pushing out all the unwanted waste that could be toxic to the body.

Holding onto what is not supposed to be kept in and around us can become poison to us. It is not everything that we consume that should remain in us, a large part that the body does not need is processed and sent out as waste to fertilize other living things that need our waste for their food and in the long run, becomes beneficial to us as food.

In the area of wealth creation, this law could be so strange to people who consider themselves to be rich. As we earlier discussed, the rich man with his money will believe that they are supposed to enjoy and keep their money for themselves, they have worked very hard to earn the money and the only thing on their mind is to see it increase, anything other than that is foolishness to their reasoning. They believe that taking away part of this money or sharing their riches will diminish it. Their self-worth is based on the size of their accumulation. All they think about is adding more to their account, seeing their account balance is adding more zeros so they can continue to answer the millionaire title and not lessen it.

A very good example of holding back what is not meant to be kept within and around us is money. No man has become richer by holding more money in his bank account this is an easy way to lose more money as that demon called inflation sets in you, the total of your money begins to lose value, and the interest rate will become nothing to smile home about. Keeping money to yourself is proof of insecurity and fear, that you will hold on to money shows that you cannot take the risk and push out the money to build more for yourself. Most rich people who keep money are also too lazy to put their skills and expertise to work, they feel relaxed and safe as far as they have the money they can see, and that is why they cannot be wealthy.

Apart from expanding ourselves, excretion teaches us to give out to the cosmos (earth). If you have not gotten to the level of giving money for philanthropy, helping to solve the needs of society, providing solutions to the pains of the poor, helping to fund research to solve a problem, investing in education, and so on, then you have not understood the law of wealth creation.

On the other hand, the wealthy mind knows that the accumulation of money and other material things to himself without pushing it out to solve problems could be poison to his growth and survival, whatever he has is for to help people and society, and to be used for his personal and business expansion. His money will be used for more research, experimentation, and exploration of new skills and knowledge for himself and those around him. With this, he begins to benefit from the ground he has given to, his excretion will become the manure for his benefits and growth.

When you understand this law and take a hold of it, you will never be stagnant, you will not become stale and stink from inaction. But the rich man will be a stingy person because he is afraid to share. The sad fact is everything around him will be undernourished and die. He will not be able to produce that much-needed energy that brings about new life. He will be irritating to those around him because he is always singing that same old song that is all about me, myself, and Ime He will become harmful to himself and a problem to others.

A wealthy man will always give out as he is enriched; his very nature is to be magnanimous. He never allows his acquisitions to freeze him in one place. He is always looking for ways to expand on others. He has a give-out and not a "to-get" mindset. As I quote Matshona Dhliwayo, "a poor generous man is greatly praised., but a stingy rich man is greatly despised". — do not have money so you can keep them for yourself alone, make money so it can be used for expansion and to solve the problems around you, that is the mindset of the wealthy.

Apart from using money as an example of what we can excrete, the words that come out from you should be a blessing, using the wealth of knowledge you have inside to encourage others to do their best in their chosen fields. You can give loud applause to those who may not deserve the credit, this will boost their morale and make them do well.

Philanthropy is not always done because the person is rich. It is often from those who have a heart for giving, you will see the love in their hearts are sincere, always wanting to make an impact. That's why the Holy scriptures narrate that the Lord loves a cheerful giver. The verse at 2 Corinthians 9:6-7 reads: But this I say, He which soweth sparingly shall reap also sparingly; and he which soweth bountifully shall reap also bountifully, every man according as he purposeth in his heart, so let him give; not grudgingly, or of necessity: for God loveth a cheerful giver.

Ordinarily, money is not meant to remain with you, it is supposed to go all out and circulate as quickly and far as possible, as it comes in, it goes out to achieve another purpose, meeting one need or the other. It is engaged to help bring more opportunities and attract more money. Just like the Endorheic lakes that whose water does not flow out of their base, attracts a lot of dirt, dead animals, and waste from the air and forest, the stagnant lakes will always smell and repel life, always void of users. The stream is always fresh with new waters, and it flows from a lot of runoffs ending up in creeks, bigger streams, and rivers, flowing downhill towards the oceans., they flow fresh water into the oceans, thus fulfilling their water-cycle duties. That is why it is imperative to study this law of excretion very well and put it to use if you want to enjoy wealth.

Growth and Development

A wealthy man is always on the grow. It might be in terms of influence or the acquisition of knowledge, it might be his growth and consistency in business or having more information about almost anything. An American businessman, Raymond Albert Kroc who purchased the fast-food company McDonald's and built the company into what it is today, is known for asking the question: "Are you green and growing or ripe and rotting?"

Are you green and growing or ripe and rotten is a deep message to communicate discipline for every age. To all those who do not know the essence of continued growth and development, age is not a factor in attaining and sustaining wealth. Many people stop growing as soon as they attain a certain age or height, they believe that end of the goal is achieved and there is nothing more to do than to relax on a rocking chair and enjoy the past glory. Growing does not have an end, so your goal should not meet its peak. Every goal must be continually renewed and expanded.

A wealthy man makes everything matter to him. He wants to know everything: everything about money matters, financial trends, and societal ups and downs. He lives in the world where he snoops for the latest information about his line of trade or business and that of many other types. He is not shaped by the world. While others are standing still, he is rising upward and moving onward. His Master Plan is constantly being revised and improved upon.

On the other hand, a rich man will always feel comfortable being stable or stagnant or just getting by. Many times, just go along to get along, not wanting to rock the ship even if the ship is the Titanic. The zeal to grow and multiply is not in their nature. They work hard to maintain the status quo and not to expand and take over new frontiers. They keep their money and properties at a risk-free level because they are afraid to lose anything or risk anything that can take away their present comfort, they have never experienced the joys of deep exploration and discoveries.

When you stay on the surface and never dive deep into big rivers or anything new, how will you know what the underwater looks like, talk alone to have something encouraging and amusing to tell people what your experiences are. You cannot refuse to subject yourself to mundane education, the higher your education about something, the better your chances of being in charge of that thing.

In my career as a Chartered Accountant, I have seen many successful organizations and individuals. All of these prospering companies and individuals have one thing in common - they are continually seeking growth and improvement. They are driven by leaders who want to be bigger and better and give mentorship that would expose all the shallowness of stagnancy. Their efforts at personal development are maximal, always thriving to be ahead of others, entering into new ideas and present-hour innovations.

Dandey Malain & co Architectural company terminated the appointment of the human resources manager who believed that the fast-growing company has arrived and is better than most architectural companies that don't have what they have acquired. They believe that they are stable and see no reason to venture out into uncharted territory as their architectural work beats every other architectural venture around their dominant cities. They are already one big name in architectural design for both private and government establishments. But because they stopped "wasting money" on frivolous expensive training and overhyped workshops for their staff, they began to face reversion, they forget that the greater the number of the staff who are well trained, the wider the cascade effect of continued success.

Rich people don't grow. They stay stuck in prior knowledge and fantasies of how great their lives will be even if they add nothing more to their already stable and glamorous standard. They have a chokehold on their assets. They don't let their money breathe, that's why they call this 'stranglehold security.'

You will notice that most rich people keep watch over their money like midnight sentries, they can account for what they have but have no clue as to how much more they could have if they would loosen up a little bit and live and explore. They work for the money; they do not let the money work for them because that could be a big risk; nothing must go wrong and dazzle any part of their money.

These people with this 'I am rich mentality' never learned better. I was talking with a friend who lives in Nicaragua, a trader of flower vases. I asked him how his business was going. His response to me was cold and the usual 'so-so'. He told me that he was making good sales though and was comfortable with his income which has helped him to cater for his family. There was no heat or enthusiasm in his voice, I could sense the agony of defeat already. He seemed like he wanted to move quickly beyond this topic.

He had more farmers coming to his small workshop to buy his ceramic wares from around the city. His designs are beautiful and have been in this line of trade for over three decades. He was able to save a little money or at least more than he had saved last year. He even managed to buy himself a space van for the distribution of his production to customers. This was all the good news and progress he had made so far as he reported to me as his altruistic financial advisor.

This was not what I specifically wanted to hear from him. He has been in this business since I was 17 years old, and is still in the same position, selling the same number of verses in the same old 12" by 8" store space. I gently pushed him further. even though the phone call was disrupted by a bad network system, I asked him to consider expansion, if he wants to acquire a flower plantation to start selling both flowers and vases. I also suggested that instead of this his usual design and model, why can't he start producing new and trendy designs? I went further to suggest learning to distribute the vases to the consumers, wholesalers, and other manufacturers instead of waiting all day for the retailers to come. He could be much bigger and richer if he can start expansion and manufacturing a newer, trendier, and less expensive version all he needed was more training and education.

His response saddened me. He said, "I am already ripe and rotten" he believed that his season has passed, and the new generation should be the one chasing after expansion and wealth. This is how many people think. They see their age as a deterrent to making new progress and following the new trends, some could even be their fears, they are already more comfortable than so many others, why should they risk the little they are already managing? With the flower vase business of this friend of mine, he could be wealthy in so many ways than one. His question of how I can start learning a new trade or coping with the troubles of expansion at this age of mine and this current economic situation could be answered by the law of growth and development. He further tore my heart by saying that he cannot allow a younger person in the same business line to start teaching him new skills.

Another petty excuse of so many people like my Nicaraguan friend is the fact that they will prefer to stay where they are because they are so used to that same routine of business, trying to make a change, or expanding will alter everything and could become the end of everything for them. Selling the vases and making what I am making now is a blessing, at least I am surviving and feeding my family with three square meals."

Fear of advancement and moving forward is the fear that keeps many stuck in their eaglet's nest, in the familiar level of poverty, thinking that they are rich, they still do not want to take a risk, explore new ideas, and give themselves to learning. Having money can easily come in any means and at a curated period, but to be wealthy means to explore and go beyond the ordinary. The comfort zone is taken out and a driving force is brought inwards.

Making money can be deceitful, it can make you oblivious to the need for more upgrades, and making you think that you are already at the peak of success could make you forget that you can run out of ideas. The skill of making money is not the same as the skill of keeping money, the latter comes with the continued development of the mind and learning more skills to be ahead. Many people make money, thinking they are doing well already. And to do well on this level you need to start feeding well, taking in nutrients from education, learning new skills, diversifying, snooping, and eavesdropping on what is happening around you. Some even become millionaires by keeping money upon money, but it is too shallow, it does not last long or make such a person financially big and independent.

But then some minds go to sleep as they handle the wheel, they relax more as soon as they hit the millionaire dollar mark, acting as if they are so content there and there is no other place they need to go. They pat themselves on the back and say, "Good job, this is where I want to be. I worked hard to get here." Right there they put a ceiling on their future earnings. Because they put the roof down on the house so soon, they have no idea how high they can go. Jim Rohn says this about that: *"Let others lead small lives, but not you. Let others argue over small things, but not you. Let others cry over small hurts, but not you. Let others leave their future in someone else's hand, but not you."*

Reproduction

This is one of the most unique characteristics of a wealthy man, a "replica". I dare say this is the characteristic that most differentiates the wealthy from the rich. It is the ability to reproduce wealth in others. The wealthy man, because of his generous spirit, gives birth to more wealthy people by adding value to their lives. In doing so he births men and women who will eventually grow to become captains and champions in different fields and areas of expertise, and with that, they begin to expand and raise others to be like them. This is the multiplier effect: raising people to raise others to be like you. wealthy people are raised everywhere, and him being the root and source of their greatness is instinctively a wealthy man. It's like he is the headmaster of a School of Greatness.

Studying an article published by the Grinnell Magazine on Joe Frankel Rosenfield, an American lawyer, businessman, and an alumnus of the school. He was one of the wealthiest men that achieved so much through mentoring and raising people. He was an instinctive mentor as Warren Buffett described him as an "extraordinarily generous and smart man" and father figure: Joe frequently reached out to young men and women of promise. One of his mentees, Fred Wittle said that Joe Frankel "really relied on his intuition, met him at his lowest point, saw his potential, and helped build a part to success never imagined.

Wealthy people raise people everywhere; they help another person grow, develop, or progress forward in their chosen career without prejudice as they are open to the most diverse group of people, every race, every socio-economic background, small towns, big cities, born in their country, born overseas, immigrant, young and old, people from small families, big families, nuclear families, divorced and joint families, anyone from everywhere, they become a great impact in their lives. They praise and celebrate the accomplishments of others and teach and guide them to greatness because they believe in them. They are never afraid to let others bask in the glow of their earned rewards; the wealthy man gives you your flowers while you can still smell them. They are eager to train and mentor others that may go on to become giants in their fields of expertise.

This is a stronghold of wealth and position, a sure-fire indication that greatness is moving in the right direction. When the wealthy man builds the marketplace, he immediately begins to empower someone to carry on from where he left off. The wealthy man grows from the seeds he has planted in the soil of his personal development. He hopes that his legacy doesn't end with him; his vision is for future generations to come, all together and growing together.

The wealthy man knows, beyond the shadow of a doubt, that there must be a decision to mate or intermingle with other like-minded people. This is the law of synergy: where two become more from where one has started. Some say the idea of two heads meeting on a problem is better than one. This is the idea of think tanks and mastermind groups.

Legendary motivational teacher and author Les Brown once said, "If you can do your idea all by yourself, your idea is not big enough." No man is an island, and no man is a self-made man; we always have somebody who helped us along the way.

Reproduction brings about a copy of what existed before. If each one teaches one from their knowledge and experience, we all will grow together. No one can be considered wealthy if they have not reached back to pull someone else up.

Sensitivity (Response to stimuli)

Author and legendary motivational teacher once said, "If you keep doing what you've always done, you'll keep getting what you've always got."

Wealthy people anticipate and rightly respond to change in their fields and surroundings. It is only foolish people who refuse to increase their knowledge to ward off the winds of change. To acquire success without end, success forever, you must continue to observe the tides and trends of progress and development around you.

No matter how good you are, there will come a time when you become outdated. You cannot be the flavor of all seasons for so long. For example, Denzel Washington is a great actor, and his many awards and accolades attest to that. But he knew that one day his star would soon give way to a 'new kid in the block', and that's why he stepped behind the scenes and began producing and directing movies, The Great Debaters, Fences, Antwone Fisher and A Journal for Jordan are a few he began to direct and produce, instead of the usual, I'll act the lead role.

We must become fully aware of the season that we are in. In cold weather, we wear woolen or animal skin clothes; and in hot weather, we wear something light. That is a way of adapting to our environment. Again, if we touch something hot by mistake, we remove our hands quickly. That is sensitivity.

During times of recession, while the rich man runs helter-skelter to hold onto their money, so they won't lose it, to remain relevant and not go bankrupt, the wealthy man grows further in search of new skills and possibilities, new trends, and more knowledge to benefit from the situation that has frozen others into panic mode.

A wealthy man is a problem solver and if there is a problem he can't solve alone, he doesn't hesitate to ask for help or assistance. This response to change is a superpower for the wealthy. They notice change quickly and don't see it as adversity: they see it as an opportunity for personal growth and development. Because they see the way, they can lead the way, and this expertise brings value and results in unending bounties for them. They don't have to advertise their greatness; they dispense it, and they attract goodwill and money to themselves. Their wealthy ways result in money in their pockets. And the services they give are always more than the buyer anticipated they would pay for. This is the concept of the "baker's dozen", which is 12 plus 1.

In summary, wealthy people believe in the symbiotic cycle of life. They never live for themselves alone; they don't keep the knowledge they have to themselves. They share the wealth of their knowledge and the fullness of their character, going forward to wherever they can extend help to others. They try to uplift others to the level of wealth their potential suggests they should be. They train and empower others to reach their aptitude. They know that money is not meant to be kept in the bank or under a mattress. Money is designed to do the best in the community, touching the lives of people and making them better than they were until the gains come back to you in good measure. And even with death, money doesn't end, it keeps working in the same turn.

Death-start of the new breed

Reverend Father Edwin DuBrill of the Agro-leads plantation, a world-class palm plantation in Mozambique, and the chief priest of the Mozambique Central Church, could be one of the best people to explain what a harvest is, when you veer into his many achievements in agriculture and commerce, he has so many years of experience he can share, especially in the cocoa plantation. The single small seed has got to die, and then there comes the root going deep into the ground, the stem shooting out, and thereafter, the tree begins to grow and then the fruit of the harvest. This is the attribute of life as illustrated in the study of biology. Every living thing must die because it has a finite span of life. As soon as the source of life is cut short, it dies, and then it marks the beginning of a new breed of seeds.

Many people are uncomfortable talking about anything that reminds them of death. Even those that are deep in religion, who considered themselves "candidates of heaven." don't want to accept leaving the sinful world for the glorious heaven. This is inevitable because it is the cycle of life. To soar in wealth, you must kill something, that is to leave behind anything that is not meant to be alive in you and with you, especially all the habits that will always hold you back.

You might have to let your old diet "die" to pursue a healthier diet that will give you the vim and vigor and energy you need to climb the ladder of success. You will have to renew your mind and yourself to be that "new person" that will have success forever. You must also want to kill that ego, that cocky, or that lackadaisical attitude.

Reverend Father Edwin gave this illustration during the start of spring at the Johannesburg planting fiesta in South Africa. The application is simply this: everybody has a seed, but the seed could be flawed. These could be the bad habits that hold you back from achieving your full potential. There may be procrastination that has taken you far off track. Fear and doubt may have taken root within you, but they must die. Anger, jealousy, irrational doubts, fear and procrastination, greed, and laziness. But until you intentionally "kill" all that and bury that, push them far from you and consciously embark on a new life, you will never reach the promised land.

I have studied the lives of many wealthy people in the world today. There was one thing that they all had in common: they worked harder on themselves than they did on their jobs. Character is key. You will never see a wealthy person who is undisciplined, that would never be a characteristic of a wealthy man. The life of every man is the product of his habits. This saying attributed to the English poet John Dryden has been quoted often: "We first make our habits, and our habits make us." In his book, Secrets of the Millionaire Mind: Mastering the Inner Game of Wealth.

T. Harv Eker simply states: "Rich people manage their money well. Poor people mismanage their money well" (Eker, p145). Apart from managing their money well, they have managed their money habits and character better. You must develop the discipline and strength to deaden the habits that distract you from becoming a success. You must avoid the pitfalls that will bring you down.

There are a million bad habits that taunt the arriving successful fellow. If you don't identify those negative habits that look simple and common but are destructive to your wealth goal, then it is time to kill them one by one and step by step. Drinking alcohol, overeating, swearing, procrastinating, biting your nails, excessively sleeping, and idleness, cracking your knuckles, hating people, watching too much TV that is not educating you for success and wealth, telling lies unceasingly, excessive shopping, smoking, staying up late, skipping work/class, and deep complaining are just a few of the habits that fill our lives.

It is just so easy to start a new habit but so hard to break an old one, why is that? New habits are developed and not earned. Until you begin to consciously keep to your goal of achieving that new habit, it won't work. Old habits won't leave you until you run away from them until you kill them, they may still find you when you least expect to see them. And, when you're forming a new habit, you don't even realize it's happening, you keep at it, you build on it, and you stand on it. wealth is not achieved by faultiness and instability; your attitude must commemorate that status you want to attain. With more power and wealth comes more responsibility.

Another area in which you must kill is the past. The past mistakes, your old life, and bad memories are mission killers, they will not let you move forward as they keep on reminding you of your inabilities. The longer you stay in that nostalgic framework, it can begin to feel like you're in a rut and shouldn't have any reason to try again. If you want to disassociate yourself from your old life with its bad memories, it may be time for you to turn over a new leaf and give yourself a fresh start, start killing something.

Your own words

· ·

· ·

· ·

· ·

· ·

Carl Sagan
"Science is a way of
thinking much more than
it is a body of knowledge."
– Carl Sagan

We learn and thrive from
each other because of our
different experiences,
skills, and beliefs. We
each have a story to tell, a
gift to share, a message to
spread, a skill to use and a
voice to be heard. That is
why we continue to learn
and use every form of
science to see deeper.

· ·

· ·

· ·

· ·

· ·

Chapter Six:
Wrong routes to riches to avoid

"The man who starts simply with the idea of getting rich won't succeed, you must have a larger ambition."

John D. Rockefeller, an American businessman, and philanthropist

---

The desperation to be rich or enjoy pleasures and the luxuries of life have made some people think of the shortest possible routes to get to the money. This desperation has reached alarming levels. Cases of crime and violence have escalated. That is only because people who are desperate to get rich quickly rarely think of the possible complications and consequences that may result from their impulsive actions. All they can think of is getting in and getting out with as much money as they can. Sadly, both the young and the old, male, or female are enmeshed in this quagmire.

Several poisoned ideas are roaming the streets, the hubs, blocks of neighborhoods, and other places. Dubious schemes abound and deadly escapades are discussed in hushed tones among people with twisted minds and perverted thinking-all in a heartless bid to obtain filthy riches. Yet, in the real sense, this desperation for riches and the attendant complications can be easily avoided. This is because, in our journey of life, we will find lots of avenues and opportunities that can be explored to become whom we were created to be and to obtain all-around success forever. It is to our benefit that we explore some of these legitimate opportunities rather than the desperado applications to get money anyway and anyhow.

The idea of passing through shortcuts and doing the wrong things to achieve them will surely bring unending regret. When desperation sets in, every kind of negative idea comes crawling into the mind. Within this time, destructive advisors may come around to mislead you, helping you build determination to take whatever risk is attached. But you must resist and face the right path because becoming wealthy is the easiest thing to achieve as it comes with thoroughness, smartness, and rightful living.

Dead End Riches Avenue

Wrong routes that may lead you into the fantasy of getting rich quickly are numerous but dangerous and have never been dependable. Too many people think they can get money by cutting corners and holding on to some nefarious means to meet their hope for outcomes; this never ends well. No one achieves greatness when they are going down the wrong path in life. Yet, we need to have some sense of the low road as we look for the high road.

Apart from the harm that is caused by doing the wrong things for money can destroy you as an individual, those morally bad and damaging habits can cause great harm also to the family setting and society in general.

After careful study of the money ideas of young people between the ages of 19 to 34, I discovered the daredevil's mindset that built an idea for them to enter into any means to having money more than their minds can comprehend. The reason why many of these young people crave this kind of money is with societal deviance, they are departing from usual and acceptable standards because they want to be recognized, be respected, and show off a standard that they can ordinarily not be able to achieve by their perception. And so, we want to look at a few routes that many of these young people had passed through to get money, many of which had failed them and made them settle in captivity.

1. Inherit It

An Italian political philosopher and historian who lived during the Renaissance; Niccolo Machiavelli once said: "...a son can bear with equanimity the loss of his father, but the loss of his inheritance may drive him to despair"

For an inheritance to pass to a beneficiary, someone somewhere has to die; this is disheartening indeed. It can be a parent, a grandparent, a benefactor, a sponsor, a guardian, a foster parent, or whoever is holding the inheritance, the so-called beneficiary of the inheritance is also waiting for the death of the testator."

Hebrew 9:16 states: "For where a testament is, there must also of necessity be the death of the testator."

The word 'testament' is the Greek word "diatheke", which means "the last disposition" or "the last will." The testament is in force after men have died. Otherwise, it has no real strength as long as the testator is alive, and the beneficiary will have to wait unless he changes his mind. But once he is dead, the Will immediately comes into effect. Sadly, for some twisted minds, their only hope, their obsession is that things will come to pass in their favor quickly, which would mean death for the testator. They want the present owner of the money, estate, or properties to die as soon as possible.

As soon as there is a mindset that riches will be coming from a proposed inheritance, they want to get the benefits of what they have not worked for as soon as possible. The majority of those who look toward gaining an inheritance is usually not ready to commit themselves to other ways of creating success for themselves. They usually never want to get money by trying to work for it or to give themselves that opportunity to build through time and perspective. Their minds are cynically fixated on the early death of a property owner, this is their sure opportunity than waiting in the queue till they gradually achieve success.

An article in USA Today gave an illustration that showed that 40% of people between the ages of 13 and 23 expect to receive an inheritance. While about 16% or less of their parents were expected to provide this bequest.

People who fix their minds and place their hopes on getting rich based solely on an expected inheritance are not threading the right path, they do so because they know that something is already provided even if they don't work. The so-called heirloom they look forward to inheriting is a product of someone else's uphill battles and endeavors, it should not be something they should be depending on.

This is only because they do not want to put their fun time to tomorrow, they want the good life now. never wanting to work for their future comfort.

This seeking meaningful employment seems like an unnecessary burden to them. Even if they go to school, they assume it is a waste of their time; their main reason for going to school is not to better themselves but to mark the time before they receive the inheritance, which they believe is due to them. They already are seeing the money in their bank account even though they have done nothing to put it there. Such people never see a need to plan for the future. In their feeble minds, they see money rushing toward them soon.

Let me say clearly that anyone waiting for or living for inheritance is a poor person. Because of their acquired bounty, some may call them rich or upcoming Richie; there is a certain amount of money supposedly waiting for them to make them copious. This is the dream they freely share with others, but it is not based on the reality of hard work. Counting on the sweat and labor of other people is a prescription for disaster, nothing but misery can come from this idle daydreaming.

Then, some other people are so impatient that they want to 'take out" their benefactors sooner. This shows how dark and empty the minds of such people are. Everything that glitters and can buy comfort is not wealth. Getting an inheritance from your parents or grandparents is not good enough for you because what you don't work for, or did not come from you, cannot bring total satisfaction, and may not be sustained.

This reminds me of a movie I watched recently, entitled "Inheritance", directed by Vaugh Stein from a screenplay by Matthew Kennedy. In the film, Archer Monroe, the patriarch of a wealthy and powerful family dies suddenly and leaves his wife, Catherine, and his daughter, Lauren, a Manhattan District Attorney, with enormous riches. But he also leaves a dark secret that threatens the love, peace, and family unity they all once knew. The inheritance ended up being the cause of the agony, death, and destruction of a once beautiful and united family. This 2020 thriller further strengthens my belief that what you do not work for will not be a venture you want to die for.

While I can agree that some people get rich when someone gives them an inheritance, and even remain rich and build on it to become great fortune for upcoming generations to enjoy, the fact remains that this is not the norm. Indeed, coming from a family that has properties and money does not guarantee that you will eventually be the owner of the fortune and assets, or that you will be able to maintain and handle it if eventually given to you since you didn't work for it and won't know the sweat and pains that built it. There have been cases in which a most anticipated inheritance has led to death, destruction, and protracted acrimony. In some cases, even before the inheritance, family members were already at loggerheads over concerns as to who will get what in the family's inheritance.

Wealth comes in so many ways and that could be a relief out of struggle and want, getting an inheritance is indeed a blessing, that someone could work so hard and lay down a good future for others, but when those who are supposed to have the focus to build their own lives, plan their future, and work to build a life are beginning to enter into a realm of laziness and selfishness, forgetting every other thing than to maim, destroy, remain selfish and never wanting to build by themselves.

Inherited riches in any form are not an assurance that they will not eventually be lost if not properly harnessed. This is because the riches are superficial; they have no roots within you, except you have been trained and taught to respect the values and the work behind them, to learn that it is even harder to sustain and build upon what was handed over to you. Conversely, whatever you acquire through knowledge and sweat can hardly be taken away from you. This is what wealth is and will multiply as you continue to maximize it, thus sustaining it.

Inherited riches are specific and limited; the amount of money or property is dependent on the dictates and whims of the donor. A beneficiary cannot get more than the donor has or is able or willing to give. This means that you cannot be richer than whoever is giving something to you, what he/she deems necessary or proper, or fair. There is a limit to what you can receive. And this will surely be the limit of what you are worth and may begin to diminish faster unless you have the plan to seize the opportunity and grow it.

Don't rely on building a wealthy life by the inheritances you received or are about to get. let your plans and goals be at the forefront and any other good thing that comes your way be a booster. If you have this kind of mindset, you will be very enlarged and successful because you would have created a solid foundation for anything that comes your way.

It bears repeating that inheritances are soft assets. They are never guaranteed. There have been instances in which an executor failed in their fiduciary duty of protecting the will of the benefactor to inherit in due time and all was lost. Also, there have been cases in which executors have mismanaged an estate and misappropriated valuable assets. There have been instances in which a testator's will was tampered with. In some cases, changed altogether to benefit another benefactor. That is why I strongly believe that counting on an inheritance to measure wealth status is a lowly manifestation.

An officer at the probate court of Ohio once told a reporter that the misuse of information and data files in the court archives has become so rampant and a constant worry for all involved in probate proceedings. Many young people who are supposed to be successful entrepreneurs, supposed businesspeople, and administrators are always trooping into the offices of the probate county courts to inquire if a probate estate has been opened. They want to know if they have a case regarding any testator that recently died and left a legacy for them or anyone close to them to inherit.

Moreover, it has been reported that the website of the National Association of Unclaimed Property Administrators (NAUPA) is increasingly inundated with people searching for places where their loved ones lived or worked to see if anything shows up. That is the extent of damage that dependence on inheritance can do to one's mentality, they hardly have anywhere else to go and make money or continue a business but wait around the city building for when a ray of sun will shine directly down on them.

Then there is the sad story of Alhaji Mohammed Baba's family that forced hot tears from so many people's eyes. I read the Al Global Media magazine that reported the case of a son who hired an assassin to kill his father so he could inherit the family assets. This news story was about a Nigerian man, 25-year-old Abubakar Mohammed Baba, who was arrested for allegedly conspiring with a friend to kill his father, Alhaji Mohammed Baba, a 52-year-old successful African businessman and petroleum product magnate. Abubakar Mohammed Baba confessed to the crime that his father's body was dismembered and put in a sack after they threw most of his remains in a canal by the Tagwa Dam, an outskirt of the town they live.

This young man was upset because his father was taking too long to die. The young man wanted his inheritance on his timetable. In his statement to the police, he believed his father's death was the only way he could realize his dreams of beating poverty in a reasonable time.

In a similar incident, 23-year-old Henri van Breda, the second son of businessman Martin van Breda, who returned to South Africa with his family, had spent several years living in Perth, Australia, where his father ran a property firm and acquired various properties to add to those he owned in South Africa and some other countries. The father and his wife, Teresa, a former IBM computer scientist were found hacked to death, along with their first-born child, simply because he wanted his inheritance which will automatically make him the second richest in South Africa, this brought forth his impatience and desire to take over the family legacy.

This could also be an eye-opener to parents and guardians as they plan and create a will for their loved ones to benefit from, that they should first help their wards to build a character and a life for themselves before they think of gaining from an inheritance.

2. Marry It

"Till death do us part" is big business nowadays. And those who are making this fake proclamation to enter a two-has-become-one-life contract in marriage just for the benefit they will get out of it are becoming too many and calamitous for society.

Some people look for easy prey, those unsuspecting love-hungry hearts that won't look before they leap. Some mistake love for an infatuation that they easily fall prey to every sugar-coated tongue; the predators, seeking quick money and a way out could take advantage of them. The strategy is to act like one is in love with the partner and play along with the game of love for some time to get what their target is afterward.

Those whose plan is to get rich with marriage are planning to kill a beautiful and sensitive organ that God created for love and life, the heart. Entering into a relationship for the sole purpose of making fortune out of it rather than finding love is sickening,

The goal of getting rich starts with engaging and getting married to rich, unsuspecting love-hungry singles from wealthy families. The destruction of life, family, and society begins here. They are getting married to get money, not to hold onto a spouse or a good home. This is one reason for the sky-high rate of divorce cases worldwide.

As of 2016, the divorce rate in Portugal was about 69% of every 100 marriages in a single year. The alarming thing is that Luxembourg had almost the same rate. And according to the Bureau of Statistics in the USA, divorce rates are growing at an increasing rate every year, never below 58% for over 20 years now. It has become commonplace for divorce cases to appear every day in court. The situation is the same in many other parts of the world. Divorce fees are getting more competitively low as every lawyer wants to get more clients to break the bonds of marriage at record speeds, within a lesser period. At one point it was "cheaper to keep her" but now it's cheaper to let her go.

Even more worrisome, studies have shown that the sole reason for many divorces was because of the desire to get financial benefits, or because the couple could not manage their family finances. There was just too much mistrust, financial misappropriation, and blatant thievery. Some of the divorces happened because one of the partners didn't get as much money and luxuries as they thought they were entitled to upon entering into the marriage contract.

Data released by a financial firm, TD Ameritrade, showed that 41% of divorces among Generation Xers (those born in the 1960s and 1970s) broke up because of money, gift, and property issues. Similarly, 29% of Boomers (people born between 1946 and 1964, during the post-World War 2 era) say they ended their unions because of disagreements over money-who should be in charge of managing the couple's finances. Some had assumed that they would gain money by marrying someone from a rich home, rather than wasting their efforts and time going into entrepreneurship or seeking some other legitimate means of making their own money. Of course, they ended up bitterly disappointed.

Financial infidelity, or dishonesty about money, usually starts when a partner is hungry for money and has resolved to achieve it by any means necessary. Such people only agree to enter the marriage contract because of the expectation of financial gains and luxuries. They were sure their partner would give them everything they wanted. When these expectations didn't bear any fruit, they began looking for an easy way out, and most often, take out the spouse to inherit his/ her riches.

Recently, there was a rumor about Iceland that has been debunked by the government but contains some important lessons for us to learn. The rumor was that the Icelandic government was willing to pay young eligible and educated men from around the world up to $5, 000 USD, as well as instant resident permits and other benefits if they could come to Iceland to marry their citizens who are still single ladies that were ready for marriage.

Amazingly, during this period, the number of men applying for visas to Iceland, in over 21 countries tripled the normal application traffic to the country. The application on the consulate website became so enormous that the site crashed 17 times in one week. This shows that many men wanted to escape their present level through marriage and shy away from their failed dreams. And so started applying as many also needed a greener pasture away from their troubled country. Not surprisingly, many of them were shamelessly scammed by fraudsters who pretended to be Iceland Immigration officials and some male acting as a lady seeking a husband. Many paid hundreds and thousands of dollars to get the marriage deal for the promised extra cash and the resident permit. Many young men paid for airline tickets without seeing the result of their applications. It became obvious that these men were in it, not for love, but the money.

Money-seeking schemes in marriage have become a large problem all over the world. Many men and women are not looking to build wealth, they want to buy into wealth. They seek to prey on rich families or well-to-do potential spouses, desperate single women or men who may not have the time to investigate their partner's loyalty deeply. A recent survey of 1,000 individuals in committed relationships revealed that 71% have committed financial infidelity at least once. They already had the mindset to benefit from the wealth of the person they planned to marry. Then they felt disappointed if they did not get as much financial gain as they envisaged. Consequently, anger and bitterness rained down on their marital home. This has led to many instances of domestic violence, and divorce. In some cases, abuse, and murder.

I was in the beautiful city of Seoul, South Korea for the annual HWPL religious conference in 2016. I had the opportunity to chat with an outspoken, jovial, and intelligent young man. I met him after the second day of the conference during a lunch break to ask for more clarification on that day's agenda. He had come to the conference from Mexico. He told me of his past marriages. It was a deep heart-to-heart discussion that we had. I told him what African marriages are made of and how the women would always give their best to ensure that their marriage worked and become successful, giving up many things and sacrificing their ego just for the man to be comfortable and king. His own story was different, he was almost a millionaire before his marriage crashed and burned. He admitted that he went into the marriage for the wrong reasons; to become a millionaire.

Nigel Rodrigues(not his real name) thinking changed about marriage after his first ever jail term, for attempted financial fraud on his wife and her estate and being a misogamist but pretended to be in love and wanted the relationship. He now realized that entering into marriage with the mindset of gaining money was not a good reason to go into it. He didn't want to live a fake and dubious life anymore; it was time to embrace love as the reason to continue in his marriage. He became an advocate of good marriages and Godly relationships after his third jail term with a rich female doctor who by luck was able to find out the plans to sell her mansion and divert her savings. He now counsels and helps marriages and young people who plan to enter into marriage genuinely. He has helped over 300 families in Mexico and the cities around his hometown and has sent many marriage counselors and clergies to training on marriage education and ethics.

He is now on the righteous course in terms of finding a purpose for his life rather than wanting to get rich through marriage. Nigel had come to the conference seeking the key to true love and authentic connection in marriage, rather than seeking riches and destroying the lives of innocent young girls who only wanted to make a happy home.

He added that he began to build up wealth for himself through legitimate means and discovered that it is the best way of life, building legitimate means of wealth is easier than thought, it also brings joy and fulfillment. Nigel now sees marriage as an institution that should be respected. He also revealed that his case was not in any way peculiar. Many young men in his country were used to pretending to be in love with young, unsuspecting ladies from rich families, attaching themselves to those who either made their fortune themselves or inherited it from their families.

The irony of this is that, even if these gold diggers eventually marry a rich partner, there is still no guarantee that they will automatically find wealth or fulfillment.

3. Steal It

The "Get rich or die trying" meme has become so ubiquitous that many youths can no longer think of embracing the dignity of labor. It has become a death trap that consumes the minds of young people so much that they want to get rich without following the principles and laws of wealth. Consequently, many have decided that instead of working to attain riches or building up themselves to become wealthy, they are violently coveting the possession of others for themselves.

Stealing is often triggered by greed, covetousness, jealousy, low self-esteem, peer and social pressure, deprivation, and much more misconduct. Poverty has been considered a "root cause" of stealing, but this is untrue. Many poor people don't steal and won't steal no matter their state of compulsion, and many are well off with almost everything going for them-who and will steal at the slightest opportunity. Stealing is a state of mind, more often than not, it is a mentality-triggered action raised by one's thinking and upbringing.

This brings us to a vital question: Why will someone want to steal to become rich? Across five experiments, a research team found out that greed was the most pertinent reason to want to steal to keep up with a standard that they are not. They see things they do not have and want to by all means make them theirs. The research fellows also pinned feeling financially deprived to be a root cause for someone to want to take from where it is abundantly available and make them theirs, it is the trigger for a range of morally questionable behaviors – from simple and little theft to white collar crimes like misappropriation, embezzlement, to destructive crimes like burglary and armed robbery.

These results hold true even though people, in general, believe they are unlikely to behave dishonestly regardless of their financial condition. The boy who claims, "All my friends are doing it" is disclosing a lot about his choice of friends and revealing a lot about himself. This is why there should be a mind-changing education program on how easy it is to be successful, which would include achieving financial wealth without doing negative things.

The irony is that being successful and wealthy in life is not as elusive as many people think. All it takes is to follow a few basic principles-many that have been highlighted in this book-with trust and faith in God for ultimate success. Those who are expecting to break into riches by stealing from others are making a big mistake because it is the easiest road path to destruction and death. Therefore, it is important to begin to educate people on wealth creation, making them understand that the pathway to riches is building up blocks of wealth. Riches are just part of the outcomes of the wealth that is built up inside us.

A student raised her hand at the Jesuit young female entrepreneurs breakfast meeting with the representative of the Ministry of Education who came to chair the fundraising event for girls' education and entrepreneurship in Los Angeles. The theme of the program was: "Is it morally wrong for a hungry and dying man to steal?" This heart-wrenching question made the hall go dark with silence. The representative from the Ministry of Education was brief in his answer as he stood up to take the microphone from the Master of Ceremony. He broke it down thoughtfully and concisely.

Many of the students were waiting for him to be for the argument since it could lead to death, he continued that though some actions seem right and justifiable and may even attract sympathy if stealing to be alive is the last option, then anybody could do it, but it takes a morally and upright person to rather die than steal. Stealing violates ethics and standards of life, whatever is against the law and morals is unacceptable in any circumstances, therefore, there is no justification for stealing of any kind and for any reason.

A classic example of what seems right but is all wrong is when someone is stealing to feed their family or forcefully taking things from one person to help another. Stealing is legally and ethically wrong, it cannot at any time be right and it comes with severe consequences. While some will want to do it because they have a "good" reason to or they have the "Robin Hood' intention to steal from the rich and give to the poor, there is no justification for doing evil for any reason.

whenever a person steals to escape poverty or to save a life, it shows that such a person had never had a good mindset and never planned to succeed in life. People who look for a way out by stealing are indeed selfish and wicked, a ready purloin. While "to take from another without the right to do so or without remorse to know that it is an act to destroy another man's opportunity to live," stolen money doesn't last because they are ill-gotten gains. The law of evaporation which works heavily with stealing states that money that comes to you by stealing has no root and it must by natural law be gone in due time.

For those people who want to become wealthy by stealing, remember that troubles come with it, those troubles can include family trouble, mental health issues, fear that torment till eternity, disgrace, and the stigma you experience after being caught. Those who steal will often have trouble making and keeping friends or business relationships because of the stigma, they will have poor relationships with prospects and future opportunities or have issues with trust because they will lose the most important aspect of good human character which is honor, integrity, and probity.

4. Lucky It.

Many years ago, I worked for a German marketing company that sold fire and burglar alarm systems in Nigeria. It was a fun job. I was head of marketing for the southwest region. I was able to meet a lot of high-ranking people in society and I was able to see the difference between mediocrity and success.

At that time, my assistant sales manager had a habit that often bewildered me. He would bring out this small, brownish smooth stone that looked like a crystal ball from his jacket pocket, roll it several times around his thick yellowish palms for minutes, and then raise his hands above his head about three or four times within an hour. As he did so, he would chant some words while closing his eyes very tightly so that I could see the throbbing veins. Just then, he would release a burst of laughter. He told me that the laugh is to energize the spirit of luck in him and was proof that he would have good luck that day.

I am still amazed until this day. I am sure that the young man, who had his education up to a first-and second-degree level could be so gullible and engage in such a superstitious practice, all in the name of finding good days through luck. Truth is, there is no such thing as becoming successful or prosperous by luck. Men don't get wealthy because they are lucky. While time and chance may occur, it is not an arranged phenomenon or something one should put high hopes on. Over 98% of those waiting on luck and surprises end up waiting all their life in vain, in regret and failure.

Like this former colleague of mine, generations of mankind in different cultures around the world have always been misled to think that they can count on luck to get ahead in life. For instance, it is believed in both Chinese and European cultures that pig charms have the power to bring good luck. Pigs are widely regarded as a symbol of wealth, good fortune, and prosperity. Thus, some people will buy pigs and keep them in sacred chambers, sometimes worshiping them, with the hope that they bring good fortune and overnight wealth.

Also, in some places, horseshoes are symbolic of good luck, power over evil, good fortune, and fertility. The horseshoe is often associated with the horse's strength and dependability. Many people believe it is best to hang a horseshoe with the open end facing upward in the room, office, or car so that their good luck will not fall out around them. Similarly, the ladybug is a popular insect worldwide.

In Germany, ladybugs are called "lucky bugs" ("glueckskaefer"). In the past, huge amounts of money were paid to forest hunters who could capture colorful insects. Some cultures believe that if a ladybug lands on your head, and you do not brush it off, you will be lucky and be blessed with anything you desire for one year, if it landed on your shoulder, you sure will see luck that day. No matter what you want to have, it will come to you in mysterious ways. It is also believed that some ladybugs bring more luck than others. This could be according to their sizes or how brightly colored they are. Some also say you will be extra lucky if you can find a deep red ladybug with lots of spots.

Some people believe that the shooting star or a falling star grants a person luck big enough to win the highest prize in a lottery or while gambling. They believe that to see a star fall is an affirmation that one's dreams have come into reality. Some saw a time when many youths would start dropping from their jobs and businesses and spend countless hours looking toward the skies, spending hard-earned money to buy binoculars to help search the sky to be the first one to see a shooting star, how hilarious!

I have to painfully admit that I had once been caught up in this foolish practice. I was a young man in my early 20s. I always had this daydream disorder that haunted me for a long time. Perhaps this was due to the poverty situation I was in at that time, and the peer pressure. I am still not completely sure if I have gotten rid of such a devilish mindset that took me away from thinking right throughout my young and active age. I will be lucky to see ten million dollars someday soon. How I come across about ten million dollars every single time I daydream is still a mystery to me, it just looks so real that someday soon, I'll get that money maybe in a suitcase that fell from a helicopter or seeing a rich man throwing a bag full of money on the road because he thought that robbers were chasing him. this hallucination almost got me to hate work and education, I began to think that I will 'blow' (become suddenly very rich) one single day and end my financial misery forever. As I continue in my strong search for this mystery money that will come by luck, where it will come from, I don't know, it never existed.

Whenever I saw young people like me having and flaunting money, fast cars, giant gold chains, and designer clothes, dragging beautiful girls alongside them, I always felt like becoming Aladdin with a lamp, and with my ginny popping out of the lamp and making all my wish come true, conjuring these things I have for a long time dreamt of to appear in my palm. I always believed that one day I was going to be richer than my friends were. The trouble, however, was that I had no reasonable idea or plan of how that would happen for me. For one, I was not ready to put my mind to work. I was not willing to summon the energy it would take to realistically pursue my dreams. I never even thought of a process to launch me into wealth and success. I wanted what the other guys had but I had to admit I was not ready to do the work.

One day while staring up at my ratty ceiling fan, which seemed to blow nothing but hot air, I began to imagine how

I was going to get rich. I started daydreaming, I started seeing myself walking through a lonely bush path leading to the city's central market, I kept looking out for the suitcases and bags that may contain my lucky money. At such times of reverie, my face would brighten up with possibility again, a smile of hope while I was still half asleep. Sometimes I would deliberately begin to walk towards every bushy path I know, where I assumed that a rich fellow who did not need money or a frustrated person would have thrown a bag of money out of his car windows, or would have thrown it, thinking he was throwing away a bag of garbage.

In essence, I was counting on luck to make me become a wealthy man, I was looking for that pie in the sky. What particularly worsened my condition was that my grandfather had once told me he became rich by luck. He was probably trying to be humble about the little achievements that made him seem like he is the champion of our clan. He taught me to always pray that I should be lucky in life. This affected me, as I thought I could indeed become rich one day, because of luck that is not guaranteed.

Sadly, this is the same mindset too many of us still have. Some will not go out of their houses without their good luck hat or necklace. Some only get lucky with their favorite spoon in their pocket. It sounds silly but this is the mindset of so many people out there. Funny enough some people attribute their reliance on luck for success and wealth to their understanding of the Bible. I remember one time when a preacher was teaching his congregation as he read from Ecclesiastes 9:11. I got home and read it aloud to myself again as if the scripture was written to confirm what he had preached in his sermon. From him, I got the sense that if I could rely on this luck he preached about, I'd never have to work again. That I would receive manna from heaven.

The verse I read said: *"I returned and saw under the sun that the race is not to the swift. Nor the battle to the strong. Nor bread to the wise. Nor riches to men of understanding. Nor favor to men of skill. But time and chance happen to them all."* This caused some war in my mind. Incidentally, this verse is what some church people use in defending their reliance on luck or breakthrough. They claim that even God gives credence to the belief that people are not supposed to toil for wealth but rather wait for their turn when the wind of exchange will turn to them.

One can only help but wonder how such people, who are supposed to be knowledgeable could fall for such deception. They have read their Bible and they know even God worked to bring the universe and everything in it into existence and that surely took Him six days to work for it to happen. Didn't the Bible say "...for God created", and the Spirit hovered in the deep"? That means that He worked to make creation happen. Interestingly, some misinterpret how God created the world, as He worked for six days and had the seventh day to rest to mean that, God had already done all the hard job, mankind need not work anymore, furthermore, that God had provided everything mankind needed so he can relax and enjoy the good things of earth. Now that man could chill on the rosy earth, the luckiest get the fattest.

The mindset of some is to have luck charms that will bring whatever was kept somewhere to them. the luck charm will either take them to the treasures or bring the treasures to them, whichever way, they are meant to have something good without laboring for it.

The successes that came through for businesspeople and their successes are not by luck, no wealthy and successful man or woman got it through luck or chance, opportunities will always meet up with preparedness.

Every success comes to be as a result of proper planning, good management, and quintessential administrative input, a move of a game changer that sees those opportunities others don't see or the things they ignored. Some people believe that rich people have simply been luckier than everyone else. I was reading through Samantha Alvis' article published in March 2019 on the topic – The deceit of luck; an article published to suppress students' dependence on luck rather than work to become successful. The argument was clear and addressed the wrong mindset that luck is the power behind every success, which is not true. She pointed out on the Outlook Magazine for the Monmouth Student University's run newspaper stating... *"Finding a job opportunity may be luck, but securing the position is hard work. Meeting someone you connect with may also be luck but turning that into a successful relationship is hard work. Luck can be a piece of the puzzle, but pictures are put together through the work."*

Can a man suddenly wake up and be lucky to become rich, of course not, lucky breaks don't happen, and personal efforts play all the role in becoming exceptionally wealthy. The role luck plays are largely faux, and if you find yourself in such a sudden room of spectacular opulence, you need to check well, it could be a daydream.

Over the decades, good luck and bad luck usually are a topic of deep discussion, and neither of them balances the other in the life of people—hardly anyone experiences a run of good or bad luck that extends over decades, it will always drop. Take lucky lottery winners, for example, most of them end up poor again just a few years after their life-changing wins because they do not have the right mindset and character for wealth. In contrast, there are plenty of examples of wealthy people, entrepreneurs, and investors who rebounded from bankruptcy within a few years because, having risen to the point of being wealthy, they still know how to make money and become the success they have always been.

Getting wealthy is not just about having a lucky break, it is far more a question of whether someone recognizes the opportunities life throws their way because they were ready for it and were rightly positioned. Lots of people get opportunities, but they simply don't know what it is, nor were they ready to grab the opportunity. Others might recognize an opportunity when it comes their way but fail to act on it. People get wealthy because they are not only good at recognizing opportunities, but they are also able to act decisively and effectively.

Some people think they don't have what it takes to get wealthy because they didn't attend university or because they did not have the right connections, some think that they came from a poor family and there were no real connections at the top echelon. But a glance at a list of the world's richest people reveals that many of this superrich were university dropouts or didn't even make it through high school, many did not have any superrich family history, and neither did anybody lay down a huge amount of money for them to start with. Attending an elite university is by no means a prerequisite for getting rich. In Germany, the study The Wealth Elite confirms that there is no correlation between school and university achievement on the one hand and financial success on the other. If success in life came down to academic business knowledge, then business administration professors the world over would all be multimillionaires or even billionaires.

That is why a person that awaits luck is an opportunist who had never prepared himself for what is next. They hang all their troubles and inabilities of not achieving what they never planned to achieve on God or their ill luck. They have misinterpreted these verses to mean that God simply expects man to not work because He made them luck-beings. They believe that becoming wealthy or successful is not by acquiring knowledge or vocational skills or even proper planning and strategizing but time and chance (luck) happen to a few that are chosen.

Surprisingly, over half of the congregation agreed with a roar of approval, shouting and jubilating, in total agreement with the preacher's pronouncement that it was all about luck. But then the preacher made a profound statement that shut everyone up. He asked, "Who has the power over everything, including time and chance?" They all replied, "God." And the pastor declared, "Then we must all accept that God is the one who determines what grace He will apportion to anybody, and He will not give that grace if such a person is not ready."

The preacher made the hushed crowd think differently and correctly. Let me say it one more time: God doesn't want us to depend on luck; He recognizes efforts and determination. What the above Bible reference simply implies is that God doesn't want us to just depend solely on our abilities alone or lift ourselves over His love, kindness, and effervescence. For it is He who shows mercy and crowns our labor with success.

5. Labor It

I started teaching high school Economics and Social Studies in 1998. I enjoyed teaching and I love the classroom. As a young graduate, it was a dream come true for me. I was fulfilled to the extent of bragging about my newfound love for my lecturers that we are now in the same category of expertise. I was teaching my favorite subjects and making money at the same time made the work look easier for me. I was determined to work extra hours for the whole seven days. I also decided to do home coaching for as many students as my father's car garage could accommodate.

I was making good money as more hours were added for each month, and the number of students increased in my home lesson. I was comfortable with my dream job I thought that one day, will become the source of much envy and I'll become very rich as I always dreamt. I saw the salary chart on the table of the college accountant after my first anniversary in the college as a teacher. He had mistakenly left it on the general file cabinet and stepped out. I used that opportunity to take a quick peek because into the books I wanted to make my heart happier that I am one of the highest paid in the school. compared to my colleagues on the same level as I am. It was then that I realized that no matter how good I was or how hard I worked and do all the extra hours that all the other teachers put together, my peanut pay is somebody else's daily refreshment allowance.

I did not like what I saw. I shook my head in disappointment and got very angry in my spirit, I immediately began to look for a way out of what I saw as a small mind, I needed to upgrade and stop depending on laboring hard to become successful.

Despite periods of economic downturn over the past decade, with businesses and factories benefiting from the profit from sales to the consumers and other government assistance, the income of the average worker has fallen drastically, compared to their expenses. According to a report published by NewPage Magazine written by the Tel Aviv-based Adva Center reporter, which performs policy analysis on equality and social justice. According to Adva academic director Dr. Shlomo Swirski, who co-authored the report with Etty Konor-Attias, *despite an increase in the gross national product, that wealth has failed to filter down to the average citizen, especially those in the labor market. "The last decade was not a good one for employees,"* Swirski told The Jerusalem Post on Tuesday, explaining that after the mini-recession, many firms made speedy financial recoveries to enjoy increases in income until the onset of the current economic crisis. In contrast, the incomes of employees and workers, especially those in the lower percentiles, did not increase and were never able to meet up with the current economic needs. Looking at the 25-page report, I called for further research into why employees, laborers, and paid workers did not benefit from the country's economic growth, why are laborers and employees never having enough to meet their needs and have a good reserve?

Swirski said. He cited the increasing weakness of the unions, and a changing labor market structure that encourages more freelancing, independents, and flexible positions. Many of those most hurt by the lack of income growth were those who earned minimum wage, Swirski said. The minimum wage for full-time adult workers has been pegged to a certain amount by law and is never or merely adjusted or increased with the economic situation or inflation, that is why you see workers and laborers are never satisfied with their financial state. "It's time that attempts were made to stop teaching the people to depend on labor and employment," Swirski said, "because if the situation does not improve then we will get caught in a cycle whereby low-income workers will not be able to afford a good life they should ordinarily have and not be able to give their children a good enough education, and that will hurt the country's economy in the future.

I realized that this young man of my age didn't have to labor, he had set everything in the right motion, all I see him do, whenever he comes to the school was smile and wave his tiny fingers at us and tell us we were doing a good job.

A drastic change took over my mind as soon as I saw that salary chart. I realized it was not hard work that made one wealthy. I would have to work smarter and make money work for me.

By June of 2001, I felt I had wasted three years laboring endlessly for monthly payments that would never make me happy and fulfilled as I thought I should be. It was around this time that I received a letter from a former schoolmate nicknamed KC. Kazeem or KC as we usually call him had started a small firm with two of his friends from school. They specialized in computer facilities management and systems engineering. They had more than 200 employees working there in the brief span of two years. He had become so wealthy he could influence the lives of many in a positive manner. His example gave me the courage to start training myself, digesting everything that would make me a success soon. I started a business of my own, and now I have a success story to share.

Permit me to give an instructive illustration: Whom would you expect to be a richer person? a man who is looking strong, well-built, and ready to work for every hour of every day, he is feeling healthy and can lift, roll, and package materials with optimum speed; sounds like he will be the best worker for his employer and may get promoted very quickly, or one who spends more time relaxing and traveling around, and has a laid-back approach to life? Of course, you would likely choose the first guy because he is stronger and works hard enough to be highly compensated. But what if the seemingly fun-seeking guy had developed the ability to think outside the box and establish a successful money-making business and employed people to work in that unique business of his? You would discover that such a man would be making money at his own pace and will. He would never be helpless because he knew how to get what he wanted. He holds his own in a leisurely manner while the other one solely depends on physical strength, hard work, and the number of hours at the job, working full time and overtime, still not going past a certain level.

You see, the first man as illustrated has his body designed to lift heavy objects, and work traditionally to reap his regular income. He might be comfortable with what he earns with all his physical strength and ability, but he might not exceed a presumed level of riches and comfort. While the second person can with his initiative and intelligence work smarter with little or no effort and enjoy unimaginable wealth and success.

Wealth is not gained from working hard, but from working smart. If riches are from hard work, then commodity movers, laborers, and those that work overtime should be the richest. But until you begin to use your head, strategize, and calculate, you won't make it to the top of the ladder. And if you do not leverage other people's time, skills, and efforts, you will achieve too little, all that your effort can produce, and you will be too small to be in the category of the big league you always desired to be in. Think big and grow rich.

To be sure, you will work hard to get rich, and the harder and smarter you work, the better your chances. As my dad would explain, "It's OK to work eight hours a day for someone else. Just work eight hours a day for yourself too, and twelve hours a day on the weekends." And that's exactly what he did, all his life.

Selling your time by the hour will not get you ahead. Human resources departments know to the dime what they have to pay per hour to acquire requisite talent. Even if you have a degree from a prestigious law school and catch on with a leading firm and can bill at several hundred dollars an hour, by the time the expenses are extracted, you'll be lucky to be grossing a third. Even if you work yourself into an early grave by billing out 3,000 hours a year, you're not, by that effort alone, putting yourself on a track to getting wealthy.

So, what do you have to know to become financially wealthy without the 'labor it' syndrome? Probably the first insight you need is that you are out to get wealthy and not to chase after money.

You will first learn how to make money with wisdom and not with muscle or work hours. How did Mark Zuckerberg make $4 billion in one day last week? How did Jeff Bezos make $6 billion in 20 minutes a couple of days ago? Elon Musk made $51.30 million per hour on July 7, 2022. Was it by increasing their hourly wage or working extra hours, or were handling the toughest machines for production? No, as you know, it was by equity. They have a network of people working together with them and using a system that works and produce what they want. If you are still searching for the best-paid job, looking for more hours and overtime, and planning to work to impress your employer to earn the award of the best and most productive worker in the organization, you are frail. If you can do something about your time, remember that You have approximately 100,000 to 150,000 working hours in your entire life (multiply that time with 20 more people doing what you are doing, what you can net per hour, and here's how wealthy you will potentially be). Your money, equity, and time can work for you 24/7 on 365 days a year, and not break a sweat.

6. Pension it

Your pension is meant to help you maintain your standard of living in retirement and help you keep a good bank account in old age, and not what you should depend on as your source of wealth. Many people are currently working a kind of job with a certain organization or government establishment because of what they will get in pension funds after retirement, they hope to live a better life after retirement, not minding whatever they are currently receiving as remuneration or the prospect of what they are doing.

A pension plan or retirement plan is a type of investment strategy which helps you to accumulate a part of your savings over a long period so that you can have a secure, peaceful financial flow after you retire at old age or when you become weak in health and mind. It is not what one should depend on and waste a youthful and vibrant life for. If what you are looking forward to is that bulk money that afterward, you could live in comfort, then, you are making a big mistake that will cost you your opportunity to prosperity.

You will discover the mindset of some people concerning financial decisions, they look forward to being able to sit back and enjoy their pension, starting up life after they get that bulk money alert, especially for those working in civil service. Their philosophy seems to be, "It is not how much you earn at this moment of your youthful age that matters, but what you will enjoy when your bones get weak and cannot work again."

Unfortunately, this fallacy has made many trade their present vibrant minds for a future that may never come to be. They seem to be forgetting that it is the present happiness and fulfillment that provides the strength to shape and prepare for a better future. See, settling for a job that takes much of your salary to save towards your pension is a big blunder.

It's all a scam like this there is no brighter tomorrow, especially if today is not solid and sound enough for you.

The alarmingly difficult experiences of pensioners in most developing nations clearly show the futility of putting all of one's hopes into pension savings. Many have ended up living in misery and penury because of this way of thinking and living. Take Cuba and Nigeria as examples. Most potential pensioners are never at ease, especially as their official retirement age or year of service grows nearby. This is because of the terrible experiences of some other pensioners. Many have had to go through the "wait-and-die" treatment often meted out to them by the Government or the pension fund administration. This probably explains why some who have access to public funds quickly siphon off as much as possible for personal use just because they know that the future is bleak, the pension fund may not come, and if it comes, they will accomplish little and not more than catering for their health services and daily living. There is no assurance that what they are saving will be there when they need it when they are totally out of the job market and rely on government social security benefits and state-funded pension plans. This is one of the reasons for rampant fraud in these countries. However, not everyone has such an opportunity or a depraved mind that seeks unfair advantages at the expense of others.

This same trend exists in almost every other part of the world: pension funds are siphoned off and pensioners are neglected and left to rot in lack and pain after their long-awaited golden years turn into their worse years when they reach retirement age. There is that promise of a good life after 35 years of service and working to at least 65, leaving those non-stop years of working behind you. Pension benefits are up to nothing good if that is what the individual is depending on. 91% of pensioners all over the world suffer depression and lack, just because the system is not created to make anyone wealthy after retirement.

Now is the time to look for something you can lay your hands on to do aside from your regular nine to five. Nothing is stopping you from starting a new trade or networking with businesspeople to help you leverage what you know and begin to build multiple streams of income for yourself and your family.

It will be a grave mistake if you are one of those who think they can make it in life if they work hard enough, through the established arrangements of the system to help you save money and get it in bulk in old age. You must start thinking beyond the box and finding your place in the arena of wealth creation. Just because you are planning for retirement shouldn't stop you from desiring to make money in every other way possible.

7. Spirituality/Magic it

"If I tell you that spirits transport money to those that chant for it, will you ever think it's a lie?", Sat Guru Maharaj Ji, made this statement at the grand master worship vigil at the Maharaj Ji temple for world worshippers encouraging the members during the teaching session to rely on spirits that can help them bring money and make them rich, rather than wasting precious time fighting to build a system or a business. Some people are not ready to use their brains and hands to work anymore, they are never applying their skills and talents to solving human problems or adding value to society but to look for the shortest cut possible to have money; praying for money to come by angels or spiritual entities of riches. Many have been brainwashed and indoctrinated to rely on supernatural provisions for money, rather than working and building wealth.

You don't spiritually attract wealth by merely chanting or praying for it. Spirituality is a practice of increasing awareness, and wisdom that is beyond human comprehension to do greater exploit in your chosen work or profession, it is not the practice of making money appear from the unknown. No one spiritually attracts wealth without 'the action'. The people who teach about spiritually attracting wealth do not get it this way. They create wealth by filming and making videos, podcasts, outreaches, writing books, leading workshops, advertising, marketing, donations, and gifts. They create wealth by selling the idea of attracting wealth spiritually.

If you are one of those that have dedicated your entire life to praying for riches, you are praying in vain. The promise they see in this method of financial prosperity is truly a mirage. Money only gravitates toward value: it flows to where the solutions to life's problems are found. Wealth gravitates to those who have the strategy to make the world better by proffering a solution and taking charge of their lives.

When Dennis Kimbro sat down to interview John H. Johnson, founder, and chief executive of Ebony and Jet magazines, for his book The Wealth Choice: Success Secrets of Black Millionaires, the first question Johnson asked him was: "Why aren't you rich?" Then Johnson went on to say: "...I realized too late that waiting for money to come by good fortune or by spiritual appearances was the greatest killer of the brain and mind. There are thousands of men and women who have lost every talent, skill, and ability to produce something good, and yet because they possess a stout heart towards godsend, they lost the groove of wealth. An unconquerable will and the determination to push ahead were lost, they are just as close to poverty as before marriage to waiting for God and spirits to bring them a fortune. Here lies the good news. Wealth is less a matter of circumstance than it is a matter of knowledge and choice. With such wealth, no one should ever be poor. You must take control of your life you must make the decisions to be wealthy" (Kimbro, p4).

Spirituality and magic are what many empty minds turn to for safety after allowing their gullibility to fail them. Some will not have the strength to seek and maintain gainful employment, but they have enough strength to fast and pray for days and weeks on end. Unfortunately, what they are praying for has no real value and will never come. They are praying that God will throw money from heaven or send someone to miraculously bring money to them. They prefer supernatural forces to rain financial manna from heaven into their pantry while they fold their hands and wait for a miracle to happen.

There is no denying the place of spirituality in the life of every man created by God. In truth, help comes from God in areas where mortal men cannot extend their reach. Yes, we receive help from God; you can count on that. But there are occasions when we have to know that there is a place beyond spiritual engagement and supernatural intervention, where getting wealthy requires much more. It requires personal efforts, high-level thinking, application of logic, and acumen along with extraordinary strategies, persistence, and much more, and God crowns the efforts with grace.

Of course, we need to pray, especially because we know some forces and powers are full of hatred, evil, and wickedness. Many of those things we will not be able to battle alone; that is when we experience Godly intervention. We also pray to make sense of the senseless and to gain ideas that ordinarily are beyond our comprehension. Yes, we pray because we know that without God, we don't stand a chance when it comes to the battle against the prince of this world, the devil. (John 12:31).

We pray for victory over death and for divine health against sickness and infirmity. We pray for comfort for those who are afflicted with incurable diseases and unknown curses. We intercede for many who are on the verge of destruction. We pray for those who are shattered and battered psychologically and spiritually. We pray for the souls of men that need to be redeemed from bondage and chains. We pray for the families and lives of people who are in danger around the world. We pray for those who are heartbroken and helpless. We also pray for courage to stand up and speak out against atrocities and all that we know in our hearts to be wrong. We pray for wisdom and understanding to seek the right things to do and to have direction. But why should you pray for money to move out of the vaults of banks into your account? That is wickedness. Or for your creditor to forget what you owe them? Or as many callous and desperate religious bigots will pray for their competitors and creditors to die because they do not want to pay back as they promised they would? Why should you pray to increase your financial bounty when you have not worked or done anything to justify such, all in the process of you getting rich?

Praying for money has never worked, especially if you are a lazy and greedy person that is seeking a short way out of your idleness, it will be the best and easiest option you pray to be true. When you work, that is when miracles happen, new ideas come, people join hands to help you achieve results quicker and easier, and God Himself sends forth insights and direction to your already focused mind. Favor is available to you at a certain time when your efforts work in harmony with God's plan for you. But if you wait on just expecting to be wealthy by chanting and praying and not folding up your sleeves for real and sincere work and putting some things in place to generate the desired funds, you might wait forever.

You cannot sit at home or in a house of worship and keep weeping and wearing sackcloth for money to come, God detests such dilatory behavior and ignoramus with a total look away. If that is the way it works, then monks and prayer warriors should be the richest people on earth. Wealth is all about strategy, hard and systematic work of the brain and brawn, and a commitment to solving human problems and satisfying human needs.

I once saw a prayer list with a young man at a religious camp meeting in Accra, Ghana. It was one of the most remembered spiritual meetings I had ever attended. The meeting ground was full. It was a 5-day retreat, and it was not during any holiday period where workers will be available out from work to attend, and not a school holiday period when I will say our young lads are all home and available to attend such a meeting. I was expecting that the meeting would be scantily attended with many people busy at work and students studying in school. But lo and behold, the average

age that attended the meeting were those young people who are supposed to be active during working hours and in the classrooms receiving lectures in the university or college.

Young men and women came to pray and seek God's help for financial breakthroughs, money miracles, and tongues of command, many of whom are not working or doing anything tangible that God could put His grace on but seeking quick help from God to make a miracle rain happen suddenly in their finances.

The retreat was tagged; *"Money from Above"* and there is this prayer list that was announced one after the other for everyone to pray about. I could not help but wonder what people pray about, whether it had become an avenue for mocking God's intention in allowing us to present our needs to Him in prayer.

Some of the prayer points I could remember as the young man with the microphone began to call out for all to pray about.

1. Prayer for immediate miracles, supernatural money miracles, and fortunes. Money from the bank should come to the one with the strongest faith.

2. Prayer for financial help and stability from God, that all the rich people in this world begin to find you and give you money.

3. Prayer for money abundance. Commanding money to come to you wherever money is resting, pray that you don't want to work again, but that money should come to you right now.

4. Prayer against my creditors, all those that want their money back should fall sick or die, and all those that owe me never find rest till they locate me and pay me my money in full.

5. Prayer for a new wallet filled with hard currencies should appear this week by a miracle in my pocket.

6. Prayer that the riches of others become mine, all their money become mine, they will have no rest of mind until they turn it up to me.

This is a typical but worrisome example of how many people have turned spirituality into get-rich-quick schemes. Even more upsetting is that this is the mindset of so many people of faith, and young people who should be using their minds in more productive ways rather than conjuring up God and chanting for money. They have been taught wrongly. This has been either by their so-called spiritual leaders or by the misleading books they have read. It is nowhere in the Bible that a man will get rich by praying and expecting miracles. God is very clear and direct that a man must work with his hands and mind while looking up to Him for wisdom, direction, and support.

Spirituality has done more harm than good to those who let it overshadow their reasoning. Spiritual work in and of itself is a way of gaining freedom from the troubles of this world, the search for God, and gains of eternity after this life, but in the minds of foolish people, it could be used as a tool to parade inefficiency. The ignorance on the side of the people who rest on magic or spirituality will make them end up compromising the effectiveness of hard work, critical thinking, and economics.

Your own words

....
....
....
....
....
....
....
....
....
....
....
....
....
....
....
....

Chris Rock
"Wealth is not about having a lot of money; it's about having a lot of options".

Taking the options best suited for you and working hard to foster your talent and career is important, the road that will take you to your desired destination may be slow but rise up to it. never take the shortest and deadliest routs, it may lead you to a dark and breathless end.

Chapter Seven:
The 15 Laws of Wealth

"The world is shaped by laws, Logic is the science of the law of thought, and so is wealth produced by laws that brings prosperity."

Oyewola Oyeleke. Author, entrepreneur,

Success is a result and not a pursuit. It is the end product of what you want to be achieved by following the rules that govern it. Financial wealth happens when you know the set laws, and not only know them but obey those laws and rules that govern them. Laws apply to everyone and are the same everywhere and at any time. Don't make the mistake that a law may be ignored sometimes or be broken without consequences, The laws that govern wealth are no respecter of your status, location, ideologies, or educational accomplishments. It is not subject to your faith or religious belief. It is a constant that cuts across every divide. These laws are what make those that obey them find the result it brings especially in the area of wealth creation. Without these prescribed laws, there is no wealth.

Success is predictable, and so is failure. Anything that is designed to function by law is predetermined by its function. It's like having a combination to a lock: if you put in the right numbers, in the right sequence, the lock will open, no matter how big or strong the lock may be. When there is law and order in a system, the laws are generally meant to be accepted and obeyed, so that there will be proper functionality. If there were a breakdown of the laws that govern a system, then there might be little or no positive results.

Every man is meant to succeed and be wealthy because laws were created to make it happen. If the laws are followed to the letter the connection will be made and the results will be achieved. Everything works by certain laws; it holds man accountable for his actions. Laws make nature alive; laws define life. Laws that hold the entire universe and are designed to function and continue by these immutable laws that hold everything together. Things fall apart when we try to create shortcuts or philosophies that contradict what the law dictates.

Successful people make themselves successful because they are smart enough to learn, know and pursue what makes things work. They instinctively follow given and prescribed laws that lead them to success. In essence, success is the result of you recognizing those basic and common laws and being obedient to those laws to the letter. The activities you engaged in brought you to where you are today. Success and failure are within the confines of rules and laws that produce them.

In February 2016, I was in New York to see a business partner who wanted to help our company get a contract approved with the New Jersey Rail Services system. The meeting was scheduled for 6 p.m. with a lawyer in the Bronx. As I journeyed down from New Jersey through the Holland Tunnel to come out at the 1-78 East, at the other side of the road, I saw a phantom traffic jam. I was dismayed because this was unusual. I had never seen traffic on that side of the tunnel this early in the morning because it is against traffic. If you were going into New York from New Jersey in the morning hours, it usually will be smooth cruising down the four-lane highway. Then, a few meters down the road, I noticed police emergency flashlights and men of the federal highway patrol were passing vehicles around an accident. They were gathered around a man whom they had handcuffed and rushing to put another lady in the ambulance. I surmised that he was the reason for the accident and the traffic jam on the other side of the road.

As I came closer to the scene, I noticed that the man had been driving against traffic on the other side of 1-78 East New Jersey seeing the way the vehicle is facing after colliding with upcoming vehicles. I was puzzled, wondering how someone could find himself driving into oncoming traffic. I drew closer and tried to get more details of such a traffic jam where there shouldn't be such, I saw that he was a delivery man with a fast-food truck. He seemed to be trying to explain why he had made an unlawful decision to drive facing oncoming traffic which resulted in a collision of several cars and trucks so he could save himself from getting late for his delivery appointment.

He was on his way to Hoboken as he explained, a city about 3 miles away from the accident scene. He was making a delivery to a pharmaceutical company and didn't want to be late to meet up, so he disobeyed the law. He was mandated to make the delivery before 4 p.m. Now it was 6:10 p.m. as I checked the time. From all reasonable estimations, it was obvious that he would not have been able to make the expected delivery time looking at the traffic we are in, but he would not be in jail for driving violations and causing multiple accidents and injuries. He decided to create a different lane by jumping into the other side of the turnpike face long with oncoming vehicles. In all indications, he had violated a major traffic law. But unfortunately, not only did he fail to meet the target, but he had also gotten himself arrested and put other people's lives in danger. He brought shame and embarrassment to himself and the company he represented. As he looked at his watch and realized the futility (perhaps foolishness) of his efforts dawned on him.

All he could do was shake his head in regret. You cannot go against the law and suffer no consequences. Every law is meant to bring order, efficiency, and success, and if disobeyed, brings trouble, loss, and misfortune.

Wealth Answers to Laws

The same scenario in the above story happens all too often in the pursuit of wealth. Wealth, as we have seen, is a spinoff of knowledge. It is governed by certain fundamental laws that cannot be ignored. When these laws are followed wealth is often guaranteed. When flouted the result, as in the above case, failure, and frustration rushed into the picture. Incidentally, laws and principles are peculiar to wealth. They govern different aspects of life and living.

Experience has shown that there is nothing not governed by a set of rules and laws. You cannot stand and walk-in midair because the law of gravity will pull you down. There is the law of diminishing returns, the law of kinetics, the law of motion, and the law of sowing a seed and reaping a harvest if you follow the proper steps for success.

You must breathe to live, don't you? You can't have a fish jumping out of the water and deciding to start living on dry land like a Chicken. A toad can't fly like a bird, they can only hop, flying is not their nature, likewise, will a tree grow legs and begin to walk around like a giraffe, the gazelle may envy the Lion and want to be like the king of the jungle, but they can never be a carnivore. And as the delivery man's experience has shown us, going against established laws can paralyze progress and productivity. There is often collateral damage when laws are not followed, consequences for disobedience to laws can be very deadly and may affect not only the lawbreaker but many innocent people that step on it. Sometimes this recklessness can cause fatal consequences to those individuals and their dreams and could be what will take their breath away. You cannot expect to drive into oncoming traffic and not cause some kind of accident or fall into trouble one way or another, this is the law of karma:

what you put out there will come back to you negatively or positively.

Working against the laws that govern life's processes and occurrences is dangerous. In wealth creation, some laws are attached to this phenomenon, which must be followed. It becomes near impossible to reach your financial goals by breaking already set laws, by not obeying the laws that govern wealth as prescribed, will bring failure and privation. We will be examining these laws in greater detail:

Law 1

Universal Law of Attraction: The Magnet Principle

Positive attracts positivity, love attracts love, beauty attracts beauty and wealth attracts wealth. This universal law of attraction explains how objects, things, happenings, accomplishments, good ideas, success, and results draw attention to it. To gain wealth, you must have all that it takes to "attract" it to you: to become a magnet for the things that need to be present in one's life to be successful. This is an amplification of the belief theory that positive or negative comes into a person's life by what they attract, this is the magnet principle. This law is based on the reality that people and their thoughts are made from the "inner pure energy" that holds what it attracts and attracts what it holds.

This law is so powerful that it takes a trained mind to fully comprehend it. Scientists have many tools available to them when attempting to describe how nature and the universe at large work. Often, they reach for laws and theories first. The mind of man can see and attract anything into the physical realm. For example, let's say you want to attract flies to yourself and repel butterflies, all you need to do is rob dirt all over your body, flies will be all over you and you will also notice that butterflies will not come close because they don't stay around dirt, but they go for good smell and bright color objects. Another example could be that you want to make friends with gangsters and chase corporate guys away from you, all you need is to dress like them, and your mode of dressing will help you achieve it.

Let us say that you need a black leather office chair. You are constantly thinking about this specific piece of furniture.

You will notice that everywhere you go from that period will be black office furniture displayed. As you are walking in your neighborhood, you will see black office furniture, in the trash, sales points, and furniture companies will all display this kind of furniture. You walk past an apartment complex you will see one that looks like what you saw in your mind. In front of the building where you live. Your mind is attracting what it has created.

A positive ready personality attracts other clubs of positivity, as it draws in healthy and wealthy people to himself, bringing positively good relationships. This is also in nature a beautiful and bright flower attracts bees to itself and causes pollination to occur. This is because beauty attracts, it attracts the attention of everything that loves beauty. Remember that whatever attracts will always bring close to it what it attracts, especially good and scarce objects that ordinarily need the power to bring them in. We can also say this concerning light. Light attracts life to itself; no living thing lives without light. Light also attracts knowledge, when light sets in, everything becomes clearer, and life becomes easier and more enjoyable to live.

This can apply to other elements like sound, smell, touch, and invariably all forces that tend to attract. Similarly, we can apply it to wealth, if you are an attractive person, with the elements that attract business minds and opportunities, you will invariably pull people that have the answers to your needs to you, businesses will gravitate towards you, money will become easier to navigate towards you and you will attract quality investments, lucrative contracts, and stellar business opportunities.

You may have noticed that most successful businessmen move in similar circles. The reason is that they are like-minded, and they have all the elements needed to achieve results. They speak the same language; they find themselves wherever they are. They come from the same perspective, they lift each other with knowledge and positivity. They are drawn to each other like magnets.

If you begin to work on your mind, your character, and your goals, you will attract into your life those things (and experiences) that will allow you to grow toward success and prosperity. You will become successful because you attract success and gravitate to a higher standard that you place yourself in. You will begin to effortlessly experience a higher standard of living and a pull of success for yourself because you are around those things and people who need what you have and must intermingle to succeed together. your success now becomes the success of those elements, and those elements cannot survive without your personality.

These people who are regarded as magnets have some elements that attract wealth; they do not speak poverty and lack, rather, their language is to succeed, big goals, great and unprecedented achievements, deep ideas, and a sense of respect for success and provider of solutions. You can't let your mind dwell on failure and penury and become wealthy. That is not going to happen; it would be against the law of wealth building. You don't just think of success, you become success personified because that is who you have become. Your thinking should be the first point of action. The reason why your mindset must be carefully aligned with the right perspective is that you should not have a fixed mindset, rather, you must have a growth mindset. A fixed mindset will not allow you to grow into your dreams, you will procrastinate and oftentimes doubt those big dreams and plans that were already warming up to meet up with opportunities.

A growth mindset will enable you to grow, develop and create as much success as a person whose mind is already made up to be what they want to be no matter the terrain.

You must be aligned with positive thoughts to open the door for the prosperity that is waiting for you when you fully open your mind. It has often been debated: when do you begin to dress for success? When you are successful or when you are on the come up? Here's a hint: sometimes you have to fake it 'til you make it.

The attraction also manifests itself through looks and charisma. You will be addressed by others who perceive you to be a certain person. You will be addressed as "Sir" when you look like that person. That's why you don't see a beggar with torn and smelly clothes walking into a five-star hotel. He can't even make it into the building, the doorman will stop him even if he is the owner of the hotel. Can you imagine a man dressed in an expensive Kiton tuxedo with crocodile-cut leather Mauri shoes, clean-shave, and smoothly groomed hair walking into a building and the doorman tells him the place is for executives only? You must begin to live according to how you want people to see you, and what you want to be attracted to you. Success begins with you, your charisma, your knowledge, and your goals. Those things we carry can either attract success and wealth or if they are negative, will repel from us the opportunities to become successful and wealthy.

The law of attraction is so powerful that it can attract either positive or negative things toward you. So, you must always be positive and do the right things to attract the right things and the right people to you. But if you continue doing the wrong things or allowing negative and destructive thinking to sink into you, then, you will only attract negativity and failure.

Law 2

Law of Respect (Reciprocity)

John C. Maxwell, author, and motivational speaker gave a beautiful illustration of how many successful and wealthy people have used this law to get ahead of the ordinary man who thinks respect is gained by demanding it and with self-pride. *"Listen and acknowledge the other person, learn from them, and address the mistakes, do not treat good things in disdain, rather keep your small cash straight, clean, and well-kept in your wallet"*. Mr. Maxwell could tell that respect is a conscious attitude of attention given to the least of things that ordinarily should be recognized. It is the practice of exchanging honor, attentiveness, and thoughtfulness with others for mutual benefit, especially privileges granted by one to another.

The last instruction from Maxwell is very simple but powerful: keeping money notes clean and straight has put those people who disrespect it in a financial mess and struggle. keeping as simple as a currency clean, properly arranged, and straight in your wallet is a financial intelligence for people who understand power and success. until you see the power that money has and give it the due respect it deserves, you may not know its value and even be able to hold on to it. What you respect will give you honor and attention, and in addition, will want to give you more of its usefulness to enjoy. Respecting your money means knowing its worth and taking care of it properly. Your relationship with money is governed by how you treat it. Money has a very important place in our lives. If we give money the respect it deserves, it will reciprocate in the same way.

Respecting the business time and appointments could look so simple and un-attacking, but it could ruin every opportunity to get ahead in the area of financial prosperity. How can you have an appointment with business associates and opportunities and not meet up with the time, how can you ignore paying for goods and services or delay the delivery of the same to your customers and think the business will strive, how can you disrespect your customers with substandard products and services and expect to get their loyalty and continue patronizing your business or product? The world of business does not joke with mutual respect, respecting the minutest things that ordinarily should be ignored could help you build a sound financial base and opportunities for wealth.

Let us talk about respect for money one more time. In a deep business environment, people that handle currency cheaply like they handle their tissue paper get entangled with losses and mismanagement. The payment for the goods and services they render will always be short, misappropriated, and unaccounted for. Oftentimes, they are unkept and messed up, some even write on the money, and some will crumple bills into the buckets and dirty containers. Just the way their office, car, homes, and even business files are unkempt. Their lives will make you know that they care less for life and everything that makes it go around. They treat everything with disdain, those things that should be important as common and lackadaisical.

Money is a spirit; it will treat those that treat it right to splendor and plenty and will curse the man that treats it badly to scarcity. When you treat things that are meant to be neatly and nicely kept without care and respect, they will begin to lose value and cannot bring anything good to you when they are supposed to. No wonder you find people who will hardly have those good things come to them, no matter how nice and gentle they are, good things become scarce for them to have just by the way they treat them, It begins to reflect with how they handle their overall financial matters and in return, showing up on their finances.

Every successful and powerful person can relate to this virtue which is hardly seen anywhere else than in people of influence and character. They respect money, they respect their office, they respect people, they respect customers, they respect other people's time, they respect successful people, and anything that shows success they respect things even when no one is watching them, and even respect animals and nonliving things. That is how important it is to align with the law of respect and diligently run with it.

As you aspire for greatness and get ready to achieve big goals, your attitude towards things begins to change, and your manners and the way you treat everything, living and nonliving will begin to change and improve. When you become friendly and compassionate, you will draw favor and grace to yourself. That is to say that when you respect success, you will get success,

Secondly, you will begin to build yourself to be Respectable: To get the utmost respect in life, you must become a respectable person. You begin to build yourself and your credibility, you become a relevant and indispensable person. This is how wealth comes, as you become the love and hope for everyone, you are of service to everyone, helping and anticipating being a source of hope and solution to the needs of man.

Listening more than you talk is high respect that comes from you to others because you are mindful of the other person's opinion, catching up with every wisdom the person has to offer in addition to the one you already carry. You become a problem solver because you can't lead others if you can't proffer a solution and create a clear road that will lead to their destination.

As you begin to develop your personality, a high mark is necessary between who you were and who you are going to be, you build self-respect for success with a lot of humility. You demand respect for yourself and give respect to others. Disrespect can wreck so many useful habits. You respect money and all the elements of wealth; then, wealth and success come to reference you, and success becomes your nature. Just as disrespect of the President is treason, so is the disrespect of wealth and all the elements of wealth are ruination.

Treachery has no place in wealth. You must be true to your highest values. Wealth gravitates toward those that respect and cherish it, and to a man that understands its true value. You must respect education to get the best of it, you must have due respect for your workplace, coworkers, and work ethics that guide your operations, or else you will ruin productivity and result. Respect and value time is golden, be on time for meetings and appointments, meet up with delivery as you have proposed to the receiver, and be on time with your payments for goods and services and your debts. Respect the feelings of others by doing the best job for them with the highest standards of quality and excellence. Esteem your network with the greatest rewards as you work with confidence and trust. Your subordinates respect you and your leadership because of the respect you give to them, no wonder your wealth continues to grow within and outside you and your business is prospering, and having much loyalty amongst those you call your team

Respect the laws that govern you and your business; you won't get far from being an unethical businessperson. Give credence to constituted authorities. As the Bible says, give Caesar what is owed Caesar (the proper authorities i.e., the IRS). "You respected my offer..." is the statement Eric Manzoni kept saying after the meeting he had with the Founder of Clerks Construction Company in Texas.

Manzoni had invited a few construction companies with great repute to help fix their leaking lavatory in the customers' toilet area. The biggest problem was that every one of the big companies rejected the request to lower themselves to take on such a small job. They described his business to the small mom-and-pop construction companies. Dr. Hank Vadju came on site and on time for his meeting with Manzoni after receiving the letter about the need to reconstruct the leaking lavatory. Clerks Construction company accepted the offer, and the founder was at the meeting at the time requested by the board. This was what made the Clerks Construction company one of the biggest companies in the field; no job was too small for them.

Law 3

Law of Nurturing (Seed Principle)

You cannot plant a seed and leave it to grow into a fruit-bearing tree by itself, every seed requires nurturing, grooming and fertilization. As soon as you hold a seed, you begin to look for the right soil that the seed will survive and produce on, then, you begin to water it as regularly as possible, adding fertilizers, manure, pesticides, and insecticides. Most seeds grow by themselves without caring for or nurturing them, but you won't expect the best harvest from such an uncared process. Most seeds that grew by themselves get withered away, some are vulnerable to death or being eaten up by birds or insects, and some produce frail, and tiny fruits on them. The same with your finances, the law of nurturing is clear and made known that if you neglect your plans and every aspect of your finances, chances are you will not get the desired result. As you begin to grow in your quest for success, you must also give attention to your financial plans to become wealthy and remain successful, learning how to plant, grow, and nurture your wealth tree is important. The money tree is a system you can imbibe to grow your finances and become wealthy, this is widely believed to bring good results and wealth to the place where it is planted. Now, even though the money plant does not grow currency, it surely shows the path on how to grow the real money plant and turn your goals into wealth.

In the early stages of your quest for wealth, you will face some difficulties and distractions. Challenging situations may make you feel like quitting, but you must develop the ability to stand strong and maintain your focus while nurturing your dreams and pressing forward. At first, you will not find it interesting to want to plant the seed that looks good for food, always, the temptation will come for you to spend your capital and as much as you have on frivolous things. Having money discipline is key in the law of nurturing, without this virtue, you cannot nurture your finances and goals into wealth.

Another area is in your watering and nurturing process, attention is needed to grow your wealth. Wealth does not happen overnight, you must till the ground, water the seed as often as possible, and take away the weed around your plant, this process requires skill and hard work, it requires attention to complete. Day and night you are alert to plan, and you become sensitive to the needs of your business or venture, clearing all loopholes and distractions.

Wealth comes in different ways. Sometimes the seed may seem negligible, but you must learn to nurture it all with diligence for it to survive and become beneficial to you and everyone. Without the application of the law of nurturing, your dreams can't materialize. Your ideas can't be implemented, and your business will never grow. Every good thing that grows in life requires tending and nurturing. When you begin to help something or someone to grow or develop and succeed, know that you have given yourself the card of fatherhood. You have started providing food, protection, and a place of shelter. Here you have taken the time to cultivate your seed. You have proven that you can nurture yourself and others.

As it is an important and necessary tool for success, you must have goals and dreams for what you want to have or become. many times, we see those dreams and goals die a natural death, not because the goals are not good enough or the dreams are mere hallucinations, but because they let them slip away, there was no anchor to hold those dreams and bring them into reality.

Nurturing your set goals and dreams into materialization is very important, it is a law that must happen, dreams and goals alone don't bring wealth, nurturing and building them does. Learn the basics and work towards creating your own 'real money tree' with a little effort, proper planning, and vision. The process is very much similar to how a tree grows. Just that, this money tree would bear wealth instead of edible fruits. Let us go through the simple 3-step process.

Sow The Seeds

It is imperative to sow the right seeds first. In simple words, create and follow the habits that lead to wealth generation. Create a budget, build an emergency fund, live within your means, and save at least 20% of your income each month. Restricted spending because of budget constraints may seem painful, but it is the best tool for wealth creation. At the same time, your emergency fund will ensure not to stash the cash in the bank and does not push you into a worst financial status in the case of emergencies. Another important factor is not to spend more than what you earn. If you spend more than you make, you can never grow rich! Instead, save a decent amount every month to accumulate a substantial corpus, without your knowledge.

Offer Nutrients for The Plant to Grow

Now that you have sown the seeds, you have to work towards offering proper nutrients for the plant to grow large. A plant needs water and light to grow big. Similarly, your money plant needs a few essential factors to grow huge, which include becoming invaluable at work, saving, and investing. Your greatest asset for wealth generation is your career and personality. Find ways to increase your value, be respectable, become wiser than you were a few minutes ago, and increase your capacity to earn big so you can help others.

At the same time, ensure to save a decent percentage, and build enough to push into the right investment channels to help your money grow. After all, money needs money to grow.

Nurture With Patience and Care

Patience yields more than force. Never expect instant results as you continue to build your wealth empire. opt for stable investment vehicles and stay focused on your business and plans, if required. For instance, mutual fund investments reap better yield when invested in a diversified portfolio for the long-term plan. Hence, patience and care are of utmost importance to generate wealth with time. This also applies to building a business or a system that will become your wealth points. Keep at what you have to do, don't give up easily, stand strong with what you have started, and push hard to achieve your aim. Successful people will never think they can be successful when they started, but it was their resilience and doggedness that brought them to the top. It may take a while to achieve your dreams, but keep nurturing them, and do not stop working and pushing to achieve your desired results.

Law 4

Law of Knowledge

A man is never greater than the available information in and around him, inside, and outside him. Knowledge is the biggest wealth creator ever, investing in financial knowledge is the best investment a person can make. You could strip away all other assets and possessions from a financially keen person, and it wouldn't take long for that person to acquire wealth and return to financial independence.

Do you agree that every man's death comes from what he doesn't know? Because if he knows the problem of his suffering and the solutions to it, he will live over that problem. A man of knowledge will always solve almost every problem and make life more pleasant and pleasurable for him and others. In the same vein, a man's success is the result of what he knows and how he applies them to life.

Knowing anything doesn't come cheaply. Knowledge demands concentration and dedication. Knowledge is an exchange: an exchange of ignorance for information, an exchange of lack of prosperity, an exchange of living in the dark and a myopic world to the bright side of life with lights of understanding that brings fame and fortune.

A fundamental law that cannot be compromised in building lasting wealth is knowledge. Socrates, a great Greek philosopher, once said, *"Smart people learn from everything and everyone, average people learn from their experiences, stupid people think they already have all the answers and never want to listen or learn."* Without knowledge whatever else is obtained will never add up to wealth.

This brings me to a story about a loving father with his college graduate son who was undergoing financial training to become an entrepreneur. There is a valuable lesson in this story. Engineer Thomas looked so excited when he asked his young son Fabian to apply for employment in his construction company after graduation. The entire family was expecting the boy to take over the company since he is the only son among three other girls and indeed the favorite. Engineer Thomas had instructed that the girls should take over the key departments and the boy should apply as a clerk and after two years, he will be promoted to work with the IT department as a system support associate. He further gave the next point of entry after another two years that he will be promoted to the office of the security and safety department to work as one of the trainees. But before he could say the next word, Fabian argued that he is old and smart enough to be the director of the company or in charge of finance and administration just like his sisters. Everyone kept their cool and silently encouraged him as they kept a worried heart that he was cheated of his rightful place as the only son with so much vigor and smartness.

Seeing that Fabian was not taking it lightly, Engineer Thomas had to explain why he was doing this rightful upbringing for his future good, he gave an example of successful men and women who through knowledge became successful in their chosen field. Elon Musk did not become wealthy because he has a nice set of teeth or because he was from a wealthy parent, he gained all the wealth by how much he know that others don't, his expertise ranges from rocket science, engineering, construction, tunneling, physics, management, and artificial intelligence to solar power and energy. In a previous article, I wrote about the knowledge of wealthy people, you will notice that all wealthy and successful people know something about everything. That is how they add up everything they know to solve other people's ignorance and need for a solution. Sergey Brin is not just a computer expert that created google with Larry

Page, he knows so much about many things that include Engineering, Mathematics, Marketing, Printing, Communication, Electrical, transcribing and so much more.

Some uncountable people have made a great mark by what they know, since this boy does not have what it takes to handle these tasks, he could not be depended on to handle the company at that level, he should learn all the skills and grow with them until he becomes a master of knowledge. We all want to be successful and wealthy, but we do not want to sacrifice more to gain them.

A father cannot give responsibility to a child that has no mental or physical capacity to handle basic responsibilities. It is the same in the world of finance and wealth. Without knowledge, there is no capacity to gain wealth from the world, or rather, the world will not allow you to handle wealth without the knowledge and ability to handle it. Until you have the mental and physical capacity to know it, see it, and handle it, you cannot claim it as your own.

All the elements of wealth function in an environment of knowledge. Your knowledge makes things work. It will amaze you that if a man of inadequate capacity is allowed to handle money, he will lose everything in a matter of time, and in the same way that if a man with skill and knowledge is given that same opportunity, he will turn it into gold and multiply the same amount of money. Each of us at one time had a vague fantasy that someday a miracle would happen, that the big pot of gold would someday show up after hard work. But year after year, life remains the same as the year before.

S. B. Fuller didn't wait for a miracle. He started his business as soon as he was out of school. He had saved some money and became one of the first African American entrepreneurs at an early age. He learned how to make soap from his mother in the basement of their house. He couldn't start the soap business until he was able to acquire more knowledge of soap making from Boyer International Laboratories, a soap-making industry that supplied most households with different lines of soap in Denver. He developed a better understanding of the ingredients that went into soap making and how to source the best materials where his customers were.

By 1935, Fuller started his own soap manufacturing business with an initial 25 dollars that he had saved and made over 1,000 dollars in less than six months. He created 30 new hair and skin care products from the same secret ingredient and built a small factory in the south of Denver. His most controversial business decision was when he mixed common brown seed and olive oil, and that simple alchemy changed his life. That simple breakthrough made him wealthy forever. In 1947, a white firm that had two successful product lines for cosmetics and facial soaps, Jean Nadal Cosmetics and H. A. Hair Arranger & Bros, sold their business to Fuller when they realized they just couldn't compete with him regarding the quality of his product.

Developing a wealth mentality requires thinking, planning, strategizing, and doing more than the required daily minimum effort to snag a paycheck. But knowledge will help you do more than just that. Knowledge will lead you to a fortune and help you keep everything forever. It is not only about making money that is important but about managing and keeping it that differentiates the wealthy guy from the rich guy. You must spend time with friends who can tell you how to get new skills and learn all the tricks of the trade, putting your mind and attention to where you can learn something and going the extra mile to pay for knowledge because it is worth it. Money invested in greater knowledge is never wasted money.

Mr. Afolabi Oyerokun, popularly known as Ftrillion, an online guru and home product magnate, was one of the guest speakers at the annual Christian leaders' convention and training of the New Covenant Christian Ministries, Bronx, New York. Archbishop Joseph called him out to the podium to give his thoughts on finances in church ministry as he gave classical examples to the attendant delegates. A registration fee of $250 was required for the one-week-long program. Many of the delegates thought that the fee was too high for a local Christian conference. But Mr. Oyerokun set them straight. His first words were "You cannot get knowledge without paying a price." In retrospect, I made a lot of money becoming a millionaire online trader because I paid the price for knowledge. Many people could not continue in the line of business because they could not face the challenges of the business. They did not pay to get the proper training to compete and win in the market. They fell off by the roadside very quickly. Those of us who took the bull by the horns and continued gulping education made a lot of money and reaped from the seeds we planted. Oprah Winfrey developed a money mentality long before she accumulated the wealth that she controls now through Harp Enterprises. Back in the day, when her friends were buying Reebok sneakers, she was buying Reebok stocks. She also paid for multiple training sessions to increase her knowledge on how to increase her wealth with that same sneaker company. While her friends wanted to just look great and expensive in Reebok sneakers, Oprah studied how to own such a company that can produce such beautiful shoes, the strategy that made the company work and made her search for that knowledge that worked for her.

He rides around New York in a Lincoln Town car limousine at age 30, suede flavored Armani suit, large diamond ring on his finger. He can afford anything at that young age. Alphonse Fletcher is a young American who spent all of his early 20's learning about the pension fund administration and the stock market. No wonder he is called the "Wizard of Wall Street." He is a stockbroker, investment advisor, and security analyst. Alphonso is respected as one of the most successful pension fund administrators of the year since 1994. He has donated millions of dollars to those organizations he got his knowledge from.

This is all to say that financial knowledge is the key to wealth and prosperity. It will not be how hard you work, but how much you know and how well you turn applied knowledge into power.

Law 5

Law of Giving and Receiving

Doing all you can do to see your money increase is always everyone's first desire, everything you know to do to get more money is also the first duty of anyone who wants to be richer. More income and higher financial balance are always the dreams of any businessperson. Seeing that your account statement is growing, and expenses decreasing is an index that you are doing just perfectly well in business; when money is coming in and nothing is going out will be a good indication of a healthy financial strategy. This can bring smiles to anyone's face anytime.

But wealth creation is a different ball game entirely, it has an order and a precept that may look incorrect to a business-minded person. It has many different rules that go beyond just gaining and bringing the money into yourself and your organization. According to the law of wealth, to increase one's prosperity capacity there must be some uncommon applications. Just like Samuel Maki, founder of Samaco Corporation and Engineering Services, wrote in a manuscript entitled "The Outspent Hands" – that book was published just after the death of the author: ...as he gave his experience with his first big money of $20,000. Though I needed more money to build my growing business and to start the construction of two water projects in a township in Harare, the capital of Zimbabwe, he said. These water projects will allow my newly incorporated and growing company to compete with the already existing and big construction and engineering companies in the Southern African region. This was the game-changer for us, we would have worked so hard for 20 years before we could get to the top of that chart or have the opportunity to do the projects we do now. Then he went on to write: "Our company was discussed everywhere in the city and among the Government agencies for the simple act of giving our first construction work for free, what we did became our breakthrough. We became a construction company of choice in less than 2 years to handle all the water projects and major road projects in over seven countries in the southern Africa region, which has never happened before."

Giving and receiving is nothing other than the flow of life— the harmonious interaction of all elements and forces that structure the field of existence. Giving and receiving are based on the fact that everything in the universe operates through dynamic exchange. Every relationship is one of giving and taking because giving and receiving are different aspects of the flow of energy in the universe. If we stop the flow of energy, we interfere with nature's intelligence. We must give and receive to keep wealth, or anything we want, circulating in our lives.

When we talk about money, we talk about currency circulation., Money or currency is derived from a Latin word meaning 'currere'- "to run or flow." The idea of acceptable means of exchange flowing from person to person." Money is a symbol of the life energy we give and the life energy we receive as a result of the service we provide to others. Like a river, money must keep flowing, otherwise, it begins to clog and stagnate. Circulation keeps it alive and vital. If we stop the circulation of life energy, if we intend to hold on to our money and hoard it for our use alone, we stop its circulation back into our lives, and you know what that means.

Money is a weapon and a defense: it must be strategically used for one's advantage. It will come to a period when your giving will be a lifestyle. Such giving will lead you to affluence. Your giving will make that way for you in unfriendly terrains. This kind of giving is that which you use to create a road map of influence and connection as seen in Proverbs 18:16 which states: "A man's gift maketh room for him, and bringeth him before great men."

If you want love, learn to give love, if you want attention and appreciation, learn to give attention and appreciation, if you want wealth and material affluence, help others to become wealthy and make many have material affluence like you. If you want to be blessed with all the good things in life, learn to silently bless those you can extend your hands of love to with all the good things in life. The more you give, the more you will receive.

There are so many testimonies of small entrepreneurs and big conglomerates about how they started their businesses, many stated that they started by giving away their first production, some gave out free products, and some gave out great services than what others in the same field gave. One way or the other, they gave out something to someone or society.

Let's take a walk back in time: King Osei Tutu of the Asante empire, the Gold Coast which is present-day Ghana. During his reign in 1701 made a revelation through the last press interview with town reporters for the British traders. At this time, the empire was bringing in those neighboring towns and kingdoms for absorption into the Asante empire. The King was given the kingship of the new regions to those that have the capacity to rule the other regions. He chose men of honor and wealth and the only criteria that could be used were for those who gave gifts and gave money for the development of the towns. Thus, giving helps you make a positive impact that will be indelible in the hearts of people and then places you in a position of unending riches and fame, success, and wealth. This is the law that governs wealth and abundance that cannot be ignored. It is a law that has what can only be described as a reversal-reflex indication. Naturally, it seems best to hoard our riches and watch over them as they increase, rather than dipping into them and giving them out and expecting nothing in return. How does it make sense to give out what you trying to build to become more? instead of just finding more ways to add to your riches, you are guided to give out. The law of giving supersedes the tendency of the natural mind.

According to this law, if you want to increase your compensation and wealth, you must increase the value of your contributions. You must do more of what others ordinarily won't do. This is what distinguishes and gives you an edge over others. You have to do what others won't do to get what others will never have. In the law of sowing and reaping, whatever we sow invariably comes back to us as a way of compensation for our respect and trust in this law. What we give away returns and in increased and better quality. It is just a natural phenomenon; it is a law, so, it must happen. If you find time to help others and help solve problems around you, if you raise others with the quality of your personality, you will get the returns of the harvest in those you poured into.

Giving promotes social connection. Studies show that when you give to others and society, your generosity is often continued down the line to the grass root and rolls up to the authorities as news and information spreads out, and invariably returns to you as wealth and fame. Every time you give attention to other people's needs and solve societal problems, seeking to help the world out of needs and problems, making out ways to create a good environment for the world to thrive, you are fulfilling the law of giving. By doing so, you are making a way for your success. Think about it. Pro basketball player Jeremy Atkinson once said that *"the waters that do not flow and are stagnant will stink and be lifeless while the flowing waters will always be useful and fresh for all to enjoy."*

Most wealthy people are so because of the many kinds of people they have raised. They poured the fullness and wealth of their personality into them. Having people, you have given attention to, pouring unwavering love to those that needed love and care, assisting the helpless and vulnerable, and freely giving out knowledge and guidance will, in the long run, be to your advantage and in return come become wealth.

Life is a circle of giving and receiving. When any party ceases to contribute, the circle will be broken, and leakages will be discovered. Whatever you are enjoying today is someone else's contribution, and whatever you are lacking today is because someone who was supposed to contribute didn't. Don't be that person who because he refuses to contribute causes leakages and problems to the circle of life and causes retrogression for themselves and the future of many. Every person on earth is here to contribute to making the world go round and make it a better place.

Giving is the essence of living. Anything that you put out that is useful will bring you wealth. Your presence is irrelevant if you have nothing to contribute. Whether big or small, we all have something to contribute and we should contribute. The system will not bring the fruit of the people to you unless you contribute to their development. In any organization, you find yourself in, contribute to its progress and growth, work hard, give your best, be punctual, be a team player and desist from complaints and negativity. In the school, in the house, in the community, in the office, in the team you belong to, in your city, make sure you are contributing. We all have something to contribute. Contribute love, instead of hate. Contribute great ideas and solutions Instead of destructive criticism, contribute positivity. Instead of being embittered by someone who offended you. contribute to uplifting the team and growing the network Instead of watching from the sidelines, get in there, and contribute. Giving is the right share of energy nobody will be able to stop as you build your fortune.

Law 6

Law of Commitment and Dedication

Until you can ignore ignorance, neglect negativity, and disregard disrespect, you are not ready for the next level. Success is not for the weak, and wealth is not for the lackadaisical, but the committed. You cannot be successful or wealthy if you are not dedicated to a cause that you believe in. There must be something you are ready to achieve no matter what it will take to achieve it. Putting your heart into whatever you have planned to achieve is the key to good results and success. Just like we see in the book of Matthew 6:21: "...for where your treasure is, there will your heart be also." And in essence, where you put your heart, which is your commitment will be where your treasure will be found.

There is no way a man can be wealthy and successful if there is no commitment of time, dedication, effort, and strength invested. Continuing your time to do whatever you set your mind to invariably means that you are completely sold out on bringing out results.

No man has ever been successful without being dedicated to his vision and plans. When you are dedicated to building wealth, you will hardly have time for mediocrity or distractions. Your attention will be focused on maximizing time, resources, and opportunities. You will not procrastinate or waste precious hours in non-productive activities.

Dedication is very powerful in the factor of wealth optimization. A man who is dedicated to duty is always a formidable force. God testified to this in the building of the Tower of Babel. The entire human race was dedicated to building a tower to the heavens and they seemed to be succeeding. That was until God foiled their plans because that was not of His program for humanity. The point, however, is that those builders were able to achieve some success because of the law of dedication that each one applied. Genesis 11:6 reveals that God saw their dedication and testified of the potential impact it was going to have. No matter how seemingly minute or unrealistic your dreams are, it is your dedication that will bring them to manifestation and fruition. Dedication is sticking to your goal until it is accomplished. Nothing can stop you. Nothing is allowed to hinder you. No matter the terrain, you just keep going.

Commitment is also an oath taken to start and conclude a cause. When you vow to do something until it's completed, that is the essence of commitment. Just like the Algerian athlete who won the first ever Arab gold medal in Sydney, Norah Buraidah Marah at the Sydney 2000 Olympics games in Australia, clinching the first gold medal for her country. She made a promise, a commitment to do her best. She returned to her country with the goal. She made herself, her family, and her community proud. She was never an athlete during her early years and her career. She stumbled into racing and made a vow to bring excellence to her endeavors. She committed herself to uncommon training, fervent prayer, and bringing home a medal, but not just any medal, the gold medal. She was not the best athlete on the field; she was told by her coach that she did not have a chance, sensing that there were stronger and better-trained competitors with good speed and years of experience than her. Many had participated in other Olympic games and had won several medals. But Norah made an oath to herself that she was going to win. She told the woman in the mirror every single morning before her training session that she is winning the gold no matter the terrain. Reporters that interviewed her after her victory said she spoke like she already knew she would win, the Tricot newspaper reported that her eyes were on the gold for the 4 months that she trained and never lost focus for one day.

Norah gave all her time, her zeal, her mind, and her strength to her running. There was no doubt that she would be successful. The stronger your commitment, the more likely you are to be wealthy and successful in your chosen field. Your success depends on your strong conviction, just like having more willingness to go out of your comfort zone to achieve success, bringing discipline, focus, and patience. When you are not fully committed to your goals and target, you quit too quickly and remain at the point you started from. You will not see any wealthy man on the face of the earth that has not given total attention to that one thing that made a difference in his life. Every successful person became so as they won in a particular field or endeavor. There is a champion in one thing that others don't have. It all started with their commitment to that thing, and that is what you must focus on if you want to be wealthy and successful.

In the same vein, the lack of commitment is one of the most common reasons why people of strength, ideas, skill, and opportunities fail to achieve their goals. Legendary football coach Vince Lombardi told a group of young entrepreneurs that *"most people fail not because of a lack of desire to succeed and be wealthy or the lack of good ideas but because they do not commit to their cause."* His football team once lost out of a very crucial qualifying game when he was head coach of the Washington Commanders football club in 1970, the team's mind was not coordinated and was so full of distractions that they were almost relegated to the second division.

Hal Elrod, a keynote speaker, and success coach is a person that has been an inspiration to many. He once wrote: "To reach levels of wealth and success you have never reached before; you must be committed at a level you have never been committed at before." My takeaway from this quote is that when you are truly committed to a goal or a target, you do all you have to do despite not feeling like it or seems as if there is no progression. You will achieve your goals even though it's getting even more difficult. You push yourself into the rain not minding the perfectly ironed suit you are wearing because you are committed to a result in a time frame. You defy sleep, break old habits, ignore comfort, and push through difficult terrain because you want to achieve your goal and get a hold of results. The stronger your commitment, the more likely you will succeed beyond anyone's imagination. Your commitment will take you away from any present state to your projected state, and this is so with creating wealth.

Commitment is not easy because it takes work. It is not something that falls from the sky or happens overnight. Rather, it's that inner focus and zeal you develop over time. It is a decision you make with a bold face and with the courage to overcome anything that tries to come your way. If you have such a mindset, and you push yourself into it, you will become wealthy and successful in due time. This is one thing that has worked for me and for all the people I have trained and counseled over the years. We have wealthy young people on our team who, without entering the lion's den to pick up gold to become rich, continued with a bold commitment to be the best in their chosen fields and came back with results and testimonies.

Most people falsely think they are on the right track, hoping they are committed to what they have planned to achieve, falsely assuming they are focused and ready to achieve their goals. But as they continue and begin to see rising obstacles, failures setting in, and defeats, they begin to give up their dreams. This is not a commitment, commitment never fades. You will never say never if you are committed to returning with the desired goal or reward. Old habits, procrastination, and unproductive activities begin to decline. They lose motivation to continue because they have tasted failure and were never committed to achieving their goals no matter what comes their way. They were never committed in the first place. When you are committed, you make a promise, take a vow, forge an agreement to do it, and get it done, no matter the obstacles or discouragements that come along.

Law 7

Law of Believing (Faith)

Whatever you believe inside you becomes real on the outside, and that becomes your world sooner or later. This law manifests from the spiritual realm into the physical. What you believe is what exists. There is a superimposition from the superior realm that affects the lesser realm which is what we see, hear, feel, taste, or perceive. My great-grandfather once told my dad who in return told me that he had over thirty-two gods that he and his kinsmen worshiped, and each one of those gods was alive to respond to their requests and prayers anytime they called for help. He could say so because he grew up believing that spirits are in those materials they have always worshipped. He saw a god in stones, trees, shoes, machetes, bottles, carved images, and clothes. His faith in those things make spirits and demons function in them and made a pact with him and all those that believe in them. He believes they are real; he has faith that it is working, and they existed and worked for them. No one can convince them otherwise that those stones and images they worship are not real, their belief in them made those things communicate with them and help them in times of their need.

In the same vein, whatever you believe strongly in, your inner man will manifest into the physical, this is a law, and it must happen that way, believe it or not. This applies to wealth creation. If you believe that you can be successful with business or investments, it will surely come to pass. If you believe that you will be wealthy and put your heart into it, you will be wealthy. Your faith is your power to make your inner desires come to life.

Many Christians, in particular, have used this principle to beat sickness, diseases, misfortunes, and satanic attacks, but have not used this in the area of their finances. The Bible is explicit on the truth that you can have whatsoever you desire once you believe in it and work towards it. (Mark 11:24).

Law is constant, and works for anyone and everyone, anywhere, and to whoever operates it rightly. Conversely, it works against anyone who doesn't apply it or who applies it wrongly. Some businesspeople have remained frustrated with their businesses and line of trade for so long because they don't operate by the law of faith. "I know my business will prosper someday" is a mere wish talk; that's not faith! Faith calls real that which isn't perceivable to the senses. Faith believes and affirms what has been seen in your desired goals and plans and has the total belief that it will succeed.

If someone who believes in his pursuit of success and wealth has a total conviction from the bottom of his heart, he declares in faith by regularly voicing his success and victory, he knows that he has started a cause that is already completed, "The law of faith requires that he keeps vocalizing his faith. The Bible says if the clouds are full of rain, they empty themselves upon the earth (Ecclesiastes 11:3). Keep using the faith you have built inside to mount pressure on that procrastination mindset, let your faith to succeed supersede the pressure of business and your faith will prevail.

Many say they believe and don't do anything, that is wrong. When you truly believe, you act. That's what faith does; it's the response or action you take based on your belief. When you say you "believe," it's not passive but active; "believing" is a word of action; it's actually "doing" your faith. That's why the Bible says, "Even so faith if it hath not works, is dead, being alone" (James 2:17). Faith requires a corresponding action; you prove your faith by your actions in working hard to succeed in business, you write out your goals and begin to pursue them rigorously. Whatever it is that you believe about becoming wealthy is revealed in your actions.

Acting in faith in your plans, goals, vision, and dreams is where the power is; that's what profits you. don't write out your plans and goals and go to sleep. Start believing in yourself that you can do it, believe in yourself that you can do it better than anyone else. The law of wealth dictates that you must believe in success, you must believe in yourself, you must believe in your abilities, and you must also believe in God who can help you fly above the ordinary terrains and give you the ability to get wealth.

It is a norm that if you do not have faith in yourself, you have started failing from the first stage of life onward, until you change that mindset and build trust in your capacity and capabilities, you will not go far. Searching deeply into the life and system of wealthy people, I discovered that the first step to their greatness is the power of the trust they have built for themselves and their personalities. They grew to believe in what they can do and saw any other obstacle as bread. Faith begins with knowing who you are and what you carry inside you. if you don't have faith in yourself, chances are you will hand over your dreams and goals to those that can achieve the result.

When we believe in ourselves, it can help us achieve our goals, manifest our dreams, and increase our well-being. But the flip side is also true. A lack of belief in ourselves means we are less likely to act, change, or push to make things better. When we expect we will fail, we are more likely to fail. The law wants us to have faith in others. But the law also directs us so we can also have belief in ourselves. Having (or not having) this belief in ourselves has similar implications as having (or not having) belief in others. For example, when we believe in someone, we're honest with them, we can count on them, and we are confident in them doing what's best for us. So, what might it mean when we don't believe in ourselves? Well, maybe we don't want to be honest with ourselves because we're not sure what we are capable of doing. Maybe we can't count on ourselves to do the things we tell ourselves we'll do. Or maybe we're afraid that we'll do things to harm ourselves instead of helping ourselves to wealth.

These are some of the key components involved in believing in yourself. Give yourself self-worth, self-confidence, self-discipline, self-trust, and strong self-belief. And see yourself become wealthy and powerful Maybe you struggle with just one of them or maybe you struggle with all of them. By understanding where your struggles lie, it'll be easier to start shifting your attitudes about yourself.

Law 8

Law of Resilience

The Spartan army was said to be one of the toughest militaries in the world to date, the wall of resilience they built with their never-give-up spirit is outstanding, they have never accepted defeat once, and that has made them win every battle. Developing a shield against enemy attack during downturns and opposing mental, financial, and emotional adversities will make you impenetrable, no matter the strength of the challenges and the sharpness of the setbacks, you will always stand and bounce back because of your stubborn stands to remain and continue. The wall of resilience must remain unbroken; that is the power of mentally strong people who can unlock the door of courage to stand strong when life's storms hit. The ability to withstand depression and anxiety in business is key. The question is, can you develop a stronger mindset for every day as you continue your business journey? It's a behavioral trait we can all develop and improve, else, we cannot be successful in that endeavor.

Some components make up. being resilient and can be developed with each passing day – competence, confidence, character, and control

Wealthy people never have a smooth road to success. There are always challenges here and there. The journey to the top consists of the good times and the rough times, failures, and successes, and oftentimes, struggles and winning. If you can listen to the testimonies of people who have accomplished great things and built lasting wealth, they will tell you that there have been times when they were tempted to give up on their dreams. But they kept on going despite the hardships and setbacks until they achieved their goals, they never say never. This is the power of resilience-the capacity to recover quickly from difficulties and failures.

At some point in our lives, we all experience some form of setback and failure. For example, this can be from losing a business deal, getting a negative result when you have put a lot to work, or lacking the motivation to achieve your day-to-day aspirations. All those examples can be terrifying and hard to manage if we fail to understand how to control emotional triggers and thoughts successfully.

The law of resilience focuses on the ability to adapt well in the face of adversity, trauma, tragedy, threats, or significant sources of stress-such as rejection from those areas we should have succeeded, disappointment, deprivation, or opposition. It relates to the determination to keep moving, even when nothing just seems to be working. There could be family and relationship problems, serious health problems, or workplace and financial stress. Still, for those who will make it, the law of resilience must be deployed.

Getting results even in the most difficult terrains means you have to demonstrate resilience and power to stand, that you must have suffered and conquered difficulty or distress during your quest for success means you are ready for wealth.

We need to explain a few things again, resilience acknowledges mistakes and errors. Making a mistake is not failure. Failing to learn and improve from that mistake is a failure. How can any of us grow without failure? Failing and succeeding are all a part of life. It is possible to shy away from trying something because of your past mistake but trying again is the brainer for wealth, rising stronger even when things didn't work the first time is healthy for your growth, and the ability to work through them until the victory is attained is what you should fight for.

Resiliency means being able to bounce back from life developments that may feel overwhelming at first. When resilient people have their lives disrupted by life situations, they handle their feelings and method of solving things in healthy ways. They allow themselves to feel grief, anger, loss, and confusion when they are lost and in distress, but they don't let it become a permanent grieving state. An unexpected outcome is that they not only heal but also often bounce back stronger than before. They are examples of Wilhelm Nietzsche's famous statement, "That which does not kill me makes me stronger." This is why resilient people usually handle major difficulties easier than others. They expect to rebuild their disrupted lives in a new way that works for them, and the struggle to overcome adversity develops new strengths in them. No wonder resilient people are successful people any day and at any time.

Resilience is more important than ever in today's world. The volatile and chaotic period we are going through nowadays will not end soon. To build wealth and sustain a good life for yourself and your family, you must be much more resilient than people had to be in the past. People with resiliency skills have a significant advantage over those who feel helpless or react like victims. In this world of life-disrupting, nonstop change. That is why success and wealth can never be complete without obeying the law of resilience.

Law 9

Law of Action (proactivity)

Sir Isaac Newton's third law of motion states that for every action, there is an equal and opposite reaction. According to this law, the action and reaction forces are equal in magnitude and opposite in direction to each other. What resonates all through this explanation is the power and predominance of action. Action is energy in motion. It starts with your ability to dream and dream big. It then involves your decisions, determination, and concrete steps toward changing a situation or improving on your current condition or achievement.

The law of action involves physical, mental, and emotional force. It could be an action towards writing out your goals, dreams, and visions or an action to begin work on proposed projects. This is the effort to begin on everything that should be lying down idle, strategizing and implementing them, it could be for you to go out and start the project or begin to meet businesspeople and prospective customers. Altogether, the law of action requires that we engage in activities that will propel our journey to success and financial freedom. There is no wisdom in sitting in a corner of the house and expecting things to happen without input on your end. Wealth will not manifest if all we do is sit and dream with our hands folded without doing something to achieve it. You cannot continue in your pity party and expect something good to happen without applying effort and action.

Wealth manifests when you consciously plan, arrange the process, and pursue the result. Action brings you closer to results. It creates the environment for new inventions and produces sure wealth, no matter the terrain. It draws commitment and hunger for success. When you begin to exert force on a particular target, it will sooner or later come to a reaction, and finally, end your wishes and yield the result you desire. In summary, the law of action simply states that a thing must be done to get a result. An act must be initiated for wealth to be created. Such acts include starting to raise and save money to start a business or an investment and going for more education to improve your skills and advance in that desired industry. Or opening up to some calculated risks to get something started, taking a bold step to send a proposal to that giant company or individual that you, ordinarily, would not feel qualified to pursue, and so on. All these are examples of action toward wealth creation.

If you want to achieve your wealth goals, you need to shift from dreaming to doing. Acting on your dreams and desires means laying out a plan to achieve your goals and putting in a consistent effort to achieve them. Over time, you can make your dreams real by working on your fears. Fear is a major reason why people will not want to act. Most of the time, it is fear that stops us from achieving success and wealth. We start to think of a million lies to tell ourselves why we cannot do it, we justify our inactions by our present financial state, the market indices, and even because there are better and smarter businesspeople out there who will shove us down if we dare try. We fear many things from failure to making mistakes to disappointment, and some of the times we give ourselves a cogent, fair enough reason to let the dream go.

You should know that whenever you dare a law, you will pay for it. And the law of action will always come to play if you want to live wealthy and fulfilled. Look around and see successful people as they bring out new ideas, new products, and new inventions, everything they achieved was a product of a dream and vision, but because they acted and brought them to the limelight, many of these dreams would have been a mere folktale.

Dhirubhai Ambani, one of India's finest businessmen said, *"If you don't build your dream, someone else will hire you to help them build theirs"*. *As* I read the touching story of how Ambani started his wealth journey, he saw opportunities that many others saw but never acted on, but he never wasted time to start. The funds were not available to start, but he started. He never had any knowledge of the kind of business he wanted to venture into, but he started. Ambani always acted before anyone could tell him that the business is risky or there are too many people selling or producing the same product. This is how wealth is built, acting in real-time before the opportunity evaporates.

Law 10

Law of Correspondence (communication)

Have you heard people say, 'I am the phlegmatic type, I am so quiet and often shy to voice my intentions or plans, I don't bother people with questions and too much talk, I don't want to be a nuisance to the peace of others? My mother will always tell us that: *"a child's inability to talk about his or her concern just started a life of collapse and deprivation."* How true this is? Because you can unintentionally begin to lose your life for your inability to speak out and communicate your needs, thoughts, intentions, and discoveries and be utterly disadvantaged by your phlegmatic nature.

It is lawful to talk and be heard, especially in the financial world. Communication is the bane of making real all you have in you to the world and knowing what the world wants in return. Without communication, there is no way you can know the problem and also proffer solutions to the needs and problems of the world, sending and receiving information, is the only way to pass what you have and receive what you need. Without effective communication, nothing is going to work, in fact, just forget about wealth. This is to allow you and those you are relating with to understand more accurately and quickly what is needed to be done and how to do the needful. Effective communication can help you foster a good working and endearing relationship between you and the environment you are working with. You must endeavor to know the terrain and communicate with it efficiently. If used properly, communication can be a crucial tool for shaping your attitude and behavior, and that of others in your wealth journey. For your success and wealth goals to be realized, you and everyone working with you must understand the expectations and what is required. Once the information is clear, it becomes the standard. it will be easier for you to work in harmony with your goals.

Furthermore, communication helps control your relationship with your environment. It makes the world aware of the various efforts you have performed and why they must get involved with you.

In the business world, there is only one way to translate your dreams into success. No matter how big your dreams and plans are, if you do not communicate them to yourself and to others that should relate to them and work with you to achieve them, then the plans are just a mirage. Whether you have a big plan for your business, or it may be a unique financial strategy, it could also be a new strategy or line of business with business partners, customers, and associates, you must get your point across clearly and in return, get feedback and information to take you to the success level.

Many businesspeople neglect or mismanage this vital tool called communication, which can either take them to the pinnacle of wealth or derail their entire operation to perambulation and stagnancy.

From another dimension, 'The invisible controls the visible, just as the spiritual controls the physical. What happens on the outside must have first happened on the man's inside. What things you tell yourself about success, those things you say to yourself about your business plans and strategies, the things you have written down while thinking and muttering, those things you planned to achieve, and the goals you have set towards getting into the space of wealth - all these are correspondences and are meant to be communicated to you first, so it will sink to your mind and spirit and they will become real to you. These are what you combine in your spirit to make things work for your good to manifest in the physical.

Oftentimes, we see successful and wealthy people have special periods of rest and meditation. It is a period of silence, which allows them to go into deep thoughts and reflections. And, in doing so, they are taken into the depths of inspiration and revelations. These individuals also read books and other educational materials, to catch up with the trends of wealth and success. Essentially, what the law of correspondence demands is that the inside must be cleansed and filled with only positive information and ideas because what happens on the inside affects the result of the outside. If you are in total bliss within yourself, then it will reflect in the physical areas of your life. If you are always talking about success, talking about new inventions, new trends, and styles, and acting successfully, the correspondence within and outside you will build up a cache of success and wealth for you.

Successful businesspeople can communicate well. A businessman should be able to form an emotional bond with his partners or customers. When they receive the right kind of communication, it can even encourage them to choose the company over their competitors. Business owners must learn how to communicate with their employees, their partners, customers, and clients effectively. So as not to lose out on one specific result.

Effective communication is the most important business skill because we must interact with all of the other components of wealth to function efficiently. A sense of confident communication is essential for a successful and productive workplace. Good communication is essential in the development of strong relationships. Listen to what the other person is saying as well as what they are feeling. Don't allow your silence to take you out of the reward, and your ego to ridicule and inefficiency.

Law 11

Law of Risk

It is imperative to know that progress and upgrades cannot happen without taking calculated risks in some areas of life. When it comes to taking risks, there's something to be said for trusting your instinct, it helps you do things that ordinarily you will not want to do. And what puts one ahead of the other is the things they did that others didn't do. But too many people confuse instinct with fear. They assume their discomfort means their instinct is telling them not to proceed. So rather than step outside their comfort zone, they avoid the risks that could propel them forward

Everyone indeed comes into the world in a safe cocoon. But once we are born, the struggle for survival must begin. Yet, we often still retain the desire to remain safe and always sheltered. The thing is, while this might have worked for us in the womb, here in the world, we must explore and experiment to thrive. Nothing ventured, nothing gained. If you choose to live a sheltered life and are confined to your comfort zone, you will never be able to experience true growth, progress, and expansion in any area of your life, especially in wealth-building. You need a good combination of exploration, learning, hunting, foresightedness, and action to build wealth, all of which make up the risk factor.

George Soros, one of the world's best Forex traders, describes the law of risk as the 'audacity' to go ahead. It is a quantum leap into the unknown, but a place where you know there is great compensation. Your instinct knows there is something big out there and you just believe as you take the plunge. Soros himself is a living example of the power of the law of risk. In September 1992, he made a tremendous fortune of over 1 billion from Forex trade, as he went ahead in taking a calculated risk at a time when everyone was shying away from the business. He knew the law was there to govern every result and he took advantage of it. Soros successfully pulled this off as other traders went into hiding, scared of losing money during the forecast of the coming of Black Wednesday. At that time, Britain was a participant in the Exchange Rate Mechanism (ERM) that required the government to interfere with the value of the Pounds Sterling against the Deutschmark. Soros was successful in predicting the outcome. Trusting his instincts, he took a risk no one was willing to take, and he made it big time.

Mentally strong people don't fear taking risks. They know taking the right risks could be the difference between living an ordinary life and living an extraordinary life. But you can't calculate risk based on your level of knowledge and the degree of fear. It means that risk-taking requires a deep understanding of the tides and seasons. You must know what Is around the corner, you must also be able to forecast the result of what you want to do and how it will turn up to a large extent. It is also important to assess the actual level of risk by examining the facts about what you are about to do. I will not ask you to take a risk that ordinarily is not worth taking or it is too dangerous to participate in. Create a list of the pros and cons and the potential risks versus benefits.

Life is all about risk. And definitely cannot survive if you do not take them. But some risks shouldn't be considered at all, these kinds of risks have never worked and are not permissible. You will not want to throw your money into a business you know is not viable and is ingrained to fail.

When you're excited about an opportunity and know you're likely to overlook the risks, ask a trusted adviser, "What are the potential drawbacks?" Talking about the downsides can help you become more rational and help you make the right decisions.

On the flip side, when you're too afraid to make a move, talk to someone about the potential benefits of moving forward. Hearing some words of wisdom from someone else may help you find the courage to leap.

The lesson, once again, is that to be wealthy, you have to take some risks-calculated risks that are necessary for you to get out of the ordinary to become extraordinary!

Law 12

Law of Focus (The straight-line principle)

When you have a goal, it is important to start on it and endeavor to finish it to get the desired result. At this point, you will need to be determined and disciplined to continue straight without wavering or condescending to roadside pressure that will set you back or take you away.

When you want to draw a straight line from point A to point B for example, you will need a lot of focus, traction, and tranquility to get your hands to draw a straight line. But oftentimes, you may need a ruler to help you draw a straight line which is far better because it is faster, cleaner, and stress-free. Working towards achieving that wealth goal, you need to head on straight till you get to that destination, and you will be needing some 'rulers' to help you keep focus as you continue this journey to wealth and affluence; you will need meditation as a ruler to keep you focused and on the straight line, you will need reminder materials like calendars, diaries, mission charts to help you look ahead and stay on track, you will also need the right people with the same focus and goals with you, dogged and passionate like you. Some other rulers you will need on your journey to success is 'the plan' of how you will move from point A to point B.

You have probably seen the animal documentary that I watched on Nat geo wild. I have watched this documentary over 20 times now, and I have never ceased to imagine the power of focus of these two spectacular animals I will be analyzing here. The cheetah is one large cat with beauty and speed that made me sit down for a bit and do some strategic analysis as to how to get a target (its prey) by the firm and balanced focus as I saw this powerful predator maneuver and attack its prey. The effort made to get its prey on one of the documentaries I watched was mouth-dropping. The cameraman that took the moment is so professional that he focused the camera to the right angles and strategically on the face of the cheetah as it prepared to kill one of its hunts.

At the bank of the stream where the wildebeest, zebras, and antelopes gathered to drink, there is this cheetah hidden under a shrub about 17 kilometers from the herds of animals, it took a while for the Cheetah to chase any of the animals. It looked for which one is best positioned for him to easily take. Which one could be most distracted and without protection from the multitude of the herds scattered on the field? The race to make its kill started as I watched closely, the cheetah raced toward the herds, running past the big and juicy ones. It also ran past the one that was closest to where it was hiding, and even the ones that did not know it was coming for the kill, it started the chase on the one it focused on from the set go. The cheetah did not check out the path it was running on if it was a rough or bumpy or thorny path, and neither did it check its legs if it was running well enough. This cheetah was looking straight at this wildebeest at the far left near the giant Giraffes were gathered as it tried to escape and do some maneuvers. The focus of the Cheetah on that particular prey was too strong for an escape. Because of its hunger for success and the focus on what it has set its eyes on, he couldn't fail; the cheetah caught the prey. Its eyes were set on that particular wildebeest' as its ultimate goal.

Now there were many other bigger juicy preys, some were closer to it and seemed to be easier to catch. But the cheetah was laser-focused on that particular prey. This cheetah chased the one he had planned to hunt down. He wasn't ready to change his mind, it was set on that particular prize. As I look at the video much closer, I saw that the cheetah never took its eyes and mind off that wildebeest until it got its prey.

Another thought-provoking and intriguing video was the Eagle documentary which caught my attention. The bald Eagle soaring from the high mountains sees a rabbit it wants to hunt. But in the video, other animals could be easier to swoop down for the kill. There were squirrels, rats, snakes, and other animals in the field that were more conspicuous, which would have been much easier to hunt down if the eagle went for them. But it traveled high into the sky diving high over the mountains. The Eagle had passed over where other smaller birds operate, it went to the topmost part to get a clearer vision and started the long slop falling straight down on the rabbit that was hidden in the thick grass and close to its hole.

I narrated these two instances to my very good friend that called himself a jack of all trades, Azeez Kubra, a young and hardworking man who has the strength of a horse to venture into any trade he hears is in vogue. He wanted to be successful by every means by trying his hands at various things. Many times, he failed woefully, and I'll tell you why.

After two decades of our friendship, Azeez was never shy about asking me to bail him out of his impecunious financial situation. He was never self-sufficient. As I previously stated, he tried his hands on so many things maybe he will be successful in at least one of them, the more he tried to dig his hands in the different holes the more the Rabbits escaped. He once started selling used books in an open market, he later added paintings to his array of products, then he sold phone chargers, kitchen accessories, and supplements on different markets in his city. It was during that period that he started selling electrical appliances, that same line of business his uncle sells at a market near his house, he thought that electrical appliances are selling well because his uncle has been making some sort of progress on it. After a while, he rented a store in a township area to start a computer coaching center, he could not continue because he had no money left to put the computers and the other things needed to continue the coaching center. It was not long after that ordeal that Azeez tried his hand at the real estate business, he didn't last long in that business either as he was shuffling his 13 different businesses at the same time.

It didn't end there; he tried some more businesses that he heard were trending. He just wanted to make money by venturing into everything that came his way and lost more than double his capital and couldn't hold any of the business in less than 2 years. He did not stop there, he started some certificate courses that could make him understand some businesses or jobs he can jump in, but he jumped out too quickly too. He also went into the field of making furniture, I think you already know how that ended up too. Not long after that, he told me that the stock market was booming and that he wanted to join forces with some guys who were making cool money out of it. Azeez did not finish starting the stock market business after looking for money to start the first trade, he had a new idea to start a petroleum product distribution business in his city near the Apapa Quays the very next week he started his furniture company. Just because he heard that petroleum products are money trees and were booming like the atomic bomb. He borrowed money from a local thrift, rented a tanker with the loan he got from the thrift and credit union, he hired two people to work with him to manage the business.

As seemed the rule, none of the businesses he ventured into worked, and none of the businesses or trades saw the light of day, he thought about the saying that " multiple streams of income give financial freedom" He thought that by diving into every kind of business or trade that comes to mind will make him rich and successful, but far from it.

I don't have to continue with Azeez's story, you have a pretty good idea of where all this is headed. Unfortunately, this is how many of us are. Violating that major principle which inherently is a major step to wealth and success. Not having a focus or direction for life is a terrible mistake anyone can make. But there is no way you are going to be successful if you do not have a plan to achieve your dreams. Focusing on the wrong things and perhaps not focusing on that one true thing will not bring the desired result, but frustration and perambulation, leading to more trouble and failure.

Chances are that you will achieve some success, but with greater focus, there are even bigger and better rewards. I heard about the power of meditation from a young monk who lives in the Connecticut Buddhist temple. I asked him what makes them sit in a spot for such a long time, away from people, objects, and activities. His response was heartwarming. There are times you have to focus on the things which are real and can only be found within you. You must look deep inside to bring certain things out of you. And the only way to get these things out is to get focused on what you envisage.

The law of focus is that string that connects productivity with results. It shows the trait of someone disciplined and resilient and ready to achieve set goals, using every tool available to get that one thing. Focus is a strong virtue because it takes away greed from the heart and sets the mind on the one thing that matters. That is why I think that the message of Jesus in Matthew 6: 21 is so true-"for where your treasure is, there will your heart be also". God also had to take away the power of focus from the children of man when they started building the tower of Babel to get to heaven 'Genesis 11:6', God said the people will be unstoppable and nothing that they have decided to do shall be impossible because their minds are one and focused on their goal.

Successful people take a niche, or a portion of the needs of the world, and hit hard on it, sometimes, they pick one thing that they know they have a comparative advantage and are passionate about and put in all their time, resources, skill, and prayers on. They become the superman of that one thing they put a grip on. They block everything else out. They don't care what is going on elsewhere, they are not ready to veer away from what they have decided to do. They keep their heads down, grinding it out until they reach their goals. They draw to themselves only the things that will serve their purpose. They focus with strength and zeal, without procrastination or distraction. They attack what they will with the full force of their intention. Such people don't return with an excuse for failure, rather, they come back holding their market share in their pockets.

Law 13

Law of Consistency

Wealth and consistency are one flesh, neatly joined together. How do you think that tiny woodpecker uses its beak to make big house holes in a tree? And perhaps you have wondered how that little flow of water from a small Rocky Fountain near the bushes comes to make a great ocean? The woodpecker aims at a spot on the bark and the heavily hardened trunk of a tree, its focus is to peel out every little chunk of the bark of that tree until it makes a hole in it. This law that the woodpecker uses to get into the toughest part of a tree with its tiny beak is called consistency, moving with accuracy on a target, and continuously on that same spot, the task is to aim and shoot a spot until the set result is achieved.

The great ocean has its water source from little flow and drops of water from a small supply portion that never stops. Little flow of water from rocks, flow from mountains, and other sources release a small and slow flow of water that forms the mighty ocean. Whenever that source dries up, the great ocean will lose its power to be called an ocean.

Consistency is the critical driver for success. Being consistent means dedicating yourself to your goals and staying focused on the things and activities that will help you achieve your goals. Consistency requires a long-term commitment from you and involves sustained effort in doing actions repeatedly until you achieve your goals. You cannot be wealthy if you are not disciplined, accountable, responsible, and focus. these are all parts of staying consistent. Consistency can spell the difference between failure and success. Being consistent can help anybody to achieve success in any field of endeavor.

Let us look around and analyze the lifestyle of wealthy people in our world today. I want to assure you that you will never see one who is not disciplined, accountable, responsible, and focus on that one thing that separated them from the rest of the world. Wealthy people have one thing they major on and built their fortune on it or through it. Seeing some examples that will make us see a good picture that you can gain from. Mark Zuckerberg was consistent on social media creation (Facebook) and built his wealth on it, Carlos Slim Helu focused on Stock trading and was successful with it, there he builds every other business, Larry Ellison is a Software developer, we all know him from this skill and created 'Oracle' the first commercially built database software company and the largest supplier of business application. David Koch has been into technical services as a Chemical Engineer, never digressed from it, and was consistently to be the leading name. Charles Koch Product development consultant. Bill Gates started as a computer software expert, and he never let go of that field till today. Michael Bloomberg cannot be taken away from Investment banking, this is the life and business he ever knows, he was consistent, and he nailed it. Warren Buffett (Berkshire Hathaway CEO) has always been a real estate Investor and has never changed his cause. Jeff Bezos (Amazon CEO): Software developer and online business owner, he has been operating Amazon for over three decades and has been successful. Amancio Ortega (Inditex founder and CEO): a fashion designer of class. He has been in the clothing line all his life and is successful. All these and many more have a trademark of what they started and continuing now. Their consistency in what they do shows us that they believe in what they do and are the best in that field.

This is how the law works, you must be focused on that one thing that you are good on, continue on it like it's the only thing that matters to you, have the highest knowledge of it, and thrive to be the very best on that aspect. Talk about your plan every day to yourself, map out strategies to make it work, and put your mind on it alone until you have become a master over it.

Maintaining consistency in everything that we do in our lives (as long as it's not consistent in making bad habits). You can make all the difference between achieving success or not achieving it. It's not easy to practice consistent action though, especially if it involves doing the same thing over and over every day and trying to be a master of one product or niche. Practicing consistency consists in playing the long game, so don't expect immediate results, you may have to continue for a while before you take total charge of that life.

The same thing to forming new habits. You must plan to stand against some things and start up the new and needed ones, and change is something that people can be hesitant to do, but you can do it if you make up your mind to. It is never too late to practice consistency, especially once we want to improve ourselves and meet our goals several years down the line. It can be tough to do it alone.

Law 14

Law of Vision

My friends, what do you see? Do you know what wealth looks like? If you have not seen how or know what wealth looks like, then you cannot own it. What you see is what becomes real and given to be in life. The law of vision is so unique in that, you can determine how big you want to be and how soon. Everyone has this special gift in them so that we can envisage and see what we will become from the very beginning. The bigness of your vision is the extent of your achievement, it comes from your inner being which can be produced in the physical.

Walt Disney saw a mouse; he was that dreamer that saw wealth, fame, and power from what another person could call a child's play or stupidity. He was able to build an empire by using his imagination, turned his dream into a kingdom where wealth lives, and made his vision the envy of many.

I remember in our childhood days, we usually saw super curved sports cars in our minds, those kinds of cars that have never been seen on the roads before, but in space. We saw and made paper flying saucers; we made impossible things in our minds that no man has ever thought of. Those kinds of robots can fly to the moon and back in a minute with rocket packs attached to its back. we imagined shoes like space rockets, without engines, usable on water and in the air, that can make us fly high from one place to another city. Something that looks impossible for any manufacturing companies to build, we had built them in our minds, that kind of pointed headlights, giant alloy rims with steel tires, super-fast bikes with fire transmission. But we see most of these things nowadays. Elon Musk had a similar vision, he saw cars without gas tanks with zero emissions and brought them into town for everyone to own, that kind of car that could also drive itself and bring dreams into reality. Now, he is wealthy.

A vision is the mental picture of the future you desire. More than just a goal, a vision is the embodiment of our hopes and dreams in a particular area; the picture of what has not yet happened, but what the future will be as you strongly hold on to it. In wealth creation, having a clear vision is highly critical. It is an extremely powerful tool to achieve the results you want.

The law is clear on this, you cannot own the future without producing it now. You must have a vision, and that is why you are reading this book. Success and wealth are the targets and to make it happen, begin to see a vision; a vision about the solution you will provide for the needs of the people, see things that you want to make happen shortly, and begin to make it a reality.

Visions are never late to see; you can start creating them now. Creating a vision of the future is a process that begins with your identifying what's most important to you and the rest of the world. It begins with describing the life you want without sparing the details. To create a vision, you should first see the needs around you and bring the solution into your mind. And to do that, you need to know exactly what you want to see in every area of life.

Let us see what it means to have a vision.

Having a vision means we have a clear sense of purpose, to see clearly that you want to achieve wealth and how you will achieve it. It means we have a much larger picture of our what, when, where, who and how it will all happen.

Visions are driven by passion and dreams, and they are reflected through real efforts to create real results.~ John

Graham *said "You've got to give yourself the freedom to dream – to use your imagination to see and feel what does not yet exist. A vision is not the same as goals or objectives; those come from the head. A vision comes from the heart."* Vision is what you only can see, and you want it to be in existence so the world could see it and use it for a benefit.

When I studied the words of Philanthropist and billionaire Ralph Lauren, a foremost name in fashion design said that *"a leader has the vision and conviction that a dream can be achieved. He inspires the power and energy to get it done."* No wonder there are so many new things popping up in the minds of people every day. People are seeing with their minds more than they are seeing with their naked eyes.

Having a vision provides a sense of purpose and direction for your life. Your vision will help you define your short and long-term goals and guide the decisions you make along the way. There has not been a single wealthy and successful man that didn't at one time or another had a vision, wealth does not come by luck or chance, but rather, through a big eye that sees things no one else has seen.

There are these 3 areas I will like you to focus your attention on when you want to start a vision.

Be Positive: Don't let fear guide your vision. Not because the law has stated that you must have a vision before you can create an outcome, so you rush into seeing things that you do not have business seeing. You must set your heart towards what you know will solve problems, see the needs of people with your physical eyes but see the solution coming in from your inner mind. Acknowledge challenges and difficulties but keep your focus on positive outcomes. According to John Graham, visions based on fear can limit your results, as you will end up focusing more on damage control rather than creating positive change.

Be Specific: A vision shouldn't be unrealistic and unachievable, but it should be bigger than your senses. You can begin to see what you want the future to be and stand on that thing you see. Be specific about what you want to happen, be specific about what problem you want to solve, and you should also be specific about when you want that vision to manifest. It should be detailed and should clarify the purpose and direction. It also must be articulated clearly so it can be understood, clearly pointing toward a specific future.

So many people lost out as soon as they begin to see overwhelming materials that do not have meaning to the situation of life. You cannot start creating a vision when you have not looked around for what the problems are. Remember what Jeff Bezos did when he was seeing the vision of amazon, he saw an empire of invisible stores that will sell everything virtually. He saw it clearly and he dived into the unseen reality, making it a visible reality.

Know what you want to see and what you want to make in the future, write it down, and give a period to it. You can also bring all those you see in the vision that will help you make the vision work into the invisible room and discuss the vision with yourself every day. The law states that vision is what brings success and wealth from the deep realm into reality.

Be Ambitious: Dream big. Your vision should be extraordinary. This is what will make it motivate, and inspire you, and something you can't give up on. You will become more excited as often as you see a vision so big and challenging that it will put you on your toes and make you fold your sleeves for real work. A good vision sets a standard of excellence and performance and forces you to stretch beyond your comfort zone.

If what you see is what your friend will say he saw ten years ago, then you have long been sleeping and having a common dream. Everyone can sleep and wake up to tell the story of how he saw money on the streets, that is not a vision. A vision should move you to tears and broad laughter, it should make you jump for excitement and want to start making things happen that men will see and marvel at.

If you have built a vision that is not big enough, it is time to re-establish it, and rewrite your old and small visions. Even better, see and write new visions that align with your big future dreams. Write a new vision that is one of expansion and awe, and in which you solve the problems of almost all the problems of the future.

Law 15

Law of Management and Administration

As we continue to learn about wealth and how it is created, the laws that govern it are given in different ways and must be understood and abided by. Without giving place for management and administration in your business and financial arrangements, chances are you won't do so well and achieve great results. Administration and management both are very significant functions for any achievable success in finance. Without management, there is no wealth, and also without administration.

There is no financial journey without putting the brains behind it that will navigate it. These two are complementary to each other, but you must understand their various functions to help you own your business and give it a proper arrangement. Running your day-to-day activities and operations effectively will depend on the structure of your administration and the ability to control your finances, your business goals and strategy, and how you manage people will depend on your management skill.

We will walk through these two and see how this law can bring success and wealth to you if you abide by the laws that govern them.

When we talk about the act of managing people and their work for achieving goals and using every resource to make wealth, then we are talking about management. You cannot talk about making success without people, they are the key to opening greater and faster results. On the other hand, administration guides your affairs. The goals you create and the style of achieving them are embedded in your administrative abilities. That is why the law of management and administration is important to building wealth. These are the concrete that holds everything that you plan to achieve. It requires a lot of manpower and mental skills.

Your own words

....
....
....
....
....
....
....
....
....
....
....
....
....
....

Theodore Roosevelt
No man is above the law and no man is below it; nor do we ask any man's permission when we ask him to obey it. Obedience to the law is demanded as a right, not asked as a favor.

The young rich ruler as explained in Luke 18:18-21 met with Jesus who asked about his commitment to the law. This young man was rich because he understands the power behind the law and the gains that comes with obeying them.

The rich young ruler was wealthy according to the Bible because of the choice he made to follow the law of wealth which is outlined for you in this book. He had no choice but to be rich because he obeyed the law. This can happen to any other person that does the same thing.

....
....
....

Chapter Eight:
Debunking Money Myths

"It's what you chose to believe that makes you the person you are."

Karen Marie Moning, American Author, New York Times Bestselling Novelist

---

There are different imbibed mindsets and beliefs that continue to ravage the minds of many and keep them from progressing and becoming wealthy. These wrong beliefs that were told to many are mainly myths and lies that have been inscribed into their hearts that probably grew up in them to become their standard for life. Perhaps amid negative protagonists, these myths were created to teach people about something important and meaningful. They were often used to teach people about events that they could not always understand, such as an image that could be true. Legends have discovered that many generations had lived with myths that shaped them to become what they were told and may probably not be erased until there is a critical cleansing of the mind. While myths are completely made up, lives are shaped by them. Imbibed from cultural and environmental backgrounds, words of parents and guardians, religious teachers, traditional beliefs, and other agents of socialization that taught things that could have been a good lesson but a negative outcome.

There is that one story that was told to you about money or wealth by someone or some tradition that stayed with you. wrong or right, you may have found the truth which has shaped your life for today, but that thought in your mind has kept you from achieving the success you should have achieved.

I have itemized some myths that were told to me by my parents and some supposedly wise seniors when I was growing up. Those tales and instructions are still deep in my memory though, causing me to reason the way I reason to this day. One of the things a wise old man told me was never to hold on to the money until the next day, or else, it will disappear by the power of genies. That this money should be given to someone older who can keep it from those spirit beings, so it won't disappear. I was told that those who are authorized and can hold money for long are parents, guardians, spiritual leaders, and other trusted adults. That mindset stayed with me throughout my young adulthood stage till I began to outgrow it. It made me not to be free with money because the spirit behind it will always take it away. A very bad and destructive mindset about money.

My thinking at that time was that my parents were passing down generational lines that must be followed, or else, money not properly handled would destroy my financial opportunities in the future. I was taught that I should rather have enough food on my table than have money in my pocket. This Affected my psyche as I grew into adulthood.

We are unveiling the truth about these money myths in this chapter because once you know the truth about what is holding you down, you can start your journey toward financial success and greatness without breaking ranks. Sometimes the things we tell ourselves are the very thing that is holding us back.

I will always be poor; it runs in the family

What many have believed to be a family line curse or linear arrangement that must be accepted has brought unending problems to some families and affected individual progress in life. What they heard about the above statement and how negatively it has affected them will determine how they fare in life. If you sincerely believe you will always be broke because that is how everyone in your family has been, you are probably correct. And guess what? What was passed down to you and what you believe about it will have a direct influence on what you will become. So, if you believe you are always going to be broke, you are probably not actively seeking ways to get ahead. You see yourself in a never-ending cycle of empty pockets. You will not only be a generational grabber of poverty, but you will also be a good dispenser of the same.

Success is a mindset, and that means that you cannot believe you are a failure and see yourself becoming a success. The inner man controls the physical reality. It has often been said, "What a man thinks in his heart, so he is." So, as you walk on the streets and do everything as a poor man from a poverty-stricken generation, you will live that life in full. You may not know how and why you are not moving forward or making progress in life, it is your belief mentality that was passed down to you as a family inheritance.

It may have been true that the family has never made financial success once, maybe you have been told that the richest person in your family almost built a house before he died. But all these are not what makes one a failure or a success, what makes the difference is your personal belief and determination.

Improving the family environment in which children are raised is vital to any serious effort to reduce poverty and expand opportunities and wealth creation. The wealth of riches Twenty-five years of extensive and rigorous research has shown that children raised in stable, secure, and well-educated in financial matters families have a better chance to flourish while those in hostile, negative mindset exposure situations are usually left in the continued poverty line.

The family structure in and of itself is an important factor in increasing wealth or reducing it and projecting continued poverty: children raised as those in a long line of poverty families are nearly five times as likely to be poor in families with exposed and wealthy structures.

Rich People Won't Let Us

If you have ever made this statement to yourself, you have indeed fixed yourself to be poor for life. Relegating yourself to the group of poor people or the masses is the first defeat you put yourself in, and to think there are rich folks out there that won't let you make headway is proof that you have placed some kind of people ahead of you and you are ready to serve them all the days of your life.

Most people won't make any headway because they continue to see rich people as different from them. Most wealthy people don't even know or care if someone is poor until you tell them that they are 'the rich" and you are "the poor" of the north side, they're just glad that they are working hard to be better than they were and are not among the masses.

 Rich people keep their eyes on the prize, they just want to keep making progress and surpassing past success. They keep at their work and don't care what others think about them. They have a heightened sense of who they are and don't let anything get in the way of them making money. The belief that the rich get richer, and keep the poor in poverty is a fallacy.

An online blog and current affairs association had a debate on this same topic on the Economist topical talk foundation. A commentator and a participant in the Rhema Ville Christian group wrote "I believe that rich people can stop hunger and allow the poor to thrive; at least a little. He continued that the reason why rich people can stop hunger and give room for the poor to survive is that, since they earn a huge amount of money, they can help the citizens of the country by pausing their income providers and providing different tools and equipment necessary for us to start doing something reasonable.

You can notice the mindset of someone who thinks that the failure of some people was made possible by those who are rich. Such mentality is common with medium and low-income earners, they believe that some people are holding them bound from making success.

I also believe that the reason why people suffer from hunger and remain poor in the world today is the rate at which they think about the rich with so much anger and resentment that they have garnered all the juice in the fruit and left nothing for them. The idea of a favored few has taken over all the good businesses and opportunities and left only the crumbs for the other 98% to scamper on.

The space for success is big and wide enough to accommodate every human being on this earth, so anyone who wants to get ahead can do so. The only reason there seems to be just a few in high places of prosperity is simply the lack of knowledge and zeal to be the best. The majority of those who would want prosperity but won't go for it continue to sink deeper into the quagmire of poverty because they lack knowledge and the drive to get to where they say they want to be. It is like those who admire the muscular physique of the bodybuilder but refuse to lift his body!

So, to go blaming the economy or the rich people in the society, or the presence of immigrants for your joblessness or poverty is a poor excuse and a trick to your mind and to that of others. It is better that you sit yourself down and reprogram your mindset. Laugh out loud and say words of inspiration to yourself. Affirmations that will bring determination and strength into your spirit to fuel your mind for success. It is time to stop weeping at that pity party you have thrown for yourself. If there is any blame for your current sorry state of affairs, that blame is within you.

The only way to wealth is to win the lottery

Suppose you do win the lottery for $1 million tomorrow. What would you do with the winnings? See, if you do not have any financial plans or goals, or any idea of what you want to accomplish in your lifetime, then it won't matter how much money you have today, tomorrow, next year, or even forever. A financial plan gets you to focus on what is sensible and possible for you. Refusing to plan will guarantee failure, no matter how much you won or inherited.

This is especially true for those that think the only way out of poverty and into financial prosperity is by winning the lottery. A former schoolmate of mine used to tell me that winning the lottery would make him rich someday. He hopes for that day to come and so he became addicted to gambling and the lottery that he became a problem to himself and society. He looked forward to the day that his friends would all bow down to his superiority. He never had time to invest in his education, and he never had the thought of doing any kind of business or working in any capacity to earn money. He always said it was all a waste of time. He just keeps on dreaming. Now, he is nowhere to be found among successful and wealthy people.

It's risky to invest or do business.

Of course, it may seem true that money in a savings account is largely safe from the ups and downs of the economy, or getting a job that is secure and brings regular monthly income, but how safe can it be? Truth is, no money kept for safety is safe, and no job is secure and regular. Especially when such money is idle and in the hands of someone else or a caretaker who has full authority and control over it. The one who has direct access to it controls the money. Rich people know where each penny of their money goes. Poor people are often surprised by how fast money seems to get away from them.

Rich people make their money work for them. They do not have their money lying around collecting some minimal interest from some financial institution. They find a venture or trade where their money can be more active. Money kept in a "safe place" is just going to be redundant and lose value over time. Even when it is kept in a high-interest savings account, it will not grow much, given that interest rates on savings accounts are typically low compared to the profit you will get if you use them well by yourself.

Even when it is time to withdraw your money from a retirement account a few decades from now, your money won't buy as much because of inflation. Investing in the stock market and other business platforms, however, have a good history of growth and returns on investment, making it an important component of your long-term investment portfolio. For example, for a young man investing for retirement, a diversified investment strategy based on time horizon, financial situation, and risk tolerance could provide the level of growth needed to achieve desired goals.

There are a variety of ways to invest. Building a diversified portfolio based on your needs and the length of time you plan to be invested can be as complicated or as simple as you prefer. You can build your diversified portfolio with mutual funds or exchange-traded funds. Or even individual securities.

You lose freedom if you become rich

What freedom are you talking about? Is it freedom from sitting in a bar with your old less busy friends, or being able to walk on the streets where you grew up from? This is the big guilt trip that gets dumped on anyone who has become financially successful and made the effort to do some things differently than their peers or acquaintances. The belief is that once you become rich, you will see your good old friends, but won't be able to walk the streets with them again. That you will no longer be able to eat the food you eat on the streets like before. Anyway, you belong to an elite exclusive club now, all those things should be off your lane.

I once overheard some young men in a game arcade speaking strongly and ignorantly against money. Their anger for riches and rich people was so palpable that they began to use bad words, railing against some prominent people. Some of whom they knew personally. They talked about how rich men were evil and how pride would not let them associate with such people as them again. One of them spoke roughly about his cousin who was doing so well with his online business and couldn't be reached like before again, he was upset with him that he associated his new lifestyle with pride. Some of them who once had a relationship with a rich person said almost the same thing about them. This spirited talk made me start doubting whether I wanted to be rich too. I mean, what's the point in being rich if you can't be with your loved ones again, and those you cared for don't want to be around you anymore too? What use would all my money be if I had to spend the rest of my life sitting alone in my white rocking chair, in my penthouse, sipping champagne, and eating roasted shrimp by myself? How comfortable would I be knowing someone was waiting for me by my front gate ready to boo me and throw stones at me, just because I happened to be rich? I have since realized that they were talking nonsense.

The only thing a rich man will lose is enemies of progress, idleness with an ill-ready lot who can't determine to move forward. The things a rich man will lose are visionless urchins that had hanged around him for too long. Don't be afraid of success and being wealthy, you have nothing to lose than all negativities around you.

Wealth space has been occupied by the destined

It is ridiculously funny when some people start saying that the space available for the wealthy has been fully occupied by the fortunate ones. There is no more room at the inn, so to speak. In truth and transparency, just like there is enough room for all birds to fly without colliding with each other, there is more than enough room for every fish and sea creature to swim around the sea without disturbing any other sea creatures. It is the same with earned success and enjoying wealth. There is no population of millionaires on the surface of this earth that will prevent you from joining the club.

I was once in a room filled with some young entrepreneurs in South Africa. They had been invited for snail farm training. Toward the end of the training, the moderator asked a simple question. He asked how the trainees would turn the lessons they had learned into building a successful business. I was shocked by the responses given by the few that grabbed the microphone to answer the question. One was a young man from Ethiopia who had been sponsored by his university alumni association. He angrily replied that he had just wanted to learn the necessary techniques that would help his father's small-scale agricultural business. He had no intention of doing anything bigger or better than that. As far as he was concerned, there were more than enough successful agriculturists in the field. He added with smug confidence that no one could make it big in that field unless those at the top passed away in death.

As if the young man's comments were not alarming enough, many others echoed his sentiments and supported his conclusions. The class soon became a gathering of disgruntled participants. This is the driving belief of many around the world. It is a limiting and self-defeating belief

that has the power to keep one perpetually bound by the
chains of mediocrity and poverty.

Investing is only for the rich

Research has shown that very few people have money invested in stocks or properties. This is because of the erroneous belief that investing in a business or stocks, real estate, or other ventures is for a set of people who have a certain background or money stocked up enough to start. Usually, those people have lots of money and went to certain prestigious institutions of higher learning. Surely not for the average person that does not have extra after expending on his income.

The bold truth is that the business world is an open space for any brace and smart thinker. Anyone can start small and become big. Wealth building is not determined by your skin color or family background. It has nothing to do with being connected to the high and the mighty.

The fact that investment areas like hedge funds seem complicated for many people is not a strong reason to stop investing or creating wealth whenever possible. There are many other kinds of investment opportunities that yield big returns like the hedge fund. So, rather than shying away from making your life better, seek more flexible and easy investment plans. Don't let fear get the best of you and keep you lower than you should be. You are an eagle and it's time for you to fly high.

maybe you're ready to ditch the weekly 9-to-5 inertia and finally call the shots. No matter what your motive is, there always seems to be one logistical hurdle stopping you: You don't have money to start or invest. It sounds like a tough situation for wannabe entrepreneurs, right? Short answer: It doesn't have to be. It's entirely possible to start and grow with almost no money whatsoever. You just need the right kind of mindset, a real vision that will open up the future, the willingness to work hard, a ton of patience, and an understanding that you'll have to start at where you are right now.

If you research very well, you will consider how these ubiquitous brands got their start. Most of them never had enough money than you have today but they started and became big. In 1978, John Mackey and Rene Lawson saved and borrowed money from friends and family to open their first store in a small house in Austin, Texas. Michael Dell started selling souped-up computers from his tiny dorm room as he juggled it with his final exams. You already know Nike founders Philip Knight and Bill Bowerman that got their business started selling training shoes from their car trunk with a $50 loan from a family member.

High income equals great wealth

Have you ever stopped to wonder about someone like MC Hammer, the famous rapper, and dancer, who sold millions of copies of his albums and performed in countless concerts and stage shows, having a net worth of about $2 million at one time? At the peak of his international Hammer Time success in the 1990s, Hammer's fortune topped $70 million. He was one of the richest music artists on the hip-hop scene during the golden age of rap music. Suddenly and shockingly, he became broke. He blew well over $70 million in less than five years.

He wasn't alone, many others from around the world came into the limelight and made tremendous money but are now broke and poor. They let careless spending, unwise investing, and poor family and money management bring them down. It is so easy to lose it all when there was never a plan for how to keep it and grow it. Having a lot of money is not a guarantee that the person will become wealthy. But a wealthy person knows that his money is just one part of his wealth. The best advice that can be given here is simply this: Develop your knowledge base and build your mindset to generate the wealth of riches that will be available to you to enjoy forever.

Money is evil

Some people believe that having money is ungodly and dangerous. Well, it is not surprising that people who hold such a bizarre view of money hardly find money coming their way. They dread the thought of money and in return money stays away from them. They become the enemy of each other as they see money leading them down a path to evil and hell. Such weak-minded people truly believe that there is something noble about taking a vow of poverty, to be broke as long as they live.

They believe their being poor makes them purer in the eyes of God and among men. They are convinced that God will provide all their needs, and if they don't have anything, it is only because God wants to rely solely on Him. All they have to do is pray for the comfort and abundance they will find in Heaven. This belief has held many supposedly religious minds in bondage. Such people will usually refer to 1 Timothy 6:8-16, which says, "And having food and clothing, with these we shall be content. But those who desire to be rich fall into temptation and a snare, and into many foolish and harmful lusts which drown men in destruction and perdition. For the love of money is a root of all kinds of evil, for which some have strayed from the faith in their greediness and pierced themselves through with many sorrows."

A careful look at this passage of scriptures reveals a different meaning from how now-minded folks understand it. Money is an innocent tool that can be turned into helpful or harmful uses. Just as a blade or knife can be used to cut meat, slice bread, chop vegetables and pull together a healthy meal. On the other hand, it can be used to stab or kill someone. It can be used in the commission of a robbery. It could be used to harm oneself. It's the same with money. It can be used to solve some problems in our lives to provide healing or a hedge of protection and comfort. It can also be used to finance evil, like for example, someone whose online gambling or recreational drug use, or social drinking has gotten out of control. The user is solely responsible for how they use their money.

The only thing that makes money evil is your thoughts about money. If your mindset can be turned away from this wrong perception and you embrace the truth that money is made and meant for good, there will be a strong pull or riches and wealth that will be drawn into your life. Your mind will be receptive to appreciation and take hold, its usefulness will be translated to having a strong desire for it and you will have the energy to attract money to you. Whatever you think is evil or negative never agrees with your righteousness. It runs away from you. If you truly value money, and the good things it can do for you and your family, money will be a treasure for you.

We all agree that we need to pay our bills, take care of our health, cater to the needs of our families, and even spend money on much-needed vacations. Money is not evil; money is from God. It is God in movement because everything good comes from Him. Every comfort is what He wants you to have. What brings comfort is money and He is ready to go along with you to get it, as much as will make you happy. He has it all because everything belongs to Him.

Money itself is not evil, it simply magnifies who you are. Money in the hands of the right person will change the world for good. While on the other hand, money in the hands of an evil person will turn the ocean into the blood. So, pursuing wealth doesn't make you a bad person at all. Neither will pursuing it make you a subpar human being.

God will provide

The Lord is not going to provide! I am not saying this because I don't want you to lean on Him. God is not wicked or uncaring. He will not take care of anything because He already finished creating and taking care of everything He needed to do. Don't get it twisted, God had done all He knows to do for this world. He is not about to go around town distributing money or looking for a good job for you. God will provide for all of my needs is what some religious people mistakenly believe and hold against the natural course of life. I must say that it is high time we stopped using God as a cover-up for our inadequacy and laziness. There is a saying that "God gives food to the birds. He cares for the sparrow and gives shelter to the pigeon." All this is true, but he doesn't drop food into their nest, and neither did He (God) make food come to them, they go out to fend for their daily food and pick shrubs and sticks to make their nests. God won't do for you what you can do for yourself. He has equipped you to do for yourself, he has provided the opportunity for you to educate yourself, start a good business or even interview for a corporate job. He has provided avenues for you to learn and train yourself on how to manage your finances better by being realistic about what you can or cannot afford. You just need to take advantage of all that has been laid out before you.

Spiritual exigency has its place, and in truth, God is still in the business of raising people from zero to hero by giving them wisdom and insight to achieve more than his natural abilities. But in all this, He has given us the ability to create our fortune and happiness. Until you take a stand and do something meaningful for yourself, God can't help you much. He will not step down from His Heavenly stool with a bag full of coins and banknotes for you to live a carefree life. What He will do is strengthen your mind and give you the wisdom to put your ideas to good use.

Money is in the lion's mouth

There is a traditional belief in some circles that the only way to get money is to face the fiercest terrain of life, using the Lion as hyperbole because it is never going to be easy to get richer but to fight a life battle. In other words, money can only be gotten from the most dangerous and deadly ventures. Another version says that there is a close connection between riches, the dunghill, and death hill. This implies that it is not possible to get rich without getting dirty or getting to risk a life.

It has become a perspective to many that one must be dubious, or a 'do or I die' affair to get money and must get involved in shady deal-making. It is such misconceptions that create wrong ideas in the minds of many people regarding money and riches. The belief here is that money is the most difficult thing to lay a hand on because it has to come through the most dangerous terrains. To lay a hand on money, you must be ready to fight, be killed or you kill. All these are all lies; money is the easiest thing to have if you play by the rules.

All you need to know about money is in this book, just seek knowledge and you will find the result which is wealth. If you still carry the mindset that before you can become wealthy, it is either you fight for it, cheat for it, accept dangerous offers for it, become dirty for it, or leave it alone to remain poor. No wonder so many people are turning their eyes away from money-making opportunities and deliberately ignoring lucrative investment opportunities, while others are going to extreme lengths just to have this money. The truth is that it is possible to make good money without doing anything dangerous or illegal.

Savings are for 6-digit income earners

This is another very common misconception. Many people believe that they can't save from their current earnings. They believe that they need to earn more to be able to save anything. The belief is that living expenses are just too high for them to consider saving. They think that it would be easier to save when their incomes rise to the six-figure income level. They believe that such an income would enable them to feel comfortable with putting a certain amount of their income to the side specifically for saving. They believe that they can only save if there is an overflow. Only then could they invest or even start a business.

But the truth of the matter is that if you don't have the discipline to save anything with the income you have right now, you will never be able to save, even when you are earning millions. This is because the mind is programmed to live commensurate with the earnings you are accustomed to.

Here is an interesting example for Reverend Chris Oyakhilome, Pastor of the Believers Loveworld Incorporated: "When our young church was getting an income of $1,600 every month, our expenses were far over $2,100. We paid rent and some other justifiable running expenses, and we never noticed anything wrong with this trend. Then, at a time we needed money to buy some equipment for the church and I asked the secretary to pay a supplier $500; she told me there was no money in the vault. "That was when I realized that we were treading on the wrong part of our finances. We were handling the church's finances wrongly. I had to rearrange our financial pattern, or else, we would continue in the financial nosedive. I told the executive team that from that day, we would be saving 50% of the monthly income of the church.

This means from that small income, of $1,600, we were to keep $800 every month in an account that must not be touched for any reason. We used the remaining 50% for the running of the office and settling all expenses incurred for each month. "I noticed the bewilderment on the faces of my secretary and other stakeholders. I knew they were thinking that I probably didn't know the backlog of debts and other issues the new strategy would create.

I knew everyone thought that I was establishing what was unrealistic and was waiting for me to reverse the decision in the following month. Well, to everyone's surprise, it worked. How it happened, I cannot explain 'til now, but it worked. "The office had to cut all unnecessary expenses. We had to open a ledger account and a petty cash book to help us manage the income and expenditure and all other accounting needs. Members also had to help by increasing their donations and giving; some gave us gifts, and many helped to sort out those minor bills that ordinarily would have made us dip our hands into the little income we got in the church. "We cut off all unnecessary transactions and narrowed our spending to what we need as a church, and not what we wanted. From that moment, we had enough money to save and invest and the ministry's finances grew so big that after two years, we already had over $100,000 in our savings account and over $28, 000 available for use in our petty cash. And we had grown so big financially ever since then, and in a geometric proportion to an income of $34, 000 monthly and a total net wealth of $1,000,000 because we had money to invest and increase our capacity."

This goes a long way to confirm that you can save at any point in your finances, and not just to save, but to also find a way to invest. There is no better time to start than where you are now. You can make your expenses commensurate with your income. Then you should begin to cut unnecessary expenses. Those wants that we think are needs and those luxuries we think are our life's hangers can be put away.

Opportunity knocks but once

Many young people have been cheated of their potential and dreams because of this limiting, and this plain wrong mentality. That as soon as they missed an opportunity or could not do well in their first endeavor, they lost faith and threw away hope never to continue again. They lose the zeal that had while growing up and nursing the ambition to accomplish their set goals and dreams begin to die an unnatural death as their mind goes into a deep sleep.

Opportunity does not only come once, but that is also a big fat lie. The fact is opportunity is everywhere and available to anyone at every stage of life. If you dwell in this big lie, you will never take advantage of the many opportunities that come around, sometimes as that one you have been expecting and praying for, and some others that will come without knowing it is an opportunity. Simply because you have thrown in your towel when you were supposed to open wide your eyes and find your cheese.

Many miss out on an opportunity and miss out on the biggest break that is just around the corner. For those who have had the opportunity to listen to successful and wealthy individuals, great inventors, or social media stars, the story is about rough times and challenges moving up the ladder of success. Many great inventors had to fail over and again, perhaps hundreds of times just to get one thing right. Many business owners had gotten opportunities that failed more times than the average person could take. But they didn't stop, and they eventually succeeded. This is because they explored all of their options. They didn't just stop with Plan A and Plan B.

While it is true that opportunity knocks more than once, it is also important to understand there are some opportunities you must grab when the time is right. You must make every effort to grab it with both hands when you know this opportunity was made for only you. You must grab it then because what you miss may be given to others and you will never see that opportunity again. There is always tomorrow but that tomorrow may not be for you. You must fight for every golden opportunity that comes your way. If you miss it the first time, you can try again, perhaps with more experience and insight this time and that might make all the difference. After that first miss, you would have gained more focus, strategy, and resilience.

Give a child candy, not money

I don't care how old or young they are, every person, a kid, or old loves that paper called money. Why? Because there is something about money that makes you want to have it. I recently attended a young child's 2-year birthday party where she received a 50-dollar bill in a beautiful greeting card, wrapped in an envelope from a neighbor from just about three blocks away as her birthday gift. The little birthday girl took the card in the envelope from her mum, looked at the envelope for a moment, brought out the money, and took a deep look at the beautiful shiny greeting card and the envelope on her right hand and the dollar bill on her left hand. Everyone was watching her as she would decide, holding both for a while, and suddenly threw the beautiful greeting card and the envelope away and put the $50 bill into her tiny breast pocket. She knew that the two papers are not the same, one was not worth keeping as it can't be used for transactions or to get something of value, but the other can get her what she wants in that value.

Knowing the worth of money is critical to making wealth, she handled the money with utmost care and importance as she kept it safely. This baby knows money and she knows it has worth. Her mother was not mesmerized as other folk who watched in awe of her understanding of money and its worth, surprised to see that the baby held on to the money and never traded it for any other thing made us understand that she has been exposed to it.

So many adults are scared to have money because they have always believed that money will corrupt them. Some are scared to have too much of it because they believe that it will overwhelm them and can even attract unscrupulous people who are more than eager to take what they have gotten away from them. Some has been taught that they cannot handle money too big for their present need. If you have been brought up that way, it is time to change that mentality.

Don't be one of those parents that will rather tell their kids or ward to go for candy and other petty things than go for money, they think it is proper upbringing but rather, it is a financial amelioration killer, it will make you detest progress and give you a strong desire to want to go for a 'hoi polloi' kind of lifestyle, to make you mediocre with success.

The more zeros, the bigger the crime

And for some, this is their biggest problem. They are chasing the six-figure income mark, thinking that this is the start of financial freedom and riches, and to those who got incomes beyond six figures, are you wealthy now? some feel there has to be some criminality at the backend of getting more money, so they don't want to go close to it. Many talks of how in the earlier days many huge fortunes were obtained through corruption and illegal means. There is the idea that these huge fortunes were built because blood was shed, or someone was swindled or a crime or another was committed.

 In the late 1800s were the "robber barons," American capitalists who built fortunes based on ruthless and unethical business practices to dominate major industries. They build monopolies in rail, steel, and petroleum. The aim was to see more zeros in their account balance, they could do extraordinary negative things to earn more money. But many people at that time feared to work more for more money so they won't be tagged as one of the barons. That mentality had crept into the minds of many generations and are still scared of wanting more money because of the stigma it had on their fore generation

But these rich fellas worked hard to be big, these "businessmen" included Cornelius Vanderbilt (transportation), Jay Gould (stocks), Jim Fisk (cotton), John D. Rockefeller (oil), and Andrew Carnegie (steel). Their fortunes were too vast to count and were becoming the talk of the world which attracted so much antagonism.

Dear reader of this book, I implore you to not allow idiocy and archaic myths to ruin your chances of becoming wealthy and big. There is no such thing as "success has a family called 'crime" this will drag you backward and make you lose opportunities. Making more money is good and worthy, it is proof of hard work and skillfulness.; the narrative should be "the more the zeros, the more the thumbs up."

"Whatever will be, will be"

From the Doris Day hit music of 1955, Que Sera Sera, "whatever will be will be" have not only landed in the lips of good music lovers but the heart of non-thinkers and mediocrity. Short and sweet of this: 'whatever' will not be; you have to make it be. You have a part to play in what your life will be. Don't leave your financial future to the rotation of a standing fan that blows in one direction and leaves the other at bay.

The idea of whatever is meant or predestined to happen will happen; there is no use trying to work hard or plan a good life if such a person has such a mentality. No one is destined to be poor in life, while another is arranged to sit on a gold box, it is by individual's efforts, strategy, and determination that will take you to the point of your state.

Creating wealth does not conform to the time and chance phenomenon or the 'what will be will b" cliche. Wealth creation requires conscious efforts to do what needs to be done to achieve success and wealth.

Just like the farmland will grow just anything on it; weeds and shrubs springing up to the farmer's surprise. This is how life situation is too, negative things happen to people than good if you let natural phenomena happen by themselves. Unless you fix things by yourself and make proper plans and arrangements of what you want and how you want things to be, the chance is, you will get nothing. Do not let that myth of negative influence rob you of your wealth and success, go to work and do new things.

"A fool at forty is a fool forever"

I was reading a friend's journal and found an article written by a freelance writer on the topic - Financial Literacy in the 21st century. How true is this popular statement, "A fool at 40 is a fool forever? The writer wrote: "A fool at 40 is a fool forever" this is very true because everyone has been either wise or a fool in life, but some will not end their foolishness as they continue in life. Well, maybe I should qualify that a bit. No one was born a fool, but you can become and remain a fool if you allow the circumstances of life to make you.

Oftentimes, we become who we are by what we learned around us, the things we see others do, and what we learn from our family and environment, that is why I tell people to "live life as though you own it because it belongs to you." It is hard to become fulfilled at any age when you are trying to live another man's life, which is foolishness." A fool at any age can be a fool forever if he refuses to let go of his foolishness. It is never too late to become wise because the day you wake up and wise up is the day you see change. It is the same as saying, "A pauper at forty is a pauper forever." The bottom line: you will never get out of the cobweb of a loser at any stage of your life if you do not intentionally become mentally mature in every facet of your life.

Putting this phrase in the area of wealth creation. Age is not a factor when it comes to wealth and finances. It is when you arise and do the right thing that you come of age. If you wake up and do the needful at age 15, then you have come of age and are ready to live the dream life, and when it is at age 80, that is when your life begins. Many people had lost their mark because of the age factor, they lose focus and throw in the towel as soon as they clock the age of 40. How sad it is to see a man that has struggled all his life to give in to fate because he is now 40 years old, how sad indeed.

I will strongly advise that you keep up the tempo of whatever you are doing or planning to do till you achieve it, you must put away the threshold of time and age that could distract you and make you miss your mark. Put a time limit away, it won't help you as it never helped anyone. That does not mean you will not set targets and periods to achieve your vision and goals, but peradventure, you still are not there yet just keep up the work and set a new period for yourself.

Success and wealth are achieved only when the result surfaces and not when you are set to achieve it. No matter your age and no matter how far you have gone, never give up your dream, never stop believing in yourself, and never count age as a disadvantage and a bar to stop.

If you are below forty and believe the above statement, I feel so sorry for you because it means you are not yet alive. Many young, sharp, and vibrant minds have gone to sleep because of this lie.

The Matchelea Boys Club had in their manifesto that they will wait until the ripe age of 40 to start a new life into happiness. They discuss in their quarterly meeting that they could continue to save money in their union account and remain unmarried until they became of that age forty, which they believed is the age of maturity and perfection.

Most of the young lads in this Matchelea Boys Club are teenagers in their prime. They were supposed to take advantage of their young and bright minds waiting for the ripe age of 40 to begin a life. What a waste! And this is how so many young people think because of the wrong ideology that was nailed into their minds. Waiting during the most active and vibrant part of their lives to pass away. Life doesn't start at 40, it starts when you are born. You can't sit around waiting until you're 40, and to tell you the truth, nothing starts suddenly at 40. Life changes over time, some get wiser with age, your priorities may change over time and life surely doesn't stop at 40 either

"All fingers are not equal"

Yes! Physical fingers in your hands are not equal but that does not make any of them valueless or ineffective in their capacity. Everyone has their area of specialization and use, and so is everyone in the area of life and finance, you will realize that all fingers are valuable for their use and purpose. Many have shortchanged themselves with this falsity, which is why I hate most of these wisdom nuggets and handout phrases, they could deceive and help us defeat ourselves at the speed of light. You are not even a finger, so why look down on yourself as if you are not up to the task?

If you reason this phrase critically, you will notice that it is a success and wealth killer, they make you submit to failure easily. It gives you the audacity to fail majestically because it could not be your fault that you failed. After all, all fingers and opportunities are not equal.

You may begin to think that some people have more brain power than others, while some are born genius, and some are born to be a dullard. Some are born into wealthy families and some, into the rich society while some are born in the slum and the third-world society. But all these don't determine a man's opportunity to either succeed or fail, it all depends on the individual's knowledge and motivation to succeed.

"What goes up must come down"

Like my uncle told me a long time ago "Don't expect to be happy and rich all the time, downtime will surely come' prepare for it". And I have believed this lie for a long time, my mindset always tells me that no one will be happy forever, so I should expect the worse to happen soon.

All laws do not function in the same direction as seen in the law of gravity. Some things that have gone up will continue to go up. You will never become younger. Your age will never come down, that is one good example. Now when you die, it will stop but that is another discussion. You can also bring your intellectual capacity up, and what you have known can never be taken from you, which means, you can expand your storehouse of knowledge without losing it. Is the price of goods coming down? Think, my friend! So, it is with your mindset towards finances. If you think that you cannot be successful, or that you cannot sustain what you have become, every time you will be pulled back. But if you see a path for yourself that says 'upward and forward only', you begin to rise to the horizon without regress. You can rise and never fall; you can be wealthy and remain wealthy and blessed forever; it starts in your spirit.

Debt Is a Tool, Avoid Credit Cards

How many times have you been told you can use debt as a tool? Dave Ramsey, author of "The Total Money Makeover," says debt has been sold to us so aggressively, it's often hard for most people to imagine having a car without a car payment or going to school without using a loan to pay for it. "Debt adds considerable risk, most often doesn't bring prosperity, and isn't used by wealthy people nearly as much as we are led to believe," Ramsey suggests it's better to instead live below your means and pay cash for the things you want.

Credit cards are viewed as the gateway to debt, and rightfully so if you don't know what it is, how it functions, and how to operate it. Thus, the popular wisdom has become that it's often best to stay away from them altogether. If you make all your payments on time and pay in full each month to avoid interest, though, credit cards can have their perks. "Many credit cards have reward programs that allow you to earn points or money back simply by using them," says Jenni. What's more, making payments on time can increase your credit score, and a high credit score can make it easier to buy a home and get favorable interest rates.

Your own words

....

....

....

....

....

....

....

....

....

....

....

George Carlin
The reason I talk to
myself is that I'm the only
one whose answers I
accept

Words can be very
powerful, and the content
can be either life or death
to those that receive it. I
have made up my mind to
listen to the good words
that will transform me
positively and do away
with the ones that will
cause me to be dispirited.

....

....

....

....

....

....

Chapter Nine:
Achieving Financial
Freedom and Control

"Rich people believe "I create my life." Poor people believe "Life happens to me."

T. Harv Eker, author of Secrets of the Millionaire Mind: Mastering the Inner Game of Wealth.

Gaining financial freedom and control begins with learning to build wealth systematically and strategically and also sustaining it. I have heard many finance instructors exaggerate the downsides of getting paid employment. They seem to disdain people who are excited about having just clinched a job they had been dreaming of or undergraduates who look forward to getting their dream jobs. They make it look like being in paid employment is something demeaning or even destructive. But the reality is that such an approach to wealth-building is not only counter-productive but is an easy pathway to poverty.

Paid employment is, for many reasons, a good foundation for building wealth and an important milestone in the journey to financial control and life in general. In fact, without going through this stage, such a person may continue as mediocre and never succeed as a financial giant.

It may interest you to know that many successful people all over the world have passed through the stage of paid employment as a place to gain work experience. By working for an employer, they discover how they do their best work. They are free to explore their best work style without having the added pressure of being a boss. This is what I call the first place of financial birth. The foundation we all get, knowing what money is, how to get it, and the things to do to get it started with working either for someone or an organization.

I mentioned earlier how Warren Buffet, the renowned businessman, was once asked how he would rise again if he was to start his financial journey from square one. The detailed answer he gave was that he would start at McDonald's. It is quite instructive that such a guru in money matters and investment would want to start being a paid employee in a fast-food company. Why paid employment? And why not start at some bigger and more lucrative companies? One would have expected Buffet to say something like, "I will want to start by establishing an online business or start a mini manufacturing company." Considering the vast wealth of knowledge and experience he already has, why would Buffet opt for a paid employee position with McDonald's? It's because he needs a platform to learn service, respect, speed, humility, and experience. He knew why he chose to start from such a cradle, probably because he had already mastered some strategies for wealth-building.

Working with a Dream

Every serious-minded employee is in his job to work for a dream. It is that dream that will translate into future achievements. Therefore, it is wrong for you to take up a job simply because of the pay. If that is the sole reason for getting a job, then such a person is a colossal failure. This explains why some finance teachers and mentors disagree that a paid job is a good way to go. They will argue that every paid employee is never going to be successful, but I disagree.

Paid employment is an avenue to acquire useful skills. The skills to be successful and financially independent do not come from Heaven. These skills are realized through training and mentorship. That is why some very successful businesses are built by those who have learned the trade as paid employees. For example, Jack Mitchell, CEO of Mitchells, a high-end clothing company in Westport, Connecticut, and his brother, Bill Mitchell, inherited the family company. After working as paid staff for seven years they were able to gain valuable experience. This was required by their parents, so they could acquire the knowledge and experience needed to run the family business. Or any other business they might desire to have in the future. From that time, it has become the family tradition that the children must work for a minimum of five years in the family business. This is after getting their university degrees. Only then could they enter fully into the family enterprise as entrepreneurs.

The five-year rule requires that every member of the Mitchell family must work for five years making minimum wages. This could be either with the family company or any other employer. The primary concern was not the amount of the paycheck, but the lessons to be learned during that period.

The Mitchell family's five-year rule of business mentorship has given every new generation the necessary business skill, work experience, and vast knowledge to win in the business world.

Another good example is H. Fisk Johnson, the current chairman and CEO of SC Johnson, a household and global company that has been passed across generations. The company has managed to keep the business in the family as all the children had to pass through the school. Then they would work for a salary for a while. Within this period, knowledge and balance are transferred from one generation to the next. For an impressive five generations now, the company has continued getting even stronger and bigger because skills and abilities are acquired from other establishments and businesses. After working as a paid staffer in different capacities, Fisk joined SC Johnson in 1987, after serving in a variety of senior-level management and marketing positions. This was both domestically and internationally. He has worked in various areas to acquire more skills, stamina, and direction in the business world.

Overview of benefits

In essence, the reason it is recommended to work as a paid employee should be for skills acquisition, experience, and direction. Other beneficial reasons could include:

1. For excitement and challenge

2. To develop your career to a certain level

3. To learn new skills and improve on current skills

4. To learn and hone leadership skills

5. To understand the structures and systems of an organization

6. To build the boldness and stamina necessary to dominate the corporate world and competition

7. To learn how people are managed at every level of work.

As you work, you understand how you will treat those future employees. Despite the aforementioned benefits, when you begin to understand the true meaning of wealth and how it differs from riches, you will understand that chasing after a job is a serious error. You are looking for a job because of seeking a good salary or wages or even the glamorous perks of certain professions. These are reasonable considerations, but you will never earn what you are truly worth. You become a slave to your employer's evaluation of you; you will only be paid what they think you are worth. This is not a growth position; you cannot fly high because there is that glass ceiling. And understand this: no one hires you to make you rich, they hire you to make themselves rich. The mantra is: What can you do for me? You have to think about yourself and know what you are worth in the marketplace of your chosen profession. You become your brand and that's where you make your real money.

In a New York Times Magazine article entitled 'Empire State of Mind', Blair McClendon writes: "In the entertainment world, people must become corporations if they want to become truly wealthy. High-profile singers, athletes, actors and so on often make their real money from endorsement deals rather than their day jobs. What separates the billionaires from their peers is that they turned endorsements into equity" (McClendon, p31).

The bottom line is an employee is paid a specific amount by his employer, regardless of what he contributes, the blood, sweat, and tears he pours out, his intellectual contribution, or the hazards of his work environment. This is not where you want to be, you are worth much more than that. Don't let the worth that others try to place on you be the final say on the matter. Know your worth!

The future of jobs

Times are changing so quickly. Everybody is not on their toes, trying to secure their future for themselves and their loved ones. But you already know, especially if you have gotten this far in this book, that the future is what you make it. You hold the keys to unlocking a bright future for yourself.

The days are long gone when a parent will call a child in the middle of lunch to ask what he or she would want to become in the future. Then if the child didn't mention some kind of high paid pensionable job (a job that probably required a degree to obtain) the parent would be somewhat disappointed. Of course, the parent would try to point the child's mind in another more lucrative direction. Usually in the fields of health, education, or business. But the days are gone when you want your child to be an expert in only one field. Simply because we must move with the times. Technology and the Internet (social media) have taken over the world of work and many industries are becoming fully automated.

According to the World Economic Forum's projections about jobs, skills, and finances in the near future, many job descriptions will be obsolete; we just don't do that job anymore. The sign of the times is that machines will take over many jobs and the Internet is where much of the business of the world will take place.

Early evidence from the World Economic Forum's Future of Jobs Survey presented in Chapter 5 of the WEF bulletin suggests that, in addition to the labor market displacement caused by technology and the recent health shock (COVID-19), employers are set to accelerate their job automation and augmentation agenda. In essence, we are not doing business like we used to do it. Times have changed, you must get with the new program or get left behind.

Moving from paid job to a wealth creator

As repeatedly emphasized, getting a paid job is not altogether bad, especially at the beginning of one's career. Trouble only begins to emerge when the job is secured for the wrong reasons. When the job is not well directed toward prosperity. The job must not be the end of the journey. Doing a paid job should not be a long-term arrangement. It should be for acquiring all you need to bring alive a new dispensation of solutions and a way to build skills and develop exemplary values. This paid job is just a stepping stone toward financial independence and greatness. That big step before entrepreneurship.

The best time to leave paid employment before entering the golden circle of entrepreneurship is when you have grown significantly in knowledge and expertise.

You will see yourself becoming very relevant and indispensable to your organization. Of course, this is usually the period that is most difficult for an employee to leave their job because of a certain level of comfort. But understand that there is no growth in the comfort zone, you were not planted to be there forever. This is the best time to make your move.

If your primary reason for getting a job was to acquire skills and knowledge you have probably reached that goal. Now it is time to press on to the building of wealth creation. Now is the time to put those competencies, skills, courage, and strategies that you have acquired to work for your benefit.

Leaving paid employment often happens when you no longer align with your employer; you have outgrown your mentor. When this happens, you might begin to feel hemmed in. You are not expanding. You are not as fulfilled as you think you should be. You are more than ready to leave the nest. You want to fly high because you know you can do more. You have developed new concepts. You have looked at your job and know that you could do it much better with fewer restrictions. It is time to spread your wings and fly. You must begin to build your own thing. You know your true worth. You know you can make more money elsewhere. You know that the current level of compensation is not commensurate with the skills you possess. You need to try your hands at something new. Also, when you start to notice your ability to lead, direct and skillfully control your work environment, you notice that you can now listen more and give more solutions to common and anticipated problems. You can push a team to great success. Now is the time for you to start your own business. You must manifest your destiny.

Your own words

....
....
....
....
....
....
....
....
....

Robert Kiyosaki
"Financial freedom is
mental, emotional, and
education process."

Graduating from help me
to 'give help' is the
master result of progress.
You are not financially
free until you own your
time, money, skill, and
people

....
....
....
....
....
....
....
....
....

Chapter Ten:
The Wealth Elements

"Without an open-minded mind, you can never be a great success."

Martha Stewart is an American retail businesswoman, writer, and television personality.

Being wealthy is not only when you have money, gold, houses, fast cars, or assets. It is about having everything that ensures a great life. It is the kind of abundance that every human being desires to have. True Wealth is intangible, but it is that variable that produces the tangibles we enjoy like money, gold, houses, fast cars, and everything else that makes life pleasurable.

Being rich is more of a spending lifestyle, but being wealthy is more of getting, keeping, and building a super lifestyle. To be wealthy is to have everything inside that creates all sufficiency and prosperity.

In this chapter, we are going to look at different categories of wealth. These are all those things that are counted as wealth, and they create those riches we desire so that we can truly be successful forever.

Mindset

The mind that is not set on the right course will go off course. Successful people have trained themselves for success. They know this is a mind game, and not about muscles. They have prepared themselves for a marathon that requires tact and information. They also invest heavily in mind-building mechanisms. When building wealth, the mind must have good control and direction, and the abundance of the mind must be good mannerisms; always think right, talk right, and assimilate only those things that are true and positive. They have no time for small talk or mingling uselessly with people of a small and negative mindset. They are always looking for that next level.

Those things that are enriching and soul-lifting are the things you must cultivate and allow to enter your mind. To be wealthy, you have to go beyond the good feelings that come from money and other acquisitions into the sacred realm of pure joy and happiness. I can recall those early years of my life. I would be sitting beside my mathematics lesson teacher in the corner of the classroom for break time "let us do the correction together". My lesson teacher was a senior student in my school, he came as an HSE (Higher School Equivalency) student. would be across the classroom after every break to have personal talking sessions. He would talk to himself and tell himself a bit audibly that he is a success, and he will begin to count the things he has promised himself to accomplish in life. Acting like he was watching the students play in the field, he would bring out magazines and journals about the biography of different companies and their founders, and how they operate. Once I asked him about all these strange things he does, he simply said – I am building my mind for wealth. I thought this is remarkable as I kept on watching him.

My extra classes lesson teacher is a smart man with so much wisdom. He made himself a success far beyond what others thought he would be in record time. He never forgot what he kept in his mind. He doesn't let the news of the day upset him. He never gives in to the news and worries of the world, he turns himself away from them quickly and focuses on what he plans to achieve in life. Affirmations are important to him. I have seen him stand in front of the classroom when everyone had gone out to play and relax during lunch break and talk to himself. He would tell himself, "I am a good man, and I will help the world see better things because I am about to shine my light and cancel out darkness."

I was privileged to notice this activity and learn from it. At first, I often felt embarrassed for him. Now I know why he did what he did. Through his self-talk, he made himself successful despite the difficult economic times in Africa. He never lacked anything. He was wealthy because he knew how to settle his mind to reach out to achieve his greatness and help hundreds he encountered on his daily journey. Now, he is one of Africa's biggest investors and business magnate. His millet and cocoa plantation industry now feeds over 20% of the West African region. He has bought a few companies and is one of Africa's richest men.

To live in affluence and power, you must have a strong mind that connects with positivity. I have defined a positive mindset to be a mental and emotional attitude that focuses on the bright side of life and expects positive results." I also looked further and believe that a positive mindset is what directs a man to where he belongs. When you make positive thinking a habit, continually search for the silver lining and make the best out of any situation you find yourself in, and push yourself to the right trajectory.

Building a good, positive, and rich mindset is important because it becomes a succession of thoughts the mind automatically thinks. It's automatic because the neuropathways or thoughts are set in the mind. Our mindsets are built when we started thinking; hearing and seeing things happen around us, and as children by how we were raised and the things that happened to us. These thought processes drive our lives bringing about behaviors without our intentional involvement. And that is why we must be mindful of our mindset.

Good name, image & reputation

There is no wealth more precious than a good name, a good self-image, and a sound reputation. They call this your brand today because your brand is who you are. Folks expect you to be consistent with that. Even before they come to you for help, they know what they are getting. Someone who has a reputation for being unreliable is doomed out of the gate. He cannot become wealthy because he cannot be consistent. No one can put their faith in him.

A bad name and poor self-image may be the result of accumulated criticisms from society. A person can be pushed down so far, he feels like he can never rise again. A good image comes from you knowing your true nature, in her book The Way of INTEGRITY: Finding The Path To Your True Self, Martha Beck defines "true nature" as "Your true nature loves things for their capacity to bring genuine delight, right here, right now. It loves romps, friends, skin contact, sunlight, water, laughter, the smell of trees, the delicious stillness of deep sleep" (Beck, p28).

A good image comes from what we make of ourselves. This is based on what we truly want for ourselves, not what others think we should have or be. I have found that many youngsters of today are offensively lazy and complacent. This can only make them fail. They rob themselves of so many future opportunities. They have no eagerness to learn. That is why it is such a challenge to teach them. Yet, they want the high life they see on television. They want to impress their peers with big accomplishments, but they don't want to put in the work. Their brand is trash. They must build themselves up to achieve a good reputation. But these days a good reputation can be trashed more easily than ever before.

This is primarily due to the Internet. One negative Instagram or Facebook comment can tear all that you've built up. And sometimes young people hurt themselves by posting content that will offend potential employers and collaborators. A single instance of bad behavior, even if you think it's not a big deal, may haunt you forever. So, it's simply best to think about what you post and why you're posting it. Things on the Internet have a forever life.

And don't ever think you have built yourself up so high you can never come down. Think of Tiger Woods. He thought he'd never get caught cheating. He got caught and lost almost everything. He lost his marriage, his sponsors and his reputation, and much of his accumulated riches. Nowadays, you must assume that you're being Googled by hiring managers, potential dates, competitors, and customers, so it's always best to think twice before you tap that SEND button.

Integrity

Integrity is what you do when your spouse or children are asleep. When you are not aware someone is looking at you or listening to you. It is what you do when your friends have left the table with their drinks and personal effects. A person of integrity keeps promises he has made to himself. For example, if he tells himself he will do 25 pushups every morning, he will do that no matter who is watching. He does it because he has made a promise to himself.

I can recall when an old friend asked a very good question during a training session in Johannesburg. This is how he led up to that question: I run a manufacturing business and a trading conglomerate which I inherited from my father. The biggest challenge is not power or machinery. It is not the infrastructure needed to run the factory. It is not even the funds or capital that are necessary to do the business. And I must say that government policies are not slowing us down too much. The biggest challenge is hiring honest staff. Everyone we hire appears to be on a mission to steal from the business. We see staff inflate invoices and under-report inventory. They record less than the actual number of units produced. The worst part is the rampant fraud we have uncovered. This was not done by a single person, but by a collaboration of more staff members than expected. They come together to steal. They all planned and strategized so that none of them can be trusted. Many of them took oaths and signed written agreements from different departments. From production to sales, down to procurement and accounts. Yet they all stole from the company. We see top management staff working with security guards to smuggle out products. Our transportation team is colluding to perpetuate these dastardly acts. There is no man with integrity in the business. It is hard to find one. There is no man or woman of honesty and dependability. No one can be trusted to handle and take over the forefront of what we stand for. We lack someone who will be our flagship and lead us to success. I doubt I can find one.

His words sounded poetic. But the sad fact is this is the reality we find ourselves in. It is a challenge to get honest people, people with integrity to work for you. Still, we look for those people because we need those people. We must build those people through our example. As it stands now, those people are as rare as pure gold. This Is the challenge of leadership: to find the people who will build upon a legacy of excellence. True leaders are hard to find, but the first thing they have to have must be INTEGRITY. So many of our current leaders have failed miserably because they lacked the will to do the right thing except for what will benefit them more than others, even when people are looking at them. We are often more intoxicated by reputation and power than character. We tend to want to be seen as successful and rich without really being whom people should see us be. It bears repeating: Reputation is what people think you are, and character is what you are inside you and beneath the eyes of God. The measure of a man is not the zeros in his bank account. It is not the places he has been, the people he commands, or the resources he controls. Nor the accolades of the crowd that tickle his ears. Even his oratorical skills, the eloquence of his presentation, and all his educational accomplishments do not fully measure a man. All this may be impressive but means nothing if that man lacks INTEGRITY!

The true measure of a man's wealth is his "IS". When you are addressed and mentioned as – he is so and so. He is good, he is kind, he is truthful and dependable. Then that is who a person is.

The wealth that will be everlasting and transferable to future generations is his integrity. Whatever a man does in secret and outside of his normal environment will be revealed and become his present-day personality. What decisions we make when no one will question us is what allows us to gain trust and respect. Having a good name is everything. It is a person's true nature, that halo that follows him. We must take control of who we are if we are to achieve success forever.

In his book Identity: Your Passport to Success, Stedman Graham writes: "Building your identity is about knowing what our calling is, learning how to do it well, and creating value in the world" (Graham, p4).

People have debated whether integrity can be counted as wealth. There was a man in the early years of industrialization and his integrity made him stand out even in the middle of a world economic recession. The story of Jon Meade Huntsman, Sr, who founded the Huntsman Corporation, a global chemical company in California. He rose from humble beginnings to become a billionaire entrepreneur. He was also a philanthropist, giving billions to all areas of cancer research. He was also the author of Winners Never Cheat- The Everyday Values We Learned as Children (But May Have Forgotten) and Barefoot to Billionaire: Reflections on a Life's Work and a Promise to Cure Cancer. He made his mark during the period when companies were eager to sell their low-margin bulk petrochemical plants. He borrowed heavily to buy such products, which created the basis for today's Huntsman Corporation. Four times his company was on the brink of bankruptcy. It was his integrity that pulled him back. He had built a name for himself when he was growing up. He mowed lawns, washed dishes, and picked potatoes. His first lesson in the importance of having a good name was when he got caught trying to steal an ice cream sandwich: he embarrassed his family and himself.

Lesson learned.

He was born into an average-income family. His family moved to Northern California so he could attend Palo Alto High School. There was the sting of poverty in his family, but he resolved to work hard and be successful. He decided to build a stellar reputation. He knew he could be successful with integrity as he was taught by his father. He was later admitted to the University of Pennsylvania. He arrived at the school in an expensive suit, $29.95 from J. C. Penny. He was dressed to impress. Later in business, when his corporation started to have cash flow problems, Huntsman mortgaged his house and borrowed heavily from banks. During this trying period, Huntsman and his wife, Karen, had to look for a bailout. After pouring his heart out to one bank manager, Huntsman was given the money he needed. Because he was known as a man of integrity, he was able to get this loan. With the loan, he was able to build a company estimated to build a company that was worth $3 billion in 2018. Later in life, he was elected Governor of Utah and was appointed by different administrations to head high-level governmental positions in the United States.

Integrity is wealth with no end. It comes from the character you build from some salient attributes which when built can never be taken away from you unless you give it up; let us take a quick peep into them.

Trustworthiness

Building integrity comes from the fundamental value of trust wherever you are. People will give up their lives and everything that matters to them for the one they can trust, and this will depend on how responsible and reliable you are. You don't need to become close friends with everyone you come in contact with to gain their trust; all that is needed is to do right, stand strong on your good ethics

When earning the medal of trustworthiness, your actions must speak for you—keeping to your promises, having high ethical standards, and holding yourself accountable for everything you say or do, even when at fault or had made a mistake.

Honesty

Integrity and honesty go together, you cannot separate one from the other, and neither can one exist without the other. The example of honesty and integrity translates into being open with your life to accountability, open-mindedness, and ensuring you do not do what will soil your name in every circumstance.

Honesty is when you do not compromise. You will not take the wrong path even if it is paved with gold. Honesty will pull you up quickly and to the status of influence and affluence.

Reliability

If the people that surround you can't rely on you in any given situation, then you are not wealthy yet., why will anyone rely on you if you do not have what it takes to make them trust you? when it is required that someone will have to constantly watch over them to ensure they're doing what they've been tasked with is no good. That's why reliability is necessary for having integrity wherever you are. It's taking the time to listen to others' requests and promptly respond to them, doing the right thing at the right time, and even being one that will deliver if the chips are down.

Not just that, but being reliable also means that your colleagues, potential employees, and peers can count on you to accommodate their needs whenever convenient for you. Since trust can be fragile, the best policy is to continue reinforcing it with a positive attitude and absolute commitment

Responsibility

Responsibility is an essential factor in having someone counted as one with integrity. No matter how simple your tasks seem, you are responsible for them alone.

A lack of responsibility is evident when you mindlessly carry out jobs. Doing so shows how irresponsible you are and breaks the trust you've built with your colleagues and peers.

Being responsible goes hand in hand with acting in a reliable and trustworthy manner. It tells your managers that they can entrust you with more responsibility if they ever need to.

To me, integrity is the greatest form of wealth. It is having everything that distinguishes you from others who don't just have it. It is the one thing that makes the world trust you and depends on you. It is developed only from the inside decisions.

Here's another story of integrity. John Lenon, director of the World Bank, told this story that touched my heart. I heard him speak at an executive event for corporate America. He became the head of a multi-million-dollar conglomerate and director of the World Bank because of the example of his father's integrity.

Lenon spoke of the arguments his mother would have with his father. His mother was somewhat frustrated because his father didn't bring home as much money as his colleagues. He was head of procurement and financial control for 38 years and never used his position to steal any money. He never once compromised his integrity.

Because he was so trustworthy that trust was passed down to his son who in return received rewards and big commendations that he would never have attained in his lifetime of hard work, and this pushed him further and enabled him to do very well in business. There were some setbacks, but Lenon never gave up.

A man of integrity may be hard to find, but we can see how they are rewarded. Because they are wealthy at the core, humanity will deliver good things to them.

Value

This is one area of wealth creation that many people never knew existed. But placing a value on you is what makes you worth your price. Our values are on full display as we show the world how we live our lives. A man's values are the basic elements found in him. They are his practices and beliefs on full display. It represents him every day in everything he does. And in fairness, it is what you call your worth that determines your value. It gets to the point where your word begins to translate into money. Your personality becomes your income. That value you carry is what you are perceived to be; big or small. It is the measure of your strategy and conscious efforts.

When you become a person of value, you have become useful and helpful, and indispensable. There is a part you play in society that no one else can play. It gets to the point that certain things won't happen until you show up. Your value is a lifeline to many people's solutions.

An Italian chef, Sic Fernando was privileged to host a billionaire's daughter and her boyfriend at the prestigious Royal Penthouse Suite at the Hotel President Wilson in Geneva, Switzerland. He served all sorts of Saffron cuisine with Fiorentina steak, Focaccia, and the super-hot zillion dollar Lobster Frittata with the choicest Italian wine. This young American couple was anticipating the time of their lives when the chef bought out a bottle of wine. He asked the servers to place it in a gold-plated chest and be carried out by a trusted waiter. This was accompanied by two other waiters. The three walked up the aisle to the young couple's table. This all amused the young daughter; she didn't think all of this pomp and circumstance was necessary. She tried to play it off as not that important, but Chef Sic was determined to present his best. He explained to the couple that the wine was a Passion Azteca Platinum Liquor, a year-old tequila inside the chest and the most expensive because of the 6,400 diamonds fixed on the bottle to boast the price as the most expensive wine in the world, costing about $3.5 million.

The couple never knew the presentation until they were shown its value. They were in awe for a few minutes, suddenly realizing that the procession was worth more than anyone ever kept in their fridge. There are so many other fine wines in the world that probably taste better and have a life stay of over 4 years but are not treated with such class. In a class by itself is the Passion Azteca Platinum Liquor or none nearly as expensive? The value placed on this wine is not the taste. Neither are its ingredients. It is not the design of the bottle, nor is the well-cultured label. What stands out is the 6,400 diamonds that adorn the bottle. And a name that only the rich can pronounce properly, and this is how value is placed. This wine cannot be served to just anybody. Neither can it be found just anywhere. Only in places that garner great value and respect. Only real money and people of influence can enjoy such a delicacy.

Wealth is not found in the gutters, neither is it found in the armpit of a poor mind. you can only find real value where there is a high demand for it. You can measure the value of something by what people will exchange for it and by how much of it is available

Most would agree that gold has always had value for all of these reasons—a component of decorative jewelry, it is sometimes used as currency or a means of exchange, and as an investment. But in addition to these concrete values, we would add another characteristic of gold, which, though harder to pinpoint, is its appeal to the human sense of beauty and glamour. And so, for any person that needs to build up value, they must do with themselves what others have not done. You must carry yourself to the sky and remain there.

The question is, what do you want to be valued with? That should be the start of your worth process. Are you desiring to be valued with money or with wealth and power? Are you desiring to be valued among the men on your block or do you want to be valued among kings and rulers of nations? Whichever value you choose, you are to determine where you are going to be placed.

You can have an incredibly rare, one-of-a-kind skill or service. But if there is little demand for it, you will be wasting away. Similarly, if you have that same kind of skill or service that the world is hungry for; your value will become high, and that translates to wealth.

Though the supply of Eastlake and mid-century armchairs on the secondary market may be comparable, the demand is not. The demand for Eastlake furniture is far less than for mid-century modern furniture. You might have five people clamoring for the Eastlake chair. You might have 50 wanting the mid-century piece. This will drive the price up and keep the Eastlake piece much lower.

While issues of provenance, size, age, materials, condition, markings, etc. may play a factor in separating the rich from the wealthy, the two main factors in determining value always are supply and demand. You can't have one without the other.

Continued Education

I can't agree less with Albert Einstein to the saying that "the day a man stops learning, is the day he starts dying" Henry Ford said, "Anyone who stops learning is old, whether at age 10 or 80. Anyone who keeps learning stays young." Continued learning is your path to not only remaining young and successful but also achieving a robust, fulfilling lifestyle.

Researchers David Cutler and Adriana Lleras-Muney report there's a large and persistent relationship between education and not only wealth but health. They found that a season of formal education can add more than six months to one year to your life span. More specifically, they discovered that the more educated you are, the lower your rates of common chronic illnesses — like heart disease, stroke, hypertension, high cholesterol, emphysema, diabetes, asthma, and ulcers.

Cutler and Lleras-Muney's research also supports the idea that being an eternal student improves your mental health, and your reasoning becomes dynamic. The more you educate your mind, the lower your levels of anxiety and depression.

 well into your so-called retirement years. Amy Blaschka in an article (Forbes online 13 August 2019), entitled Four Reasons Why Travel Is the Best Education, shows that stepping beyond the classroom can ensure personal transformation and career growth. According to Amy traveling increases your wisdom because it:

- Broaden your horizons
- Inspires your creativity
- Helps you connect better with others
- Challenges you to grow

Education means more than acquiring knowledge. It is what empowers people to develop strong personalities and to make them become socially and economically active. It is the addition of understanding to all you learned formally and informally. Education creates a kind of society and people, two of Asia's fastest-growing economies, India, and China, show that education has clear economic and social advantages. A third example: In the 1950s, South Korea was in worse condition than many African countries are today. Continued education in equal proportion and access for men and women, old and young, have contributed to a decrease in infant mortality rates and to an economic transformation that created a boom. The lightning-fast development of the Chinese economy suggests that there has been a real hunger for education, and nearly every Chinese person under the age of 25 sees education as a key issue and lifestyle.

The same goes for reading and learning new skills, as you get educated in the mind and soul, your horizon broadens. Education is perhaps the most powerful weapon that you could use to change your world, it keeps the mind young, sharp, and active so that they can contribute something of value to the world, and produce wealth for their carrier.

Plans & Strategies

A tree will never bend for you to climb it. Climbing a tree must start from a desire to climb, you start the climbing process from the ground and gradually and systematically move up. True success will never lower its standards to accommodate you. Rather you must raise your standards to get up on the success line, so to speak. If you don't know what success is (for you) how can you possibly create it? Success is different for different people and no one person is the custodian of success (pregnancy for example) is the joy of one person but might be another person's catastrophe. That's because success (or failure) is not so much about the situation or circumstance, but how one reacts (or feels about what has happened). That's why one man's trash can be another man's treasure chest.

To create success, you must first define it-and far too many people have not. You must be clear about what you want or don't want in this life. Clarity is the fuel for energy and excitement. This energy and excitement produce momentum. Momentum produces behavioral change. Behavioral change produces different results and eventually, the internal vision becomes an external reality.

God provides food for every bird, but not for its nest. Manna from Heaven had to be picked up; it never fell into the mouths of the Israelites. Today, you must rise to the challenges ahead of you and begin to plan and strategize on how to achieve success. It is time to face your fears. Determination and Focus turn ordinary people into extraordinary success stories. You can be the next success story. Carefully plan your next move and put all your strategies to work for you. Success is yours if you claim it.

Health & Wellness

Health is such a broad word. It means so many different things to so many people. But when you look good, you feel good and when your physical body is in good shape, then you can achieve better and beyond boundaries. Many are chasing after success, working so hard and unstoppable while ignoring other dimensions of their lives, which are their health and wellness.

Take care of yourself. You are no good to anyone if you are confined and sick or ready to drop dead. Eat right, drink right, and live in harmony; that is the path to a good life. And remember to be grateful for what you have by caring more for it and God will give you more to enjoy. Work towards what you want, but never achieve anything at the expense of your health, your salvation, or your family. What is the point of having success if you can't enjoy it due to illness?

When it comes to your health, it should be paramount if you want to live a wealthy and successful life. Increased risk of ill health, injury, and death can put one out of the game forever. It can negatively impact the quality of your life. It may also damage the productivity of your company and your family's prospects, productivity, finances, and reputation-all which can be difficult to recover from. Living successfully is related to consciously working on your wellness, paying rapt attention to it and making time for regular exercise, and preparing a healthy diet every day.

The book of Proverbs in the Bible states "Health is wealth" which means that one's health is the greatest wealth. You have been given this vessel and it is yours for this lifetime, so why not take as good care of it as you can? Of course, we cannot be perfect, but if 90 percent of the time we are doing our best to enjoy good foods, exercise, manage stress, sleep well and at the right time with the adequate quantity and supplement, when necessary, we are going a long way toward caring for this beautiful body that we have been given.

Health is the state of a person's physical, mental, emotional, and social well-being. A healthy body is unstoppable when it comes to achieving anything. When the mind is healthy and alert, it will always navigate good health culture, giving attention and realizing that we are here only because of God's grace.

Skills

You are creative and as such, create what people want. This age is so digital and fast-paced that you will become indispensable when you have something unique that the world needs to get rolling. Put what you have on the table, do not bury your talent, God will ask what you did with them. Did you bury them or make them grow? Your skill is your gift and how you protrude that gift to the world matters. Your talent comes to you by birth or training, whichever way, it is that ability that separates you from others. This can be your opportunity to become successful in your given endeavor.

It has been said often: Your talent is God's gift to you. What you do with it is your gift back to God. Let me remind you what Jack Ma, founder of the fast-growing online marketing company, Alibaba, said. I am delighted to amplify his words because he has something big in him that he can tell us, right? He's the richest man in China. It's a huge company.

Jack Ma puts it this way: "You know, when my grandfather was alive, he worked 16 hours a day, 6 days a week, and he felt very busy. Me, I work eight hours a day, five days a week, and I feel very busy. My children will work three hours a day, three days a week, and they will feel very busy."

He says that every single muscle power job will be eliminated by technology. And he goes further to say that every single knowledge-based job will be eliminated, as well--maybe not as quickly, but it will be eliminated. And he predicts that whenever you have these kinds of ruptures--and he thinks that this is a major rupture, the way that artificial intelligence and technology is moving, there is a major rupture coming. And when that happens, his interpretation is that skill and intelligence will keep the few afloat.

Your skill can not be overthrown by technology or machines. What you know and can do better than others is your power to continue trending and be relevant in a fast-moving world. Old methods will evaporate, muscles will fail men, and only skills will enable make man to continue to live.

Your own words

....
....
....
....
....
....
....
....
....
....
....
....
....
....
....
....
....
....
....
....
....
....

Albert Einstein
"The value of a man should be seen in what he gives and not in what he is able to receive."

A good man holds himself accountable, takes responsibility for his actions, does what is right regardless of popularity, maintains the highest integrity, and harbors values and respect for all.

A man of success is seen with some spectacular virtues, these virtues make him who and what he is.

Chapter Eleven:
Buy the neighborhood, not the building

"Your world is your living room, it is in all continents, and it all revolves around *your neighborhood.*"

Martha Stewart - American businesswoman, writer, and television personality

---

If you want opportunities to knock, build doors, and if you want events to unfold, build bridges. This is an aphorism to let you know that you can create opportunities and not only that, but you can also create your moments in different folds and different dimensions. Success is not fortuity, but it is by design. The more opportunities you create around you, the more expansion you can get from it. Your success is not complete until you have the world in your hands. You must be sure that you have made the necessary impact to see a changing environment, then you can relax on your happiness and enjoyment in splendor. Your goal should be to make others comfortable and complete, that is why you must strive to be big and wealthy.

We have a lot of poor people around us, those who are hungry, those in need, and many destitute. The solution cannot always come from the government or help to come from some organizations, that is why you need to be big and wealthy so you can be a solution to the needs of many. why should you have money, and your marriage is in disarray, why should you have money, and your children don't want to see you, why should you have money that your neighbors cannot be at peace with you, what kind of prosperity is yours that your brothers and sisters cannot come near you? Your money is now making you lonely and sad. I don't understand why your influence is on you alone, instead of society and your sphere of contact.

You are making it better than when you encountered the circumstances. You are adding value and improving the lives of many, those you meet every day and those privileged to meet you. You cannot change the world if you are not capable of first impacting your neighborhood. That means you must have the wherewithal: intelligence, morals, and ethics to touch lives around you and make everything better for the world.

Robert Jenkins, Chief Education and Associate Director of Programmes at UNICEF once said, "The greatest power is people power." And when you have people power, then you have political power and it all adds up to economic and social power which translates to wealth, and in addition, you become an authority. All these transcend to wealth in every ramification, that is why the wealthy are called the hook of the network ring. That one connection that brings and holds every individual with different backgrounds, abilities, skills, and talents together to achieve the greater goal.

A professor of economics addressed a group of young bankers at the international conference of certified accountants in Zurich, Switzerland during the 2018 bankers conference about the financial reports used as a case study of one of the richest spiritual bodies in the world. Those young bankers' best guess about the Vatican's wealth when they were asked about it was put at about $100 million to 30 billion. But it was more than their projections. It was over

$30 billion to $35 billion at the end of that financial year. Of this massive wealth, membership contributions and gifts to the spiritual body alone ran to $14.6 billion. This means about 68% of the wealth came from

followers and devotees of the Catholic church. You can imagine that their estimated net worth comes primarily from their followers and members, others are from ownership of properties, including churches, schools, presbyteries, hospitals, nursing homes, offices, tennis courts, and telephone towers to mention but a few. But the bane here is the power that came from the people.

There is nothing more powerful than having people power. This is where wealth comes from before anything else. Money is not the greatest measure of success, network is. Warren Buffet, American business magnate, super investor, and philanthropist, once said that true success in life is "When the number of people that believe in your dream is higher than your dream itself, and until they begin to dream the same dream you dream, believing in your dreams that all they want is for it to come to reality." It is also having more people you want to have on your side, believing in you as the light that shines in their path.

When you look around and what you see is the people that are ready to stake their lives for you. That they believe in you and are ready to run with you. That they believe in you and are ready to build their dreams around yours. That is what having "People Wealth" is all about. This is also called leadership which comes from foresight, it primarily is from the way you treat people rather than the way you want them to treat you. You may have come across people who called themselves "rich" and don't want to be associated with the masses. They don't mingle with mere mortals whom they believe will bring them down from the top of the shaky ladder of their success. They seem to forget that the "people" around them are readymade wealth that can never be bought with money. They are the ones that preach, "If you do not have rich friends in your circle, go make new ones." They think they are better alone in their mansions, building more affluence for themselves. No man is an island, and you can never be a success without the people. They are the circle that makes you a champion. You can never be big without a network that provides your net worth.

Since neighbors live right next to you. You must know that human beings do badly when isolated from others. They need to be a part of a community to thrive. They're the best people to watch over your life and property and everything that belongs to you when you are not around. That is why you cannot afford to stay isolated. Neighbors unconsciously watch you and subconsciously learn your habits and most times can pick up pieces of who you are. How they can benefit from you and at the same time help lift you or break you. Either of which you have culled for yourself. There is safety in numbers. If multiple eyes and ears proactively look out for one another. It creates a safer community for all.

The best way to get world information is from local knowledge. Some people on your street have probably the information you need for your business to thrive and prosper. Or you may have people that can convert your network just by strolling by you. You don't even notice them. Your neighbor and the people in your sphere all have ears and thousands of eyes. Meaning they know the ins and outs of the place you planted yourself. They are the people you need daily. No single person should be overlooked or made common. They could be the synergy you need. Every knowledge they have can be passed onto you.

Neighbors have great value. Neighbors might give you a heads-up about what snakes you might see during the summer. Let you know where it floods when it rains. Or where the best local cafe is. They might be the ones to tell you where to get the cheapest suppliers of the products you have been playing to produce. Neighbors have value.

Dealing With Difficult People on your way

We talk about buying the neighborhood and not the building. It won't be as easy as buying a family of dogs and training them to follow you on the street. It is persistent care and genuine love, knowing full well that you will meet difficult and pain-in-the-neck kind of people on the way. Always remember that you will meet difficult people everywhere in the neighborhood. This is at work, at school, on the streets, in the marketplace, amongst the family, and among political parties and affiliates. Even in religious gatherings like the church. It doesn't matter the number of good things you do; you will still meet difficult people in life. But the bottom line is to have everyone in your kitty doing your bidding and having your back. They will mock you. They will criticize you. They will discourage you. They will fight you and speak negative things about you. Many will tell lies about you or even steal from you. They will threaten you and so on, but all great men come across difficult people in their journey of life but made them better and useful for their success, and that of others.

Difficult people are easy to come by. They will be around you all the time. And that is why you must learn to deal with them rather than wrapping yourself up in your blanket, trying to live a self-pitying and secluded life. This won't lead you to success and wealth because you need people on your way to the top. This is where you begin to realize that your success is in people. Your desire to attain stardom is more valuable than money and any other material possession. You will relish relationships and do everything you have to keep them all. Still, these immature people need your help. Some are wounded and seeking help, some are seeking revenge against you for being the superhero and the solution provider. Those people will come your way with jealousy and seeking relevance.

You will meet the proud and cynical who never want to see anyone above them. Those who are failures in their life pursuits, looking for people to go down the fall with them. That is why you must learn to be above board, having all the strategies of leadership and winning in your mind. As you begin to spread your relevance and win your way through people, you will encounter challenging people who will not want to deal with you. Some will pretend to be true but are pretenders. What does the presence of these kinds of difficult people mean? It means there is a great ability within you to change a perspective and to use such fellows to your advantage in your ongoing journey to success and wealth. It also shows leadership qualities in you that must be harnessed. It means you have great potential, and you must overcome them. It means that despite all that you have gone through with difficult people, you are on the right track. Start building a strong dynasty, and get the people to your side, it is called networking.

Learning to recognize potential in people is key to building your network. Your network becomes bigger and stronger, you become heavy with capacity and influence. It will not only be that you can recognize the potential in people, but that you can also trust them to build a dynasty with them is key to true leadership and wealth. This means you are giving out responsibilities for people to handle, releasing information to make them grow with you, and training and retraining them to continue the line you have created, so they can have the chance to prove their abilities all by themselves as they in return help you build your dream. This transfer can only be done with the quality of your personality. This is the power to win and become influential and wealthy.

As you begin to choose men without looking at their background or having personal likenesses of one to another, you will begin to raise those who have the willingness and potential to grow. Some people have a lot of potential that are hidden under their skin, you will never know what they carry until you bring them on board your team. They must be identified and raised to be useful to you.

To bring up people, you must see their abilities ahead of them. You must know how to bring people in, how to raise them to become, and train them to navigate into your ideology and what will make them better people will raise the giant within them. Looking at the scriptures, 1 Chronicles 12:1-40, we saw King David raised mighty men of war from people who were described as 'mere men'. Those David's mighty men were once destitute, sickly, and impoverished, and were financially dead and bankrupt. It was these same men David raised to become the helpers and warriors of the great king. This made him the most feared and respected king in the region at that time.

David's wealth grew and his fame became loud to the skies because of these mighty men he raised from the zero level to be heroes. They became men others dread and fear. Imagine when your lieutenant is respected and honored just like a king is honored, How do you think they will honor the king himself? People will respect and honor you more. Not because of your money but of the power of those that are following you. The network you have built is the highest height of your power, where influence and prosperity is.

When you raise people, they become your currency. They become your power. That makes you "the eye of the ring." Learn to believe in people and never give up on your dreams about them. Remember that every person is a potential chest of riches. When you misplace that person or devalue that person, you have thrown away wealth.

There was this fellow I met on the train to New York. I was coming from a pastors and discipleship training in Staten Island, New York. He told me a story after he introduced himself as an investigative writer for the New York Times. He spoke so unguardedly, like a newly purchased parrot. He told me about a young writer who wrote his first book a year after he graduated from high school, he wanted to launch it on his 21st year birthday. He needed funds to launch the book, and the thought of how to raise the money occupied his mind. As he approached a cleric in his community to help him with some money from the church.

On his visit to the cleric, he explained his need and asked for assistance from the church. The cleric was interested in the boy's accomplishment and wanted to help and immediately asked him how much he would be needing for the book launch. After all the discussions and planning, the cleric told him to take out a piece of paper. He brought out his pen from his white cassock and asked the young man to write down 10 people he knows who would give him $1, 000 each for his book launch. This would amount to $10,000, which is what he needed to have the successful book launch that he talked about.

Surprisingly, after a long pause, blinking his eyelids like the mouth of a choking lizard. He could not think of two people he could count on to help with such an amount. He said the people he knows would not part with such an amount. He didn't have that kind of relationship with anyone, not even his immediate family.

The cleric told him in plain words, "It is not enough to have talent and skills. You must understand the power of building valuable relationships." Your network is directly proportional to your net worth. It is the value of the people you have that make your little efforts become an accomplishment. You alone can write a book. But you cannot publish it alone; you need a team for that. Relationships are currency. It is a stream of income, and in fact, it is the biggest wealth dimension accumulator, everything in this life reproduces based on relationships.

Many people are talented and hardworking. But you have to know who they are. Take the story of Joseph. He was in prison and the king didn't know he was an interpreter of dreams. It was the cupbearer who told the king. This shows the power of relationships.

Who are the people in your neighborhood, at the office, and your religious gatherings? Your old schoolmates and acquaintances are far more important than a push away. The security man or the young boys and girls you see on the next block or street might be the ladder to where you are headed in your business. The lady in the church that you refused to treat well might be a decision-maker for that government agency that you are about to send your proposal. Sometimes, it takes just a recommendation to change your struggling story to a success story. Kingmakers don't always look like kings. Still, they can help you gain the crown. People will defend you and stand by you when they realize that you value and respect them.

Maya Angelou once said: "I've learned that people will forget what you said, people will forget what you did, but people will never forget how you made them feel." Your greatest achievement should be raising achievers. Your greatest trophy should be the tears you wiped away from people's faces and not what you acquire materially.

I tell people that if you make money and become wealthy and successful, make people your biggest investment, and plug into their dreams. The people you help today are the future business leaders of tomorrow. They will defend you and stand by you and honor you. They will always carry a good report about you. Nothing makes life sweeter than making people happy.

Many people use and trample on other people to make progress for themselves. They take people for granted and minimize their relationships with others. Messing up bonds, disregarding another person's relevance because of their present financial worth or level. All these will tell in the future. These are the people that will tell what is sticking onto your shirt because they want you to look good at all times. They are the ones that will chase out any stray fox from climbing into your backyard. No matter how rich or influential you become, you will never remain there without the support of regular people. You must invest in social capital. The people around you are the wealth that will last forever. The very visible assurance of your achievements that will keep you on top are these people. It may be your son or daughter, your friends or associates, or your business partners. It may be your mentees or the people around you. It could be people you haven't met yet. These are the people that will be counted as your currency when every other thing fails. They will pick you up and never let you down.

This level of building wealth through the team doesn't happen by accident. It requires commitment, effort, and a level of repetitiveness known as practice. When we build a team of people, morale will often show just how well things are working and the importance of teamwork. High-functioning teams can be proof that you are reliable, stable, and ready for the future.

As you buy the neighborhood, building men will begin with the respect you accord each person. You respect every individual contribution, show your appreciation, and make sure they know that their effort has the potential for real fulfillment and success and their effort is important and highly appreciated. you can build and sustain a happier network, with a good sense of accomplishment from being a part of you.

Your own words

. . . .

. . . .

. . . .

. . . .

. . . .

. . . .

. . . .

. . . .

. . . .

. . . .

. . . .

. . . .

Michael Jordan
"Talent wins games, but
teamwork and
intelligence win
championships"

teamwork helps build
strong bonds between
people and communities.
Having one big family is
built by compassion and
love, giving so much to
each other, and
developing a better
understanding of
individual strengths,
weaknesses, and personal
traits. Through stronger
relationships trust is built
and communication

. . . .

. . . .

. . . .

. . . .

. . . .

. . . .

Chapter Twelve:
Developing a Wealth Mentality

"Ability to solve problems is the bane of success and the trait of a great leader."

Colin Powell, American diplomat and Secretary of State

Each of us at one time -or the other has indeed built the vague fantasy that someday a miracle will happen. We believed that the big pot of gold and diamonds will after the tussle with contenders eventually become ours and that after this big break, we will never suffer or have to work ever again. Some are waiting for that miracle to happen and are probably still waiting. Then some have a different kind of mindset, they have developed the will to make things happen, and they want to create a system for the present and establish a legacy for a great future.

You cannot have a certain kind of mentality and be poor or average, you cannot be rich in your mind and be chasing after how to break through or how to have money. The richness of your mind will direct you to where you ought to be, what you ought to do, and how you ought to do the things that will produce results for you.

When you begin to have the 'I can do mentality' that is when your journey to success begins, you will begin to live, talk, and live in that kind of life that the wealthy live. The success and the I can do it mentality are the outburst of a trained and disciplined mind. It is time to change your thinking and renew your mind if it is still filled with fear and disruption. You will start building the success mindset by first having the desire to be a problem solver, you want to lift others by first building yourself to grow big and wealthy.

What makes you say the things you say and make you do the things you do is the result of what you have built inside you, the way you do things is through your mindset. But until you begin to think rightly, talk rightly, and act rightly, your ideas and absorption will only place you in a variable condition, not until you grow big in your mind when you have that ever-succeeding and ever-achieving mindset, wealth will be easy for you to achieve.

Montpellier rugby club president and Entrepreneur of the Year, Mohed Altrad, survived on one meal a day when he moved to France. He was born into a nomadic tribe in the Syrian desert to a poor mother who was raped by his father and died when Mohed was still very young. Altrad was raised by his grandmother who would not let him attend school in Raqqa, the city that is now the capital of ISIS. Despite opposition, Mohed struggled by himself and attended school anyway. When he moved to France and attended the university there, he knew no French and lived on one meal a day. Still, he went on to earn a Ph. D in computer science. He worked for some leading French companies and eventually bought a failing scaffolding company. He transformed it into one of the world's leading manufacturers of scaffolding and cement mixers in the world, the Altrad Group.

In a television interview with a French journalist, he said that learning to speak and write French was one of the factors that made him wealthy. He has been previously named French Entrepreneur of the Year and World Entrepreneur of the Year. His net worth grew in time to over $1 billion.

Mohed further explained that he built the future he is living now by the thoughts he had. He had never thought that he was going to be poor or disadvantaged, he has always known that he will be so prosperous and very wealthy. He said, " I knew that I would buy up giant companies and build a business that will outlive my fifth generation, I have always seen myself to be a super-duper success".

Indeed, no one could take what he has built for himself inside him, no economic situation or family background could hold him down from succeeding. And it is also good to know that no one showed him how his future will be, in fact, his situation as a growing kid pointed to poverty and the lower class menage.

Some so many people have built wealth in their system before they brought forth all that they own now. Fighting to have a good job or a business is not the jumping-off point, rather, it is the mentality, the frame of mind toward success, and the intellectual ability to start, run and build a system that will produce the line.

One must remember and take to heart the words of Indian steel tycoon Lakshmi Mittal who came to wealth from humble beginnings and now is worth over $12.3 billion: "Hard work usually goes a long way, those days, people work very hard to achieve the good life, but now you have to work even harder and simpler as you build yourself and especially your mindset because that is what will make you become wealth personified."

A 2000 BBC article reported that Arcelor Mittal, CEO, and chairman, who was born in 1950 to a poor family in the Indian state of Rajasthan "established the foundations of this fortune over two decades ago by building his personality. He afterward started doing much of his business in the steel industry, the equivalent of a discount warehouse." Today, in his seventies, Mittal runs the world's largest steelmaking company and is a multi-billionaire businessman. Many times, he could have gone bankrupt, but because money was just one aspect of having true wealth, he kept bouncing back bigger and better. This was mainly due to the quality of his personality; he was too rich inside for him to fail; another indicator of his true wealth.

What you think, speak, and perceive is what you attract in your life, and so the mind must be trained and directed to go the positive way. If you perceive greatness, great things follow, if you perceive wealth and success, you already know what will follow. Over the past few years, I have been working on my mindset. I can tell you it has been a journey. I have always been the "pessimistic" kind of person, the one who sees the "glass is half empty", a tendency to see the worst part of things. Life experiences and the circle of where I was raised as a child into adulthood led me to this mindset and by default, it stuck so that whenever I was faced with a challenging situation, I could think of the worst that could happen. But began to learn how to change my mindset from the negative to the high positive, I have been blessed with the best teachers and a life coach. I accredit most of my mindset change to my pastor, Reverend Chris Oyakhilome, and the so many other well-built personalities that pushed me. Now, my mantra is "Forward and Upward only"

There are steps necessary to apply to be able to build this wealth mindset. And as this is done, the journey into wealth and success will be a smooth and uncinched roller coaster ride. Let us dissect those steps.

Start Creating pictures

As you begin to read books, you improve your memory, communication skills, focus, and empathy. The first step to creating a sound, positive, and wealthy mindset is by educating it, good books can help you cultivate such a positive mindset. There's a book for every situation and direction, you need to find and read them voraciously. This will help your mind create pictures as it sees different opportunities and strategies of great minds who wrote them. This picture is necessary as a guiding light and a target for you to run with because when you decide to take the run, you will know the steps to take and the track that leads you to the finish line ribbon. The picture of your success will anchor your progress and

You can also create a success picture when you meditate. Meditation is when you ponder deeply about something, you take hold of what you want to see and begin to build it inside you by thinking deeply about it. Oftentimes, you will have to think about that particular situation alone and for a long time, letting all other things melt away. You take away every other matter from your mind and ponder, ruminate, and think about that particular thing you want to build inside you.

Meditation also means to mutter "Hagah" in the Hebrew language – that is talking under the tongue or whispering silently about something for a long time until it becomes a part of you. You cannot talk to yourself about success for a long time and not begin to live it. Muttering brings a picture and a reality to your mind, you will begin to master what you say as your present reality, any other irrelevant and unnecessary thing won't be able to engage your mind again, you will only begin to see and live according to what you have seen and spoke.

Make positive affirmations

Your words affect your mental state more than you may realize. When you say positive words to yourself and the things around you, you become calmer and more confident. Your words can influence how you think, and how you do things, so it's important to always talk positively about yourself and the future you want to create.

People don't easily agree that the life that they are living now was a result of the things they have said in the past because it is. Words are spiritual, they travel far and so fast to create what is spoken about. Instead of talking about irrelevant things, why not pause and allow yourself to make your words count? You can begin talking to yourself and your future even right now. The words you say will become the wealth you will enjoy tomorrow.

You can learn to speak positively by including positive affirmations in your daily routines. Start each day by saying something positive about yourself. For example, saying 'I'm going to have a good day or 'I'm going to achieve my goals today, are great ways to begin talking positively and rightly.

Wealthy people have often used this strategy to build their future and the state they are in, no wonder they will never say what they have surpassed, rather they will talk about what they want to achieve "the next big thing"

Focus on your strengths

Rather than thinking about your limitations, focus on your strengths. Your strengths are your power, for both the physical and mental functions, and so it must be harnessed. They make you enthusiastic about success because you know that you have what it takes to achieve it. It is beneficial to consider how to use them to tackle challenges than sob like a sucking child with the things you cannot achieve. Note your strengths and find ways of using them every day. Improve your mood by adding more result-oriented actions to your life.

Building a wealth mentality requires you to be positive always, desiring to conquer dreams and make them a reality. Wealth creation requires a positive and strong mind that can take a hold of anything that comes its way and keep it.

We all have our strengths just the way we have weaknesses, but the wealthy man will grab his strengths as his priority and strong points and throw away the weaknesses and the inabilities into the gutters, they mean nothing to him and should not be a distraction. You should never think of what you cannot do or maybe you will never win, but rather have your mindset towards your skill, your strong points, your achievements, and your result; there should be this 'win only mentality'

Love and have a passion for success

It is never true to want to die for what you don't like. And it will always be true that you will want to give up everything to have what you love. If this is what it is, then you must love success, you must desire it and have a strong passion for it so you can have it.

The mind is the custodian of passion, it could be for love or hate, but when it comes to building wealth, you must first have a deep love for it so you can go headlong to harnessing it. Your mind will begin to build up passion towards it and will make you align towards achieving it.

A strong hunger for learning new things and wanting to become a success on TV made Leonardo De Caprio a world-class entertainer, unafraid to take on challenges, he had a passion to become an actor or a marine biologist. His passion to be a movie star made him become one of the best in the world even at the young age of 13, he made a respectable impact in acting which brought fame, wealth, and success. His love for acting made him stay on this desire that nothing else interests him much, even those in the acting realm where he has worked with several stars respected his talents and passion. The 13-year-old knew since the age of 3 that he wanted to act. It was an outlet through which he said he could exercise his creativity and "show a side of myself that a lot of people don't see."

Imagine being able to design clothes for people all around the world. she didn't realize that she had a passion for fashion until she was 9 years old in fourth grade. When there is free time available Folorunsho Alakija, the richest black woman in Africa will most likely look through magazines, put outfits together, or even sew little samples. There are a lot of facts that I didn't know about fashion design before, but now I know, just because of my love and passion for it.

Success and wealth come with many responsibilities such as working long hours & weekends, keeping up on the latest trends, and denying oneself some pleasure just because of the passion to succeed.

Your own words

....
....
....
....
....
....
....
....
....
....
....
....
....
....
....
....
....
....

Johann Wolfgang
Von Goethe
"A man sees in the world
what he carries in his heart".

Life can be hard and
challenging. To cope with
hard things, be effective and
successful in life, or simply
experience extraordinary life
and adequate well-being, we
need resources, *inner
strengths* like resilience,
compassion, gratitude , and
other positive
emotions, self-worth, and
insight.

Chapter Thirteen: Arranging a Wealthy Tomorrow

Arranging a wealthy tomorrow does not throw away the functioning of today, it is important to be conscious of how your present moment is by critically analyzing what you have and what you have achieved so far and then begin work for a better tomorrow.

No matter what present level you are, you may want to know that you can still achieve great results and be wealthy and successful. The journey to that life of abundance and happiness begins that very moment you make up your mind that it is doable, and it is now. You need to be sick and tired of where you are to make a change for the better. It comes from a mental decision with deliberate action into your decision.

Your question may still be "I want to be better than how I am now, but I don't know how!" Success is inherent and it is that thing we strive to become. From the moment we spark up the idea that we want to achieve a better life and to the time we acknowledge that it is possible, to the moment we start our first move. The whole process is meant to move you forward in life, build you up for a better future, and make you a strong force in the world's system. But how do you start achieving such a feat?

Mother Theresa made a statement at the city of Calcutta in East India a few years before she died, "Yesterday is gone. Tomorrow has not yet come. We have only today. Let us begin." This statement will put anyone who desires a good tomorrow on their toes, with no room for time wasting. Tomorrow is the next day that must be planned for and should be better than what you are or have at the present. If you want to be a better person, you must strive to make your next move a big hit. That means you must be ready for success. Start by opening up yourself for business every day if you have been working sparingly. Activity is the key to productivity, you need to find new ideas, find new prospects, make new friends, broaden your contact and database and make them your customer or network. You must begin to recruit and build your future in whichever field you are driving on. You need to start doing something out of the ordinary and start seeing tomorrow as you want it to be.

A great future does not come if you do not start molding it today. What you do now can drastically change your future for the better. Think about anything in your past that you would have liked to change if you could. Begin to write them and proffering a possible solution to them. The things you can do to make them come to pass are in your hands and mind, and you have the opportunity to navigate through them.

When you are in an empty room, your ability to see a beautifully decorated arrangement starts right in your mind and not in your naked eyes. It is after the decoration is complete that you will see the beauty with your physical eyes. You make positive changes to your empty rooms with the right decor by seeing from the inside. Your ability to see bigger and clearer pictures comes from your mind and this will help you create that future you always desire. Feel free to share what changes you see and will make to yourself as often as you can to ensure that your past does not challenge or equal your future.

Time To Start Is Now

Sulking and regretting past errors or inadequacies could make you get even worse and more frustrated. There is no better time to make the required change and improvement than now. Anthony Robbins said in one of his blog quotes that "Your past does not equal your future. What matters is not yesterday but what you do right now." This statement is what everyone needs to start any match. If we make real efforts to actively make positive changes right now — despite how the past was, our chances of success in the future are going to be much higher.

It is the things you do today that will affect your tomorrow. You will have to plan and make deliberate changes in your life immediately. Follow the steps in this book to have a great future. Especially in this age of rapid technological advancements and online business successes, there are many other things you can use to prepare yourself for a great future. As you are one of those who want to be successful and wealthy, you are more motivated and determined to chase your dreams. You have more people to spur you on as they also run this same race as you and mentors who have been where you are right now, with more experience than you have, all these are there for you to look up to and help guide you. Your drive, passion, and commitment are at their peak. This generates an increased motivation to unlock your dreams into reality.

1. Define your values

What tomorrow will be for you is determined by how you value it today. My mum will always say that "the eyes of a man that will see clearly in old age will not start hitching and bringing out rheum in his young age" – that means, if you want to have a good future, it will begin from this very moment. Make sure you know not just what you stand for but also what you don't at the very start of your journey.

Being true to yourself will give you inner peace. Make a list of rules that you are going to live by. These will give you an indication of what your values are. They will be the guarding steps to what you want to achieve. At least, you will want to do well for yourself by bringing out the best in you and the best things you want to achieve. For example, if one of your 'rules' is 'I must never tell a lie Then you value honesty. Or if one of your rules is 'Never be rude to others then you value politeness. And if it is to follow your set rules accordingly, then you will value consistency.

Once you think you've defined your value, check to see if they are your values. Look at how you make decisions daily. Do they truly reflect your values and what you want to achieve for the future? If you break your 'rules' and you feel upset, guilty, or distraught, then that rule most likely reflects your values.

Oftentimes, I talk to myself as if I was talking to another person, loudly, I will call my name as loud as hearing myself clearly – "Oyewola, remember what you have in the pipeline and go for it, you must achieve big success, you must do greater things than you have previously done. Never compromise quality and the values you have set for yourself" This has worked for me on different occasions. I have set my values and they are working well because they are good. I have talked to myself consistently about what I have written down and set as my values.

Your values will set you on the right path. And this should be at the start of your journey. Personal values shape whom you perceive yourself to be. It may even heavily affect something as trivial as your attitude towards another person and even help you navigate well in life by making decisions. It can help us find our purpose, ease decision-making, increase our confidence, and guide us through difficult situations. Values bleed into your personal, academic, and professional life. For instance.

2. Set your goals

Set your ambitions in line with your goals. Where do you see yourself in five or ten years? Remember that it is your future you are working on. What can you do now that will help you achieve these ambitions? If you see yourself at a certain kind of level, research the kind of skills that you need to take you there. Find out how you can acquire them. These ambitions are your set goals that must be met.

Think about what you want to achieve, when you want to achieve them, and how you will accomplish them. Setting up your goal should revolve around what is important or priority to your success, maybe your priority is to build new friends and new relationships with people who are going to be your business partners. Those who will be your business and your likely network in the future. Or maybe your priority is to better the community in some way. Maybe your passion is writing, or your passion is academics.

Research how you can make your passion fulfill your goal. You most likely have an idea of a 'dream future' it must start with the kind of goal you present from the beginning. Plan your goals. Break down your goals into smaller, manageable steps. Find out what you'll need to do to achieve each step.

Your goals and ambition may change over time. You only have control over your actions, not your circumstance. Make sure how you react and respond to your circumstances as you reflect on your values. So long as your ambitions stay in line with your values, you will have a great future.

3. Be efficient

Remember that the quality of work you put into an hour is more important than the number of hours you put into the work. The quality AND quantity of your work matter. Sometimes working for a long time on something gives you the illusion that you are getting a lot done when you haven't had a productive hour. Being efficient doesn't have to mean overworking to achieve a result, it is not a boring or overused period, it is also not a hyper-focused workday with bleeding eyes and heavy legs for a long hourly workload. It simply means re-focusing your schedule, spending the day the right way, and getting stuff done.

Be open and honest with yourself about the quality of what you are planning for your future. If you need help, ask for it. Other people might be able to give you better tips on how to do something efficiently and effectively.

Write down everything you complete in a half-hour so you can see how efficiently you're using your time.

Start each morning by prioritizing your to-do list. This will probably mean moving those dreaded and difficult tasks to the top (you know, the things that have to get done first and quickly) and moving all the fluff things to the bottom.

Another way to track your efficiency is to log the time you spend on each project. As I say to my business students, "Log your time at the beginning of every task period, writing down how much you spend on each task and activity. Track everything you are doing from scratch to end. This will allow you to notice and see where the majority of your time is being spent and then make any necessary adjustments.

Never waste time on unnecessary things. Every minute and every hour should be important to you. remember that you are working towards tomorrow's prosperity, and it is not a baby task. Eliminate distractions and focus on the task at hand. This might mean turning off the television or putting away your phone while you work. You can also try to streamline your work process by finding ways to do things faster or more efficiently.

4. Question yourself

Whenever you set out to do something in life, be sure you know your reasons for doing it. It's very easy to slip into 'autopilot' or to do things just because others are doing it or because they're telling you it's the right thing to do. If you do not lead your life with purpose, you are less likely to achieve your goals.

Questioning yourself will require monitoring the way you think and the things you do. Negative thinking styles will hinder your efforts to achieve your goals, and that is the best time to think big and ask yourself if you are tailing the right path.

Be sure to do this every night before you sleep if not constantly throughout the day. Self-monitoring will become habitual over time and make you see tomorrow even more clearly.

5. Build a network

Build a network of people you can rely on for business, partnership, advice, and support in the future. This includes your friends, people you work with who are higher in the command chain than you are, your peers, and your mentors and teachers. Look to those with more experience than you for advice on how to work toward the future you dream of. Even if your idea is something that they don't have personal experience with, they can still give you solid advice that applies to you.

Remember that your network is your net worth, if you are going to build a solid financial future, you need to build people, make them your own and let them have trust in you. Building a good network of people be it personal or professional is a good thing. It's not as complex as it seems, but it does require resetting your approach in a few ways.

I do not only advise having transactional networking where you establish connections ONLY if they have value but make connections with people that will become your people power In the future.

6. Establishing and maintaining good credit

Don't Borrow Easy Money, Credit cards are so easy to get these days and the fastest to trap you down. Unfortunately, most people use them as though they never have to pay that money back.

However, credit cards can be good to use if you are disciplined. If you pay your credit debt on time each month, you will quickly rack up points that you can convert to cash or low-interest rate on transactions. So, there is an incentive in having credit cards. But that's not for everyone who will abuse it because it will abuse you in return since most people don't have the self-control necessary to use their credit cards wisely.

To arrange a wealthy tomorrow, you must start building credibility today. Start raking points now, and increase your credit score as quickly as possible, this will be your advantage tomorrow.

7. Harness the power of compound interest

In this section, we are going to be learning everything about compounding interest in wealth creation and the future. We are talking about what will create that future for you.

Benjamin Franklin described compound interest by saying, "Money makes money. And the money that money makes, makes money" this is so simple but deep.

If you are starting to build wealth, there is still time on your side. An often-cited roadblock to getting this started is the lack of discipline to know the difference between your capital and your profit.

Albert Einstein also once called compound interest "the 8th wonder of the world," and for good reasons. He said, "He who understands it earns it, he who doesn't pay it." Given the choice, we want to be the ones who earn it.

For many, the first time you see a compound interest example, you are inspired. I have included a powerful example below to demonstrate how much investment growth accumulates over time, compared to the amount you are saving in your bank account or your private purse.

By saving small amounts of your extra – profit from your sales or business, the money you got is not meant to pay your bills. These monies are redeployed into what produced them in the first place, thereby increasing the value which in turn brings more as it is invested again and again. This is where compound interest becomes your superpower. Automating these savings from here and there, each of these separated money is reinvested to bring more money for you. It is arguably the single biggest impact decision you'll make in building wealth and preparing for your future. Because of the natural discipline that it creates for you as you put back your profit and the other money you gained from different sources together, it makes it hard for you to stop this beautiful path down the road. You will see yourself desiring to increase the money your plow back into the business by a bigger sacrifice and there, your expansion is unbroken.

Have your money work for you well those are the big ones make some more money you all have amazing skills you'll have extreme technical skills if you're under 30 there's something that you can do build someone that has brick and mortar business, build a better website for someone, get on Shopify put your own products online, help others with social media whatever you want to do write a book just make more money when you're young get it to work in compounding power of interest so I want you to make it and I want you to start investing one of the things that under 30 people do is they buy what they want when they have some money because they haven't been able to do it and you forget to invest for the future very simple get a compounding calculator you put $25,000 away you put $200 extra a month away for 30 years invested at around 10% if you're better investor you might get 15 or 20 you'll be worth seven $800,000 by doing one thing right make 25,000 young put it away invested you'll be rich best thing that you can.

wealthy people act, think, and behave differently. They make and invest; make money and invest over and over again, this method is going to change your life and make you successful without blinking. With money and every currency that you make, It doesn't matter how small it may look at the start, you should put some of the money away right into an investment or into your existing business. Right here, I am not encouraging you to put your money into a bank account and let it lay there with the hope that it will yield much and make you wealthy in the future because it won't yield much for that future that you dream about. Saving money in the bank is not the best idea when it comes to growing your money. Bankers don't like this statement, but I have to say this truth to better the lives of the reader.

Compound interest grows your financial standard, assets, and investments exponentially, meaning interest is based on the return on the original amount and the accumulated interest invested and what it has brought back to you in a multiplied amount.

Wealth is Bread and Butter

The financial gurus call it bread and butter. This is what we all know as buying and selling which is the first and main source of income for every financially independent person. There is no financial independence if you are not selling something to someone, be it goods or services- life revolves around what you can give another person in exchange for a reward.

I made a post on my website blog post on achieving wealth with ease at www.homefrontcorporation.com. "If you don't have bread and butter you will wait for others to feed you". The Solution to being financially stable and independent is to have something to supply others and in return enable you to earn from it. Anything that makes money circulate unhindered is the goods and services supplied and received. When you hear people use bread and butter as an illustration of real-life financial situations, they are talking about what they do to enable themselves to earn a good living.

If at this stage of your life, you are still waiting on a wage or salary to live the life that you want, then you are still under the bridge. No matter how big the paycheck looks, it will never be enough to care for your needs. Not until you sell to others to receive profit, which is that extra income. No matter how small the profit on what you sell is, it is the difference you need to live above the norm. Wages, while they can pay for most of your expenses, have one drawback. They are always a fixed amount. Worse yet, the deductions that come off your check keep increasing while your wage stays the same. And if you do happen to ever get a raise, you could fall into a new tax bracket and take home less than before. It's happened to a lot of people and isn't very funny.

Profits or commissions, on the other hand, offer more than a wage could ever hope to give you. The reason is simple.

There's no limit to how much profit or commission you can make. That's why wages can only earn you a living, but profits will make you a fortune.

Oftentimes I see people that have a complete disconnect between their goals to be wealthy and the necessity of knowing the place of selling and or providing services to people. People talk to me all the time about how they want to be wealthy and financially independent and then I bring up the idea of sales or providing a service and immediately they are turned off. "I'm not interested in what I'll start cracking my brain to start" or "Oh, I'm not a salesperson in nature, I prefer the constant paying job that pays my bill and help me cater for my family. Today I want to address the importance of selling so that you can master it and create wealth at will.

You must have a product or service to be relevant and successful in life apart from your other job or profession. Wealth does not come by prayers or fasting, not even by the level of your education or by the strength of your bone, but by the product that you produce to solve a need or a service that you render that will solve someone's problems.

This is the time to know what your bread and butter are. What are you selling, or the services you can provide to others to make you have wealth in return? You cannot fold up and think the only means to become okay is to have a stable daily or monthly "constant" income than exchanging tangible solutions for wealth in return.

Your own words

....

....

....

....

....

....

....

....

....

....

....

John Guare
"It's amazing how a little tomorrow can make up for a whole lot of yesterday."

Can you think of a way to become richer by tomorrow that doesn't involve any struggles, headaches, embezzling, or manipulations and with minimal to no effort? If you haven't figured out the answer for yourself yet, then you really need to start exercising your creative mind.

....

....

....

....

....

....

....

....

....

Conclusion

"All riches have their origin in the mind. Wealth is in ideas-not money."

Robert Collier, American author of self-help books

If you have come this far in this book, then you have made tremendous progress in your life already and have shown a serious commitment to achieving true wealth. You are all about controlling your destiny and changing the world for good.

By now you should be aware that your personal financial goals and choices will also become an example for other people looking up to you. You are the prime example of a broader economic change within your sphere of influence and the world at large.

Always remember that the wealth you cannot imagine cannot be real for you. Albert Einstein said: "Imagination is more important than knowledge because there is no limit to imagination, the limit to knowledge was imagined." And that which is not flowing in and through you is not going to become wealth for you.

Dear Reader, I believe that this book has opened your eyes and helped you see beyond the concept of trying to be rich and chasing money in hopes of becoming comfortable and secure for the future, rather it is who you are and what you have made yourself to be. If your wealth is not sustainable and not coming out of a grounded-in-wealth mindset, it is not true wealth.

About the author

Oyewola Oyeleke is a Financial and Accounting professional. He had his Post Graduate Degree in Financial studies at the Ladoke Akintola University, Ogbomosho, and an MBA degree in financial management at the same school. He is a member of the Institute of Chartered Accountants of Nigeria ICAN. He also is an associate of the National Institute of Marketers of Nigeria, (Chartered) NIMN.

He is the senior pastor of Christ Amplifier Ministries INC and the host of the popular syndicated radio and television Bible teaching program, **The Amplification,** which is broadcasting internationally.

Oyewola is the CEO of Homefront Corporation USA, He founded the online hosting company, **kicksdomains**, where hundreds of sites on the internet are hosted and promoted.

The author is an Accounting and Economics teacher spanning over 2 decades in different schools and colleges and has mentored over 30 young professionals in business and entrepreneurship. His business has helped 13 businesses start up and grow into big businesses.

He is married with kids.

Made in the USA
Middletown, DE
25 October 2023

41313345R00205